New Frontiers of Educational Research

More information about this series at http://www.springer.com/series/10795

Yuhong Du · Zhijun Sun

Research on Compulsory Education Financing in China

Springer

Yuhong Du
Faculty of Education
Beijing Normal University
Beijing
China

Zhijun Sun
Economics and Business Administration
Beijing Normal University
Beijing
China

北京师范大学985工程"世界一流教育学科与中国教育"创新基地经费资助
Funded by Innovation Base Fund of Beijing Normal University 985 project "World Level Education Discipline and Chinese Education"

ISSN 2195-3473 ISSN 2195-349X (electronic)
New Frontiers of Educational Research
ISBN 978-3-662-47829-5 ISBN 978-3-662-47830-1 (eBook)
DOI 10.1007/978-3-662-47830-1

Library of Congress Control Number: 2015946584

Springer Heidelberg New York Dordrecht London

Printed on acid-free paper

Springer-Verlag GmbH Berlin Heidelberg is part of Springer Science+Business Media (www.springer.com)

Acknowledgments

After more than a year of hard work, the consultant team completed their research work and a written series of high-quality survey reports. Looking back on the research and study process, support from various parties ensured the success of the project. Our thanks first go to the Finance Department of the Ministry of Education, International Cooperation Department of the Ministry of Finance, and the Asian Development Bank for their guidance, support, and help. For the setting of research objectives, project management, and project activity coordination, we received guidance and help from many officials and experts. We especially thank the Deputy Director of the Finance Department of the Ministry of Education, Mr. Tian Zuyin; Deputy Director Mr. Hu Yanpin; Division Heads Mr. Zhou Jian, Mr. Li Yongzhi, Mr. Yu Yunfeng, and Mr. Zhao Jianjun; Division Heads of the International Cooperation Department of the Ministry of Finance Ms. Wang Wei and Ms. Wang Guangzhu; and Ms. Amy SP Leung, Mr. Robert Wihtol, Mr. Wu Lan, Mr. Fei Yue, Mr. Eisuke Tajima, and Ms. Mila De Leon of the Asian Development Bank for their support and help.

The success of the project was also dependent on guidance from Professor Mun C. Tsang from the Teachers College of Columbia University, USA and Professor Rosalind Levačić from the Institute of Education of London University, UK, who provided great help in research design, tool development, and other related international experiences, guaranteeing that the research project finished smoothly with an international perspective. Thus, we would like to express our heartfelt thanks to these two international experts.

We also thank the Departments of Education from four sampled provinces for their support. Our thanks go to the Deputy Director of the Department of Education of Heilongjiang, Yin Xiaolan, and the Deputy Division Head Zhang Runlin; Division Head Pan Weichuan and Mr. Lin Tao from the Department of Education of Zhejiang; Division Head Hu Xing, Division Head Zuo Fei, Mr. Wan Lifei, and Mr. Zhu Aiguo from the Department of Education of Hubei; Mr. Wang Wenxiang and Mr. Wen Yihai from the Hubei Institute of Educational Science; Division Head Liang Jiabin, Deputy Division Head Nong Hankang, and Mr. Wei Haitao from the

Department of Education of Guangxi Zhuang Autonomous Region. From the very beginning of the project, all of these provinces provided detailed reports on the implementation of new mechanisms and put forward many constructive suggestions on revisions for the project team in terms of research design. In the actual process of investigation and research, these provinces also made great efforts in collaboration and arrangements. Our project would not have been completed without the support from the Departments of Education of these provinces and support from investigated counties and schools.

As the leader of the consultant team, I also thank my colleagues who participated in research design, all research activities, data analysis, and report drafting. In the process of our research, we tackled difficulties with a unified effort—not only finishing the research work but also forging profound friendships. Thanks to all of you for your cooperation and professional dedication.

My thanks also go to the graduates from the College of Education Administration of Beijing Normal University, whose enthusiasm and energy also contributed to the innovation of the project research.

My special thanks go to two graduates of mine, Li Tingting and Wang Shaoyi. As administrative assistants on the project, their responsible, careful, and meticulous service and highly efficient organization ensured the smooth progress of project activities. Thank you for your great support.

Finally, I sincerely hope that our research will benefit improvements of the long-term fund guarantee mechanism for rural compulsory education. I should also apologize to the families of my colleagues and their assistants, who sacrificed their summer holiday and Spring Festival holiday for data analysis and project work to ensure that out project finished on time. Thanks also to the families for their support.

May 2008 Yuhong Du

Contents

List of Figures

List of Tables

Executive Summary

The Reforms in Compulsory Education Financing Project was technically assisted by the Asian Development Bank (ADB) to help China's Ministry of Education improve the Fund Guarantee Mechanism (FGM) for compulsory education over the long term.

The project was executed by the Financial Department of the Ministry of Education, with the College of Educational Administration of Beijing Normal University serving as a consultant. The domestic experts included Yuhong Du, Guoliang Chen, Zhijun Sun, Zhenzhu Zhang, and Zeyun Liu. The program has invited Professor Mun C. Tsang from the Teachers College of University of Columbia and Professor Rosalind Levačić from the Institute of Education of London University to serve as international consultants. Professor Yuhong Du was the team leader.

The project started in March 2007 and ended in June 2008. Due to time limitations, the consultant team selected only four imperative problems in the implementation of FGM instead of studying the details of all aspects of rural compulsory education financing. The four problems focused on approaches to the appropriation standard of non-personnel expenditures for primary and junior secondary schools in compulsory education, student assistance policies in compulsory education, the equity in compulsory education finance, and the monitoring and evaluation of FGM for compulsory education.

Since 2005, the Chinese government has fully implemented FGM for rural compulsory education, which is a milestone achievement in the development of Chinese rural compulsory education. China has achieved the goal of having rural compulsory education funded by the government. According to the renewed Law of Compulsory Education, FGM for compulsory education mainly includes the following six aspects:

1. Guaranteed mechanism for teacher salary
2. Guaranteed mechanism for non-personnel expenditures
3. Guaranteed mechanism for construction and renovation
4. Guaranteed mechanism for student assistance

5. Division of responsibilities of governments at various levels
6. Improvement of school budget management

However, implementing and developing this new system will still take quite some time.

This report is the culmination of a 1.5-year study by the College of Education Administration, with an aim to determine effective strategies to perfect FGM. The report is comprised of six chapters. Chapter 1 reviews the transformation of the compulsory education finance system and policy in China and summarizes the challenges facing the compulsory education finance in China. Chapter 2 is an attempt to clarify the approaches used to calculate non-personnel expenditures. Chapter 3 analyzes the student assistance policy and estimates the living costs for low-income boarding students. Chapter 4 calculates several indicators on education equity, evaluating the effectiveness of equity policy. Chapter 5 presents a framework that was designed to monitor and evaluate FGM and discusses a way to establish a monitoring and evaluation system for education policy in theory. Chapter 6 presents international experiences on compulsory education finance, particularly the non-personnel expenditure and equity issues. Professor Levačić provided an international experience on non-personnel expenditure in compulsory education and Professor Mun Tsang provided advice and shared international experience on education equity.

Chapter 1: Finance System and Policy Review of Chinese Rural Compulsory Education

The finance system for compulsory education experienced three phases: decentralized financing and decentralized management, the county-centered system, and the fund guarantee mechanism. The implementation of FGM is a milestone achievement for rural compulsory education financing, but FGM still needs long-term efforts to perfect such a new system.

In the 1980s, the central government established a decentralized fiscal system, based on which a decentralized administration and finance system for compulsory education was shaped. According to the decentralized compulsory education system, rural compulsory education was funded by the county government, township government, and farmers. However, after 1994, tax-sharing reform resulted in a contradiction between the decentralized education finance system and the centralized fiscal system, causing financial difficulty for rural compulsory education, including teacher salary delays and dilapidated school buildings.

To eliminate the centralized fiscal system's negative effects on rural compulsory education, the central government provided some assistance projects for rural compulsory education, especially for rural compulsory education in poverty-stricken regions. However, it was not until 2005 that the central government started to implement FGM to resolve the financial difficulties faced by rural compulsory education via institutional reform.

Although China has made huge achievements in universalizing compulsory education, the development of compulsory education still faces many challenges after FGM, including the inadequacy of total expenditures for rural compulsory education, low standards for non-personnel expenditures, a lack of funding for teacher training, low standard of living subsidies for low-income boarding students, a disparity of resource allocation between urban and rural areas, financial disparities among regions, a lack of a long-term guarantee mechanism for physical facilities of rural compulsory education, and the crowding-out effect of multilevel governments.

Chapter 2: Study on Non-personnel Expenditure Standards

Rural compulsory education lacks teaching and learning resources and cannot provide adequate curricula for students. The main reason is that the government does not provide adequate non-personnel expenditures for rural compulsory education. Non-personnel expenditures for compulsory education include expenditures for regular operation, teaching activities, equipment, and logistic services.

Adequate non-personnel expenditures are an important guarantee for school to improve education quality. Since FGM, the non-personnel expenditures for schools have been guaranteed and improved remarkably. However, these expenditures are still not enough for schools to provide quality education.

China has achieved a goal to popularize nine-year compulsory education but currently cannot provide quality compulsory education for all. To provide quality compulsory education for all, the government must allocate adequate funds, especially non-personnel expenditures, into rural compulsory education. It is also urgent for governments to issue non-personnel expenditure standards so as to implement FGM effectively. However, in China, there is little research on the estimation of non-personnel expenditure standards. Our study developed an item-specific integration approach (ISIA) and explored the standards of non-personnel expenditures by a cost-function approach.

Item-specific Integration Approach

In this report, the item-specific integration approach (ISIA) was designed to estimate non-personnel expenditure standards. ISIA is used to calculate the standard for each item of non-personnel expenditure, based on the standards of school operation issued by the government. Considering the school differences, adjustment coefficients were calculated. These coefficients give full consideration to the school scale, class size, school type (boarding school or not), geography, climate, and local price, among others.

The expenditures for equipment, special materials, and books are calculated in accordance with the standards of school operation issued by the Ministry of Education. The expenditures for training, labor union, and welfare are calculated according to the required proportion in expenditures ruled by policies. The expenditures for the stable materials consumed by schools are calculated according to 92's Ration. Other expenditures are calculated according to professional judgment and the successful school approach.

Non-personnel expenditure standards for a prototype school were estimated in this study. It was assumed that the scale is eight classes and 300 students for primary schools, with 12 classes and 540 students for junior secondary schools. The standard for rural primary schools is 345 Yuan per student per year, which is 9.8 % higher than the national average in 2006; the standard for rural junior secondary schools is 495 Yuan, which is 3.5 % higher than the national average in 2006. When non-personnel expenditure standards are calculated for each school, the standard must be multiplied by the adjustment coefficients.

What needs to be emphasized here is that the minimum standard was calculated using the 2006 price index. Education production is quite flexible. The demand for school non-personnel expenditures is much larger than the minimum standard. In reality, the study shows that non-personnel expenditure in half of the provinces is already higher than our minimum standard. This is because not enough attention was paid to the cost differences across regions due to varying levels of economic development. Another key issue here is the changing mechanism of non-personnel expenditures. The changing mechanism needs to consider the price fluctuation and government requirement for education quality.

Cost Function Approach

The study also estimated the non-personnel expenditure per primary school student by the cost function approach. The cost function approach means that the demands for educational funds are not only influenced by the features of students and schools but also by expected student achievement.

In the cost function equation, the dependent variable is the per-student non-personnel expenditure; independent variables are the students' achievements, students' features, and school's features. In this equation, using students' achievements as the independent variable, it can be technically possible to determine the non-personnel expenditure standard considering the education quality. Students' features and school features help us to estimate the non-personnel expenditures for different schools by controlling these factors.

Student achievements are based on standardized math and Chinese subject test scores. Students' features include the amount of students and the proportion of boarders. The school's features include the per student school building area, per student books, ratio of students to teachers, well water or tap water, heating or not, and teacher's salary index.

The data used in the cost function model are the actual non-personnel expenditures of a sample school; however, these expenditures are not enough for schools to operate well and provide quality education. Therefore, the non-personnel expenditure standards estimated by the study are lower than the actual need.

Chapter 3: Study on Student Assistance Policies in Compulsory Education

The financial burden of a family has been a major obstacle preventing children's access to compulsory education. To remove this obstacle, the government started to construct a student assistance system in 1986. In 2001, the central government implemented "Two Exemptions and One Subsidy" (TEOS) in western poverty areas, which symbolized that a perfect student assistance system had been formed in compulsory education. TEOS refers to exempting from textbook fees and miscellaneous fees, as well as providing living subsidy for low-income boarding students.

From 2001 to 2007, the beneficiaries of the two exemptions expanded from low-income students in poverty areas to all students in rural areas. In addition, the one subsidy now benefits poor boarding students in all rural areas, not just in poverty-stricken areas. TEOS has had several effects: a large number of student dropouts returned to school, students transferred from private/urban schools to public/rural schools, and the financial burden of rural families was truly reduced. To some extent, we can say that financial burden is no longer an important obstacle to school access.

Findings

Since autumn of 2007, Two Exemptions have been available to all rural students, and the standard for the One Subsidy has increased to 2 Yuan per day for pupils and 3 Yuan for junior secondary school students. However, we found that TEOS still faces some challenges, as follows:

1. There are some differences among miscellaneous fee exemption standards, which leads to new inequities.
2. The free textbook policy only covers textbooks for the national curriculum. Local curriculum textbooks and ancillary materials still need to be purchased by the students' families.
3. The allocation of the free textbook fund has some problems at each level of government. Some provinces with a high percentage of poor students get a low percentage of the free textbook fund, while the coverage of free textbooks is higher in provinces with less indigent students. In some counties, free textbook support does not favor poor families because the method to select the students is not clear and objective.
4. Both the coverage and standard of the subsidy are very low. For example, in Rong'an within Guangxi, the subsidy standard is 150 Yuan per student per year—much lower than the real need.
5. The subsidy does not benefit non-boarding indigent students. These poor students also are faced by living cost burdens, which may lead to them drop out of school.
6. The method to select students for the subsidy is not perfect and needs to be improved urgently. After this policy extends its coverage gradually, if the method is not perfect, One Subsidy will deviate from its targeted groups.

7. The number of students in the appropriation formula for Two Exemptions is the statistical number from a previous year, so fiscal appropriation do not meet the real demand.
8. TEOS does not cover private school students and children of migrant farmers.

The government should perfect several aspects of TEOS before Two Exemptions are provided for all students. First, TEOS should use a scientific method to select targeted students. In addition, TEOS should benefits all targeted rural students, especially those in private schools and urban schools, via an education voucher. The government also should issue uniform non-personnel expenditures instead of miscellaneous fees. Finally, the government should not only provide national textbooks but also local textbooks and learning materials.

Estimating Living Cost for Poor Boarding Students

The most urgent issue the government is facing in the implementation of TEOS is to improve the standard of One Subsidy. Originally, the standard of One Subsidy was just 1 Yuan per day or even less than 1 Yuan, which is too low to meet poor boarding students' need for living expenditure. For the government to supply poor boarding students with adequate living subsidies, we estimated the boarding student's living cost, which includes expenditures on meals, transportation, and accommodation. The study used sample students' data and Rong'an family data to calculate living costs. Based on the sample students' data, the average living cost is 150 Yuan per month for primary school students and 232 Yuan per month for junior secondary school students. According to family data, our estimates were 123 Yuan and 185 Yuan per month on average, respectively.

Although the standard of One Subsidy has increased to 2 Yuan per day for pupils and 3 Yuan for junior secondary school students since autumn of 2007, it is still much lower than the real need for living expenditures.

Chapter 4: Study of Equity in Compulsory Education Finance

Equity is a basic criterion to distribute educational resources and evaluate the effect of education policies. Education equity also should be the ultimate goal of the government. However, in reality, the inequity problem becomes more and more severe. From 1994 to 2000, financial disparities in compulsory education gradually expanded (Yuhong Du 2000; Mun C. Tsang and Ding Yanqing 2005; Wang Rong 2005 and etc.).

The financial disparities in compulsory education between rural and urban areas and among regions become one aspect to which the government, public, and scholars paid increasing attention. Since rural Tax-fee Reform in 2000, and especially FGM in 2005, the central government has made great efforts to reduce financial disparities in compulsory education. Rural compulsory education has been the top priority in government education investments. The central government enhanced financial transfer payments to the central and western regions.

In addition to the trends in disparity, we are also concerned with the equalization effects of education policies. It is not a problem that the rural area and the central and western region get more support from the central government, but the exact equalization effect of these policies is unknown. Our report tries to evaluate the equalization effect of these policies, examining educational equity from three dimensions: horizontal equity, fiscal neutrality, and vertical equity.

Findings

The inequity is expanding in some provinces: It was also found that financial disparities have been increasing in Guangxi and Hubei in the past 6 years. The disparities in Heilongjiang and Zhejiang showed wavy trends, which alternately reduced and increased. Although the central government and local governments have increased fund inputs into compulsory education, especially rural compulsory education, to enhance horizontal equity, the real effect of those increased fund inputs just slowed the pace of horizontal inequity expansion. The education resources for compulsory education are still not enough and the distribution of education resources lacks a horizontal equity mechanism.

The horizontal inequity of different education resources has different reasons: Intra-county inequity and inter-county inequity have shown different trends. It is difficult to put forward a unified policy suggestion to reduce horizontal inequity for each education resource in different regions. Horizontal inequity could be better reduced according to the real situations in different regions.

A local government's preference has important influence on education equity: In some provinces, the horizontal inequity of junior secondary education is much lower than primary education. However, in other provinces, the horizontal inequity of junior secondary education is much higher than primary education. From this perspective, the government's preference is very important in education resource allocation decision-making.

Inequity also occurs in terms of fiscal neutrality: The study also found that the Gini coefficient for per student education expenditure within the county increases when the per student expenditure increases. Therefore, economic development cannot solve the inequity issue. The government should pay more attention to the equity aspects when increasing the per student education expenditure. We also found that the per student education expenditure across counties is highly related to economic development. Therefore, the higher-level government should take more responsibility if we want to reduce the disparity across the counties.

To achieve fiscal neutrality, the central government and provincial governments should construct a reasonable transfer payment mechanism to reduce financial disparities across counties, even across provinces. Also, local governments, especially county governments, must change its current funding delivery mechanism for compulsory education.

A large difference still exists between rural and urban areas: For primary education in Zhejing and Heilongjiang and junior secondary education in Guangxi and Zhejiang, a large difference still exists between rural and urban areas in per student education revenue, per student fiscal appropriation, per student regular expenditure, and per student non-personnel expenditure in some provinces. However, the same differences narrowed for primary education in Guangxi and Hubei and junior secondary education in Heilongjiang and Hubei. At the same time, the difference for per student capital equipment value was the largest. In all, there is still a long way to go to reduce the difference between rural and urban areas.

There are five approaches to reduce the disparities in compulsory education: balancing the delivery of fiscal appropriation, standardizing the education input to reduce horizontal disparities, designing equity-oriented transfer payments to reduce inter-county inequity, improving intra-county equity, and providing more education input for rural compulsory education.

Chapter 5: Monitoring and Evaluation System for Rural Compulsory Education Financing

Monitoring and evaluation (M&E) is the key to successful implementation of a policy. The FGM is no exception. When central and provincial governments put huge amounts of money into rural compulsory education, whether the money is used well in practice and has the expected impact highly depends on the M&E system. Although there can be some inspection arrangements from the upper-level government, the inspection can only deal with case issues. The inspection cannot provide systematic, objective, and robust data for the overall situation or a detailed assessment for the implementation and effect of the policy. An M&E system can provide full information about the policy implementation and the policy effect. Based on the full information, stakeholders can get enough information for the policy adjustment and the policy evaluation. Our study aims at set up a framework for the FGM in order to monitor the implementation and evaluate the relevance, effectiveness, and efficiency of the FGM. Focusing on this issue, we designed an M&E framework for the FGM.

The Framework of the Monitoring System

The FGM mainly includes following six aspects: a guarantee mechanism for teacher salary, a guarantee mechanism for non-personnel expenditures, a guarantee mechanism for construction and renovation, a guarantee mechanism for student assistance, the division of responsibilities of governments at various levels, and improvement of school budget management.

According to the contents and objectives of the FGM, the study suggests a monitoring system framework for a guarantee mechanism for teacher salary, a guarantee mechanism for non-personnel expenditures, a guarantee mechanism for construction, a guarantee mechanism for student assistance, and division of the government's responsibility on various levels. The framework of the monitoring system consists of principles, monitoring bodies, monitoring contents, and monitoring indicators. The principles are legality, publicity, and scientificity. Monitoring bodies include educational administrative departments, legislative institutes, and other stakeholders.

The aspects being monitored include the TEOS implementation data, non-personnel expenditures, repair and maintenance of school buildings, and teachers' salaries. According to the objectives of the FGM, we designed monitoring indicators for those four aspects.

The Framework of the Evaluation System

To improve the quality of rural compulsory education, the central government has directed much more funding into rural education since the beginning of the twenty-firstst century, especially since the FGM in 2005. Although the funding from the central government is increasing year by year, the amount of funding for rural compulsory education does not increase significantly.

The main reason for this phenomenon is a crowding-out effect: after the central government increases fund inputs for rural compulsory education, local governments reduce their fund inputs. To find out whether the crowding-out effect exists, we designed static indicators, dynamic indicators, absolute indicators, and relative indicators to evaluate provincial and county government funding. However, we cannot use these indicators to evaluate the local government's effort of funding compulsory education because it is very difficult to collect accurate data.

School Budget

School budget is an important part of the FGM. Whether education resources can be used effectively is decided by school management. That is why the school budget received more attention after the government increased funding of compulsory education. Therefore, our M&E framework tries to examine the budget process and the budget methods of schools. Based on the data from the implementation of school budgets, we evaluated the function of school budgets to see whether the school budget in practice can play the role that the government expected.

Field surveys on school budgets found that budget planning does not yet reflect the real and reasonable need for funds. Worst of all, the majority of schools and education bureaus at the county level have not realized the significance of budget compilation for improving administration and increasing financial efficiency.

Chapter 6: International Experiences

Mun C. Tsang and Rosalind Levačić served as international consultants for this study. They provided international experiences on the reduction of financial disparities in basic education and on approaches to calculate non-personnel expenditure standards.

International Experience with Non-personnel Expenditures

Professor Levačić outlines her experience with non-personnel expenditure standards in the report. The report starts by setting out international classifications of education expenditures, thereby identifying what constitutes non-personnel expenditures. It then outlines key indicators on non-personnel expenditures in relation to other education expenditures. As non-personnel expenditures finance the acquisition by schools of learning and other physical resources, the measurement of these is considered next, focusing on surveys. The next section of the report summarizes evidence on the importance of non-staff resources for achieving educational outcomes in middle- and low-income countries. This shows that the provision of learning and other physical resources generally matters for students' educational attainment. The next section considers international practices in the allocation of non-personnel expenditures for compulsory education, focusing on experience with specifying benchmark standards for adequacy. Then, the report provides a short discussion of general principles or criteria for designing formulas for the allocation of funding for school resources. The report concludes with recommendations for the project drawn from international experience.

International Experience on the Reduction of Financial Disparities

Professor Tsang, the consultant on education equity, presented experiences in reducing financial disparities in primary and secondary education. There was a clear overall and significant reduction in inequality in per-student expenditures in primary and secondary education in Australia, Brazil, Spain, the United Kingdom, and the United States. Inequality increased in Germany but was rather stable in Japan. He also introduced changes in the financing of primary and secondary education by governments at different levels. Although those countries have different share structures for financing primary and junior secondary education and have centralization/decentralization of government funding, they have achieved significant reductions in financial disparities. There is a mixed relationship between the reduction in financial disparities and the share structure or centralization/decentralization of government funding.

Chapter 1
Finance System and Policy Review of Chinese Rural Compulsory Education

More than thirty years after reform, China has made remarkable achievements in economic and social development. China's gross domestic product (GDP) increased from 364.52 billion Yuan in 1978 to 24.6619 trillion Yuan in 2007. Per capita GDP increased from 381 Yuan in 1978 to 18,665 Yuan in 2007, with an average annual growth of more than 9 %. Fiscal revenue increased from 113.226 billion Yuan in 1978 to 5.13 trillion Yuan in 2007. This pace of development has been called China's "Miracle." With the rapid economic growth, China has also made remarkable progress in education, especially compulsory education. The popularization rate has been increasing year by year and facilities have been gradually improved.

However, despite the fast economic development that occurred for 30 consecutive years, China is still a developing country with a weak economic base. The status quo of a dual society has not changed, and the gaps both between urban and rural areas and among regions are still wide. According to statistics, China's total rural population accounted for 56 % of the total population in 2007. Therefore, the development of farmers, rural areas, and agriculture is key to China's economic and social development. For this purpose, the Fifth Plenary Session of the 16th Party Congress of Communist Party of China (CPC) in 2005 clearly put forward the strategy of "building a new socialist countryside." Governments at all levels should intensify inputs in agriculture and rural areas, expand public finance coverage in rural areas, strengthen public services of the government in rural areas, and establish a permanent mechanism of industry to promote agriculture, with urban areas assisting rural areas.

As an important part of rural development and a main approach to improve the quality of the farmers, the development of rural education has become a key point of building a new socialist countryside. Popularization of high-quality nine-year compulsory education at a high level has become the top priority. How the educational finance system guarantees the healthy development of rural compulsory education is the core focus of this research. This chapter reviews the development of Chinese compulsory education and its finance, outlines the features of educational finance in the major phases of compulsory education development, briefly reviews the major projects carried out in recent years in compulsory education, and finally analyzes current problems in the finance system of rural compulsory education.

Y. Du and Z. Sun, *Research on Compulsory Education Financing in China*,
New Frontiers of Educational Research, DOI 10.1007/978-3-662-47830-1_1

1.1 Development of Compulsory Education in China

1.1.1 Development of Compulsory Education

By the end of the twentieth century, China finished the historic task of achieving popularization of nine-year compulsory education and basically eliminating illiteracy among young and middle-aged people (called "Two Basics" for short). The national per capita years of schooling has reached 8 years, exceeding the worldwide average. By 2006, the number of counties that have realized Two Basics reached 2973, an increase from 2573 in 2001, accounting for 96 % of counties in China. The population coverage of Two Basics reached 98 %. From 2001 to 2006, 11.363 million young and middle-aged illiterates have been removed from the illiteracy and the illiteracy of young and middle-aged people has decreased to 3.58 %.

In 2006, there were a total of 341,600 primary schools in China, with a total admission of 17.2936 million and a major increase in rural areas. The total number of enrollments for primary school was 107.1153 million. The net enrollment ratio of primary school-age children has reached 99.27 %, (99.25 % of boys and 99.29 % of girls). The number of primary school graduates reached 19.2848 million.

Also in 2006, there were 60,885 junior secondary schools (including 335 vocational schools) in total, with admission of 19,295,600 students, enrollment of 59,579,500 students, and 20,715,800 graduates. The gross enrollment ratio for junior secondary education was 97 %, up 2 % from the previous year. The promotion rate of junior secondary school graduates was 75.7 %, up 6 % from the previous year.

Efforts have been made in a variety of forms in rural and poor areas to eradicate illiteracy as an important measure against poverty, especially in groups of young and middle-aged adults, women, and people of minority ethnicities. From 1994 to 2009, 94 million people in China have become literate, which is a great contribution to the decrease of illiteracy worldwide.

With regard to faculty, the ratio of qualified full-time teachers in primary and junior secondary schools has been increasing. In 2006, there were 6.12 million teaching staff in primary schools in China, among which 5.5876 million were full-time teachers. Full-time teachers acquiring qualification certifications in primary schools accounted for 96.34 % of full-time teachers, up by 1.12 % from the previous year. The guarantee mechanism for teachers' salaries in rural primary and junior secondary schools has improved, which played an important role in keeping teaching staff.

Concerning the facilities, in 2003 the government began to allocate new educational financing into rural areas. As a result, school buildings and other physical facilities of primary and junior secondary schools have been obviously improved. Distance education and information technology have been introduced into rural schools, making it possible for students of rural areas and remote areas to enjoy more and better educational resources.

In 2006, the floor area per primary school student in China was 5.47 m^2, up by 0.94 m^2 since the 4.53 m^2 of 2001. In 2006, the floor area of teaching buildings per primary school student in rural China was 5.51 m^2, up by 1.02 m^2 since the 4.49 m^2 of 2001. In 2006, the floor area of teaching buildings per junior secondary school student in China was 6.40 m^2, up by 1.71 m^2 since the 4.69 m^2 of 2001. In 2006, the floor area of teaching buildings per junior secondary school student in rural China was 6.40 m^2, up by 1.72 m^2 since the 4.68 m^2 of 2001.

In 2006, a total of 53.49 % of primary schools had stadiums (gymnasiums), 47.44 % had qualified sports facilities, 42.43 % had qualified numbers of musical instruments, 47.74 % had qualified art facilities and 52.75 % had qualified mathematics and nature experiment equipment. In 2006, a total of 67.76 % of junior secondary schools had stadiums (gymnasiums), 64.74 % had a qualified number of sports facilities, 56.99 % had a qualified number of musical instruments, 55.59 % had art facilities, and 72.73 % had scientific and laboratory equipment. All indicators improved over the previous year.

1.1.2 *Increase in Expenditure for Compulsory Education*

With continuous economic development and an increase in the ratio of fiscal revenue in GDP, governments have made more efforts in financing education. The total expenditure in compulsory education in 1993 was 59.3 billion Yuan, which increased to 400 billion Yuan in 2006—a 5.75-fold increase. The total expenditures for rural compulsory education increased from 35.1 billion Yuan in 1993 to 217.7 billion Yuan in 2006—a 5.21-fold increase (see Fig. 1.1). Fiscal appropriation for compulsory education increased 8.12-fold from 33.4 billion Yuan in 1993 to 304.3 billion Yuan in 2006, of which the fiscal appropriation for rural compulsory education increased 8.24-fold from 20.4 billion Yuan in 1993 to 188.1 billion Yuan in 2006 (see Fig. 1.2). The growth in fiscal appropriation for compulsory education,

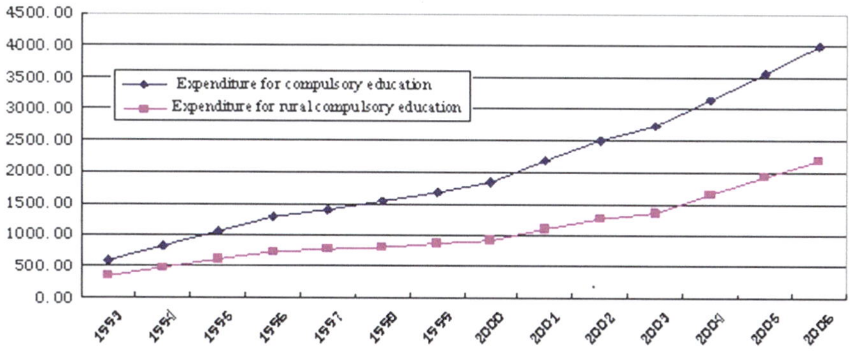

Fig. 1.1 China compulsory education expenditures in total and in rural areas, 1993–2006 (Yuan, in 100 million)

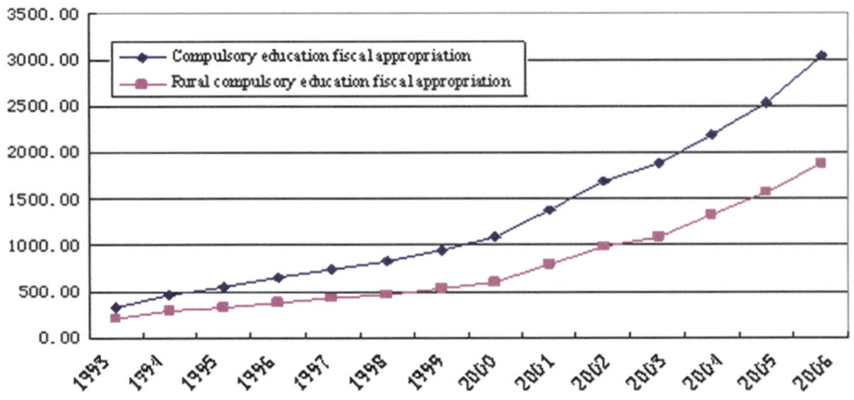

Fig. 1.2 China compulsory education fiscal appropriation in total and in rural areas, 1993–2006 (Yuan, in 100 million)

especially for rural compulsory education, has exceeded the growth of total revenue. The growth of total fiscal appropriation enabled the proportion of fiscal appropriation to total revenue of compulsory education to increase year by year, from 56 % in 1993 to 76 % in 2006; the proportion of fiscal appropriation for rural compulsory education in total revenue increased from 58 % in 1993 to 86 % in 2006 (see Fig. 1.3). These data show that efforts made by governments for compulsory education, particularly for rural compulsory education, have been greater each year.

Along with steady growth in the total expenditures, meanwhile, expenditures per student and fiscal appropriation per student in compulsory education were also increasing annually (see Figs. 1.4, 1.5, 1.6, and 1.7). The expenditures per junior secondary school student increased from 552 Yuan in 1993 to 2669 Yuan in 2006—a 3.83-fold increase. The expenditure per rural junior secondary school student rose

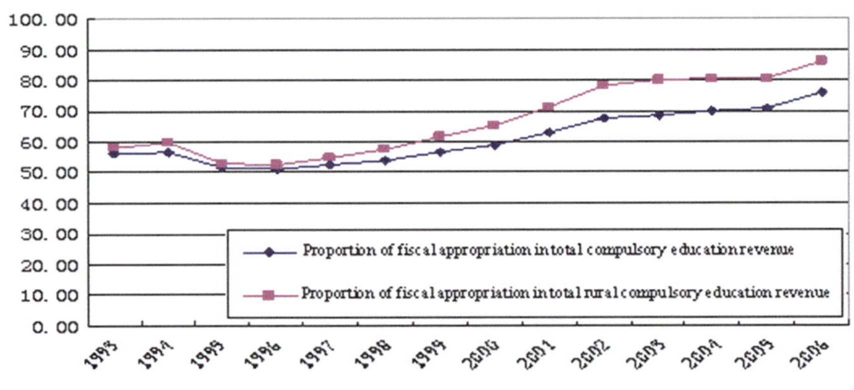

Fig. 1.3 Proportion of compulsory education fiscal appropriation in total compulsory education revenue in China, 1993–2006 (%)

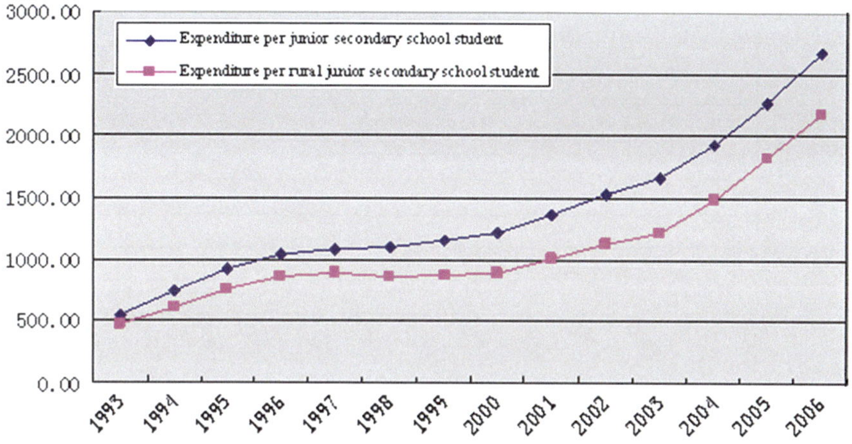

Fig. 1.4 Change in expenditure per student in junior secondary school in China, 1993–2006 (Yuan)

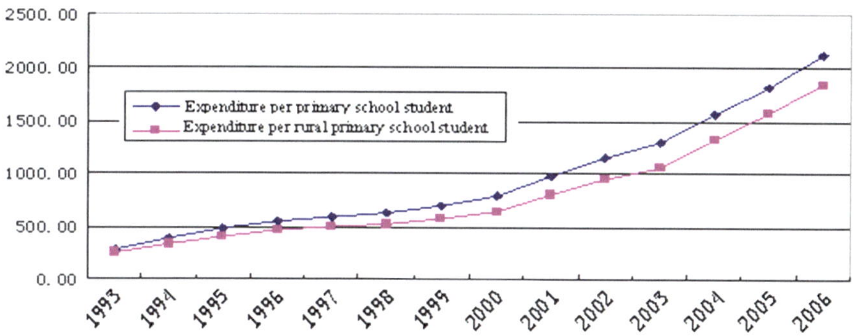

Fig. 1.5 Change in expenditure per student in primary school in China, 1993–2006 (Yuan)

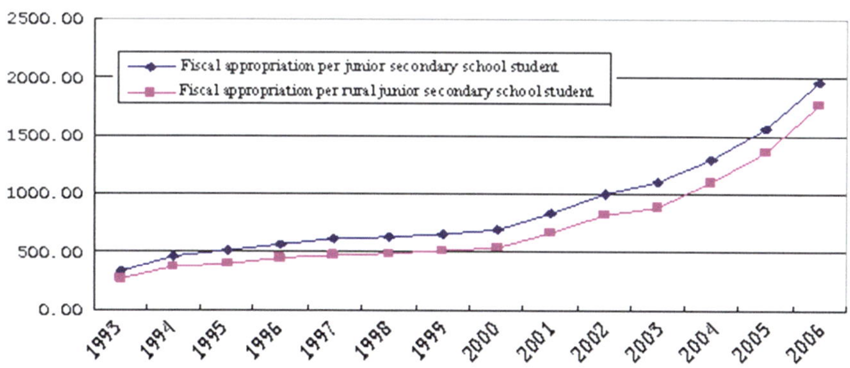

Fig. 1.6 Change in fiscal appropriation per student in junior secondary school in China, 1993–2006 (Yuan)

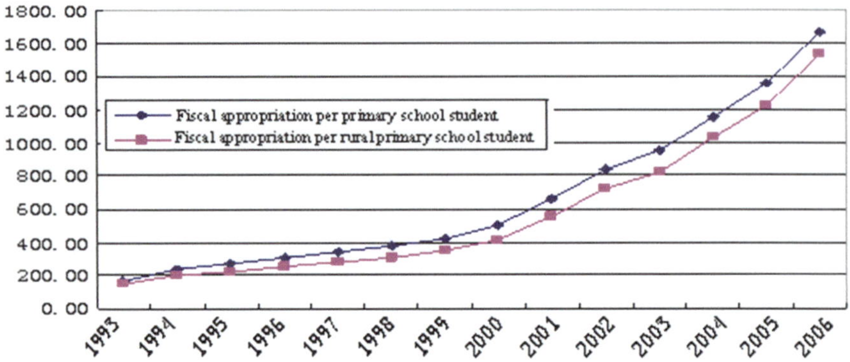

Fig. 1.7 Change in fiscal appropriation per student in primary school in China, 1993–2006 (Yuan)

from 473 Yuan in 1993 to 2190 Yuan in 2006—a 3.6-fold increase. The expenditure per primary school student increased from 278 Yuan in 1993 to 2122 Yuan in 2006—a 6.63-fold increase. The expenditure per rural primary school student rose from 250 Yuan in 1993 to 1847 Yuan in 2006—a 6.38-fold increase. The fiscal appropriation per junior secondary school student increased from 332 Yuan in 1993 to 1963 Yuan in 2006—a 4.9-fold increase. The fiscal appropriation per rural junior secondary school student rose from 275 Yuan in 1993 to 1764 Yuan in 2006—a 5.42-fold increase. The fiscal appropriation per primary school student increased from 168 Yuan in 1993 to 1672 Yuan in 2006—a 8.85-fold increase. The fiscal appropriation per rural primary school student rose from 147 Yuan in 1993 to 1531 Yuan in 2006—a 9.4-fold increase.

These statistics demonstrate that expenditures on Chinese compulsory education, especially rural compulsory education, have been growing rapidly. Meanwhile, the proportion of fiscal appropriation in total inputs has also been on the rise, representing a change from "people's education financed by people" to "people's education financed by government".[1]

1.2 Transformation in Compulsory Education Financing System in China

A focus in rural development has been the popularization of nine-year compulsory education at a high quality and high level. To ensure the continuous development of rural compulsory education, a long-term effective and stable expenditure guarantee

[1]People's Education Financed by People refers to 50 % of rural compulsory education expenditures from the government and another 50 % from non-government before 2001. People's Education Financed by Government refers to expenditures in rural compulsory education, which have been nearly 90 % from the government after 2001.

mechanism should be established. In China, since the Reform and Opening Up policy, reforms in the fiscal system have been deepened gradually. The compulsory education finance system was also reformed after fiscal system reforms. The responsibility of investment for compulsory education at all levels of government has been more clearly stated. Also, compulsory education has been incorporated into the scope of the public fiscal guarantee. Reforms in the Chinese compulsory education finance system have undergone mainly four phases, as described in the following sections.

1.2.1 Decentralized Financing and Decentralized Management

In the initial phase of Chinese economic system reforms, in order to mobilize the initiative of local governments, a transitional system reform of fiscal all-round responsibility was started in the early 1980s under the idea of decentralizing power and granting interests. In February 1980, the State Council decided to carry out the fiscal management system by compartmentalizing the scope of revenues and expenditures and responsibility contracts at various levels. It divided income into fixed income, fixed share cropping of income, and equalized income by categorizing and share cropping. The fiscal expenditure was mainly divided according to the affiliate relations of enterprises and institutions; local fiscal expenditure is limited to the designated scope based on their revenue and localities were responsible for fiscal balance.

In 1983 and 1985, the governments carried out a two-step profit-tax reform, and state-owned enterprises began to pay tax instead of submitting profits. Meanwhile, some new types of taxes were also launched to further improve the tax system. Since 1985, adjustments have also been made in the fiscal system, compartmentalizing categories of taxes, designating scope of revenues and expenditures, and adding responsibility contracts at various levels. In 1987, a contract managerial responsibility system was carried out in China; the fiscal system did not match this system in some aspects. In 1988, fiscal contract system reform was carried out, which made local governments independent interest bodies and formed the decentralized fiscal system.

To match the decentralized fiscal system, the basic education finance system began to carry out decentralized financing and decentralized management reform. In 1985, the Decision on the Reform of the Education System by the Central Committee of the Communist Party of China set forth the principles of decentralized financing and decentralized management. The Compulsory Education Law of the People's Republic of China was promulgated in 1986, which set forth that under the leadership of the State Council, local authorities shall assume responsibility for compulsory education. In particular, county governments, township governments, and even villages assume the responsibility of financing rural compulsory education. County governments and township governments assume managerial responsibility. The State Council and the local governments at various levels are responsible for increasing the recurrent expenditures and capital expenditures needed for the implementation of compulsory education, and the expenditures must be fully guaranteed. Therefore, managerial responsibilities and authorities of governments at all levels for compulsory education were specified more clearly and local governments were mainly responsible for raising expenditures for compulsory education. Rural compulsory education basically formed the model for financing schools at three levels of county, township, and village and administered education at county and township levels. Fiscal educational expenditures were mainly borne by county and township fiscal revenue. Under the compulsory education management system, the local authorities assume responsibility for compulsory education, which is administered at different levels; county and township governments played a key role in guaranteeing expenditure inputs in compulsory education.

Raising school revenue through multiple channels has been another feature of educational finance reform since the 1980s. In multiple channels, government input is still the main source of compulsory education expenditure; the non-government source is supplementary to government input. The major channels of nongovernment resources included educational surcharges (the Notice on Raising Expenditure to Finance Rural Schools in 1984, the Provisional Regulations on Collection of Educational Surcharge in 1986), expenditures collected from farmers, encouraging schools to create income, and mobilizing social expenditures to develop non-governmental education, among others. The Outline of Chinese Education Reform and Development released in 1993 and Law of Education promulgated in 1995 further clarified that the state shall establish a mechanism based mainly on fiscal appropriation and supplemented with various approaches to raising non-government educational expenditures.

To guarantee the increase of education expenditures, these two documents also regulated increase and ratio requirements for fiscal appropriation: the increase of the fiscal appropriation to education should be higher than the growth of the national economy and fiscal revenue, educational expenditures per student should increase yearly, and teachers' salaries and non-personnel expenditure per student should also increase proportionally. The percentage of fiscal appropriation of education in GDP in 2000 was to reach 4 % and the ratio of fiscal expenditure in education should reach 15 % on average in the Eighth-Five Year Period.

1.2.2 The New Problem of the System of Decentralized Financing and Decentralized Management Due to Tax Sharing Reform

To strengthen the macro-control ability of central government, China began to reform the decentralized fiscal system in 1994; this reform is referred to as *tax sharing reform*. The main contents of the tax sharing reform were "three sharing and one return." The first "sharing" refers to specifying the expenditure scopes of the central government and local authorities. The second sharing is to specify the scope of income of the central government and local authorities, concerning the different kinds of taxes. The third sharing is to establish the State Administration of Taxation and Local Taxation Bureau to collect taxes for the central government and local authorities. "One return" refers to establishing tax returns from the central government to local authorities. This reform also considers classifying the responsibility between central and local governments.

The main achievements of the tax sharing reform were the establishment of new relations between state and enterprises, state and individual, and central government and local governments; creation of a unified and fair competition market for the microeconomy; establishment of a tax sharing framework suitable for requirements of a market economy; stabilization of fiscal allocation relations between the central government and local governments; mobilization of the enthusiasm of central and local governments; formation of a stable growth mechanism for fiscal revenue; realization of remarkable growth of fiscal revenue; and enhancement of the macroeconomic control ability of the central government.

The tax sharing system expanded the revenue of the central government, but it did not adjust the central government's expenditure structures. As a result, the fiscal situation of the central government became better and better, while the fiscal ability of local governments, especially the county-level governments in poor regions, was further weakened and unable to take up the responsibility of compulsory education financing to some extent. In the late 1990s, the problem of delayed salaries for teachers in rural areas around China was centralized as a reflection of the contradiction. To achieve the objectives of the two basics in 2000, although the central government strengthened fiscal transfer payments to local governments and implemented many education projects, such as national compulsory education projects in the same period in national poverty stricken regions, the fact that basic educational fiscal revenue in rural areas had been in difficulties remained unchanged.

1.2.3 Rural Tax-Fee Reform and the County-Centered System

Since 1999, China began to carry out rural tax-fee reforms gradually. The main contents included removing various fees that had been levied on farmers, such as township administration fees and expenditures raised for rural education; removing the slaughter tax and some other taxes and burden of farmers; and adjusting the policy of agricultural tax.

The tax-fee reform in rural areas has benefited farmers and effectively improved the income of farmers. However, because this reform removed two important channels of rural education investments—rural educational surcharge and educational expenditure raising—it has made significant impacts on inputs into rural education. Taking 2002 as an example, the rural educational surcharge decreased by 9.8 billion Yuan since 1998 and the rural raising-expenditure has decreased by 3.5 billion Yuan since 1998.

Although central and provincial governments have gradually enhanced transfer payments from the Ninth Five-year Period to alleviate that gap, there are still many problems preventing rural schools from regularly operating that could not be solved by these schools, which leads to difficulties for rural compulsory education. To solve the problems in rural educational expenditure guarantees, the State Council promulgated the Decision on Reform and Development of Basic Education in 2001, proposing the establishment of a county-centered system. The new system has two obvious features compared with the previous system. First, both central and provincial governments should enhance transfer payments towards county-level governments. Second, it clearly states that county-level governments are the major administrator and provider (county-centered) of rural compulsory education. The salaries of teachers will be paid directly by county-level financial departments. The main educational responsibility of a township government is to serve as an assistant to county-level governments. The new system mainly aims to remedy the financial gaps as a result of tax-fee reform and guarantee the timely payment of teachers' salaries.

In 2003, the State Council convened the first national meeting on rural education since the founding of the People's Republic of China, clarifying the strategic position of rural education in national education, making a significant and important decision on increasing educational input, and deciding on new increased expenditures mainly inputted into rural compulsory education. In 2004, the Chinese government initiated a plan to make nine-year compulsory education universal and to eliminate illiteracy among the young and middle-aged in the western region (2004–2007), launching a distance education project in rural primary and junior secondary schools, and implementing a policy to provide free textbooks and subsidies to poor students. In 2004, the Ministry of Education promulgated the Plan for Education Development 2003–2007 and further implemented the compulsory education project nationwide in poverty-stricken regions, as well as a project of renovating dilapidated school buildings in primary and junior secondary schools.

1.2.4 Fund Guarantee Mechanism for Rural Compulsory Education

Since 2005, the financial system reform in China has focused on the alleviation of burdens of farmers. As an important measure to reduce farmers' burdens, the central government issued a series of policies of alleviating the educational burdens of farmers and further established a public financial framework and put forward a new guarantee system for rural compulsory education.

On 24 December 2005, the State Council promulgated the Notice on Reforming the Fund Guarantee Mechanism for Rural Compulsory Education[2] (hereafter called "the notice") to establish a fund guarantee mechanism for rural compulsory education. This fund guarantee mechanism is generally called "item-specific and proportional sharing." Item-specific and proportional sharing refers to dividing education expenditures into some certain parts, such as teachers' salaries, non-personnel expenditures, capital expenditures, and student assistance. In each part, the central government and local government share the expenditures in proportion. The notice clearly put forward that, from 2006, the tuition and fee for students of rural compulsory education in western areas would be exempted. The new Law of Compulsory Education promulgated in 2006 further clarified connotation of the new mechanism. The fund guarantee mechanism of compulsory education should include six key points: teachers' salary guarantee mechanism, non-personnel expenditure guarantee mechanism, school buildings construction and renovation guarantee mechanism, student assistance guarantee mechanism, specified responsibilities of governments at various levels, and school budget systems.

In 2007, according to the implementation plan of the new mechanisms, exemptions from tuition and fees were expanded to central and eastern regions; meanwhile, the policy of providing free textbooks was expanded to cover all rural students and living subsidies were provided for low-income boarding students. In 2008, the non-personnel expenditure standard was further improved, with average non-personnel expenditures reaching 300 Yuan per student per year for rural primary school students and 500 Yuan per student per year for junior secondary school students. In addition, the living subsidy for low-income boarding students were evenly shared by central government and local governments. The expenses for renovating school buildings will also be shared by central and local governments, with an annual input of about 7.5 billion Yuan. According to the current depreciation of school buildings, it will basically meet the demands of renovation of school buildings in rural compulsory education.

The implementation of the fund guarantee mechanism for compulsory education is a milestone in Chinese rural compulsory education development. It clarified the responsibilities of governments at various levels for compulsory education, incorporated expenditures for compulsory education into the scope of financial guarantee, and realized the important transition of people's education financed by governments in rural areas. However, as a new mechanism, it still needs long-term efforts before complete implementation and improvement.

[2]Fund Guarantee Mechanism for Compulsory Education is short for "new mechanism".

1.3 Key Compulsory Education Projects in China

The number of enrolled students in compulsory education in rural areas has reached nearly 150 million. From any point of view, the focus and difficulty of compulsory education should be on rural areas. Meanwhile, rural compulsory education is crucial to overall economic and social development in rural areas. Since 1995, in order to speed up the progress of popularizing nine-year compulsory education in poor areas, the central government and local authorities have input a large of money to carry out some major projects to develop compulsory education, which has achieved better effects.

1.3.1 National Compulsory Education Project in Poverty-Stricken Regions

To help poor regions speed up implementation of compulsory education and promote the progress of local people, the Ministry of Education and Ministry of Finance jointly carried out the first phase of the National Compulsory Education Project in National Poverty Stricken Areas (hereafter referred as the project) from 1995 to 2000.

To implement this project, the central government invested 3.9 billion Yuan and local governments input 8.7 billion Yuan, totaling 12.6 billion Yuan. The first phase of the project covered 852 poverty-stricken counties in 22 provinces, among which 568 counties were national poverty stricken counties set down by the Seven-Year Program to help 80 million people out of poverty.

With governments at various levels having attached great importance and full support from the society, particularly people from poor regions, the first phase of the project was finished completely by the end of 2000 and reached its planned objectives. The major achievements include the following:

1. The process of Two Basics in the central and western regions was accelerated. By the end of the first phase of the project, 428 counties among 852 counties in the project have passed Two Basics.
2. The physical facilities of compulsory education in poor areas have been remarkably improved. By the implementation of the project, 384 new primary and junior secondary schools were established and 28,478 primary and junior secondary schools were renovated and expanded totally. The floor area of primary and junior secondary schools in project counties increased from 13 billion square meters to 18.8 billion square meters, with an increase of 58 million square meters. The rate of dilapidated school buildings decreased from approximately 10 % to less than 3 %. Approximately 6.53 million sets of desks and chairs, more than 100 million volumes of books, and almost 400,000 items of teaching equipment were newly purchased.

3. The teaching level of teachers has been largely improved. In 5 years, the number of trained primary and junior secondary school teachers totaled 466,000 person-times and trained principals totaled 72,200 person-times, improving the qualification rate of primary school teachers to 94 % and of junior secondary school teachers to 87.7 % in project counties. All principals of primary and junior secondary schools are qualified in terms of academic credentials.
4. The distribution of primary and junior secondary schools has been improved. By the implementation of the project, the number of schools in project counties has decreased by 16,700 and the number of students increased by 3.2 million. The average scale of schools has reached 168, with the ratio of students to teachers being 22.7:1. Enrolled students in junior secondary schools have increased by 1.53 million and the average scale the of school has reached 660, with the ratio of students to teachers being 18.2:1.

By the end of 2000, after the first phase of the project, there were still 522 counties in China that had not popularized nine-year compulsory education, covering a total population of approximately 124 million. It is a more arduous task to achieve the objective of popularizing nine-year compulsory education in these poor areas. Therefore, the central committee of CPC and the State Council decided to further carry out the second phase of the project in the period of the Tenth Five-Year Plan. The central government invested 5 billion Yuan and local authorities input 2.36 billion Yuan, totaling 7.36 billion Yuan. The specific transfer payment from the central government would be inclined to western regions, which accounts for more than 90 % of specific transfer payments. The second phase of the project also focused on the renovation and construction of teaching buildings. It also strengthened teacher training and offered new programs, such as the provision of free textbooks and equipment for information technology education.

According to the plan, 10,663 primary and junior secondary schools in the 522 project counties would be newly constructed, renovated, or expanded (4062 newly constructed and 6601 renovated or expanded). Of these, 6928 are primary schools that would be newly constructed, renovated, or expanded (2431 newly constructed, 4497 renovated or expanded) and 3735 are junior secondary schools that would be newly constructed, renovated, or expanded (1631 are newly constructed and 2104 are renovated or expanded). Primary and junior secondary school principals and teachers to be trained would reach 467,000 person-times, with 16,000 sets of equipment, 205 million sets of desks and chairs, and 23 million books and materials purchased. A total of 1.14 million sets of free textbooks were provided to primary and junior secondary school students. Almost 20,000 rural primary and junior secondary schools (14,770 primary schools and 4940 junior secondary schools) were equipped with information technology education and distance education facilities.

1.3.2 Project of Dilapidated School Building Renovation for Primary and Junior Secondary Schools

To speed up the renovation of dilapidated buildings of primary and junior secondary schools, the State Council decided to carry out the Project of Dilapidated School Buildings Renovation for Rural Primary and Junior Secondary Schools around China in 2001. From 2001 to 2002, the first phase of the project was successfully implemented in rural areas, for which both the central government and governments of provinces (autonomous regions and municipalities) allocated special appropriation expenditures of 5.2 billion Yuan. Among the expenditures, 3 billion Yuan was allocated by the central government. A total of 17 million square meters of dilapidated buildings of rural primary and junior secondary schools were renovated. In 2003, the state started the second phase of the project for the rural areas, deciding that the specific transfer payment of 6 billion Yuan would be invested from 2003 to 2005. This would basically eliminate the D level of dilapidated school buildings for rural primary and junior secondary schools throughout the country.

1.3.3 Rural Boarding Schools Project

To achieve the objective of universal nine-year compulsory education and eliminating young and middle-aged illiteracy in western areas by 2007, a guarantee expanding scale of compulsory education counties targeted by Two Basics and removal of the bottlenecks preventing popularization of compulsory education in western rural areas, central, and provincial governments were jointly implemented in the Rural Boarding Schools Project. Namely, it took about 4 years to construct, renovate, and expand a quantity of boarding schools as the mainstays within rural junior secondary education from 2004. Meanwhile, it aimed to speed up the pace of renovating and expanding boarding schools and to make sure all students who needed boarding could study at boarding schools. The special appropriation expenditure of 10 billion Yuan was mainly allocated by the central government. By 2007, of the 410 targeted counties, 317 reached the goals of making nine-year compulsory education generally available and basically eliminating illiteracy among young and middle-aged adults. The proportion of the target groups attaining these two goals in the western region increased from 77 % in 2003 to 96 %.

1.3.4 Two Exemption and One Subsidy Policy

Two Exemption and One Subsidy (TEOS) refers to exempting students from tuition and miscellaneous fees in compulsory education, providing free textbooks for students from families with financial difficulties, and supplying living subsidies for indigent boarding students in poor regions. In 2005, TEOS was first implemented in 592 national key poverty-stricken counties and then expanded to western rural areas and some of rural areas in central China in 2006. Since the spring of 2007, TEOS has covered all rural areas, benefiting 150 million primary and junior secondary school students in rural areas and concretely alleviating the educational burden of farmers. Taking the western region as an example, miscellaneous fees have been reduced by an average of 140 Yuan per year for a family with a primary school student and 180 Yuan per year for a family with a junior secondary school student. Under the free textbook policy, costs have been reduced by an average of 210 Yuan per year for a primary student and 320 Yuan per year for a junior secondary school student.[3] Moreover, the exemption of miscellaneous fees in urban compulsory education has been added to the agenda and will be gradually implemented.

In 2006, a total of 184 billion Yuan in government appropriations for rural compulsory education have been used to exempt 52 million students from tuition and miscellaneous fees in compulsory education in western regions and some areas of central China, providing free textbooks for 37.3 million students from families with financial difficulties, and supplying living subsidies for 7.8 million boarding students in poverty.

1.3.5 Project of Distance Education in Rural Primary and Junior Secondary Schools

To improve the quality of basic education in rural areas, the state decided to carry out a distance education project in rural primary and junior secondary schools to transmit quality schooling resources and teaching methods to rural primary and junior secondary schools via Video on Demand (VOD) of teaching disks, VOD of satellite teaching, and computer classrooms. The Decision of the State Council on Further Strengthening Rural Education introduced the distance education project in rural primary and junior secondary schools, to proceed on the principle of "overall planning, pilot anteceding, making breakthroughs in main areas and implementing step by step."

Since 2003, the central government has supplied 1.344 billion Yuan from central finance and treasury bond expenditures for the pilot program of modern distance education for rural primary and junior secondary schools in central and western China, under the rule of local governments being responsible and the central government providing the appropriate subsidy pursuant to the economic development level of different regions. Particularly, the pilot regions in western China mainly depend on investments from the central government with support from local

[3]Statistics are from website of Ministry of Finance: www.mof.gov.cn/news/20070228_2118_24475.htm.

governments. The special appropriation expenditures from the central government account for two-thirds of the total for pilot areas.

Efforts will be made to equip about 110,000 digital disc teaching systems in rural primary schools, establish about 380,000 video stations for satellite teaching in primary schools, and establish and equip about 40,000 computer classrooms in rural junior secondary schools in 5 years, so as to alleviate the burden of schooling resource leanness and insufficient teachers in rural primary and junior secondary schools in the western region and promote teachers' qualifications and quality education. With regard to the Modern Distance Education Project in Rural Primary and Junior Secondary Schools, the central government and local governments have inputted accumulated expenditures of more than 11 billion Yuan to set up a distance education network covering all rural areas in China, making it possible for primary and junior secondary school students in central and western regions to enjoy quality teaching resources. By 2006, approximately 8 billion Yuan had been invested into the modern distance education projects of rural primary and junior secondary schools in China, covering more than 80 % of rural primary and junior secondary schools in central and western regions and providing more than 100 million primary and junior secondary school students with access to quality educational resources.

From the beginning of the Ninth Five-Year Period, the central government has constantly strengthened financial support for rural compulsory education. The implementation of these projects has made nine-year compulsory education universal in poor rural areas and improved educational quality. Meanwhile, these projects were implemented in the background of transformations of the rural compulsory education finance system and were reflections of these transformations to some extent.

1.4 Main Challenges in Compulsory Education Finance in China

1.4.1 The Inadequacy of Total Expenditures for Rural Compulsory Education Has not Been Resolved

After the implementation of the new mechanisms, the expenditures inputted into rural compulsory education have been improved remarkably. However, total expenditure is still inadequate. Because rural tax-fee reform did not increase the income of grassroots governments, there still exist some finance gaps for grassroots governments, meaning that the financial guarantee of rural compulsory education is still at a low level. Particularly, due to the limitation of financing in some regions, schools cannot appoint new full-time teachers and only employ temporary teachers whose salaries are lower than full-time teachers.

1.4.2 Teacher Quality and Teacher Training Are Crucial for Further Development of Rural Compulsory Education

Since the implementation of new mechanisms, the operation of rural schools has been guaranteed. However, treatments for teachers need to be resolved urgently. The salaries of rural teachers are generally lower than of urban teachers; in particular, local allowances for rural teaches have become a more urgent problem. Teachers' incomes in some areas are even lower than before implementation of new mechanisms. However, the implementation of rural compulsory education in high quality and at a high level mainly depends on quality teachers. Approaches to improve the treatment of rural teachers, strengthen training for rural teachers, and formulate related supportive polices to improve the quality of rural teachers have become a bottleneck for further development of Chinese compulsory education.

1.4.3 Adequacy of Non-personnel Expenditures Needs Improvement and Growth Mechanisms Needs Perfecting

With the implementation of new mechanisms, the non-personnel expenditures for rural primary and junior secondary schools have improved remarkably. However, whether the non-personnel expenditure standards are adequate or not still needs to be tested in practice and further theoretical research. Currently, non-personnel expenditure standards are not adequate for teacher trainings and related expenses of boarding schools. Take the boarding schools' related expenses as an example: More staff resources will be needed for dormitory management and catering. These resources normally are not included as formal staff and their salaries are mainly from non-personnel expenditures. Non-personnel expenditure standards as implemented may not meet this demand.

1.4.4 The Standard of Living Subsidy for Poor Boarding Students Is Relatively Low and Expenditure Guarantee Needs to Be Further Strengthened

Although the state planned to implement a policy of equal sharing of subsidies for poor boarding students by the central government and local authorities, and the sources of the subsidy have been guaranteed to some extents, the subsidy standards are still low compared to the living costs for low-income boarding students. The coverage, subsidy standard, and expenditure sources still need further clarification and strengthening.

1.4.5 The Resources Allocation Between Urban and Rural Areas Is not Balanced and Per-Student Expenditures for Rural Schools Are Much Lower

Because China is still a developing country, city-oriented social and economic development policy, which had been carried out for a long time in the past, has led to an obviously dual structure of urban and rural areas in China and conspicuous differences in education between urban and rural areas. Taking the year 2006 as an example, the expenditure per urban and township junior secondary school student in China was 3479 Yuan, while that for a rural junior secondary school student was only 2190 Yuan—1269 Yuan less than for urban students. The expenditure per rural junior secondary school student was only 60 % of that for an urban and township junior secondary school student. The expenditure per urban and township primary school student in China was 2855 Yuan, while that of rural primary school student was only 1847 Yuan—1008 Yuan less than for urban students. The expenditure per rural primary school student was only 70 % of that of urban and township primary school student. Unbalanced educational resources allocation between urban and rural areas will have an impact on human capital accumulation for rural areas and a further impact on the balance and equality of income distribution in the long term.

1.4.6 Differences of Expenditures Per Student in Rural Primary and Junior Secondary Schools Are Comparatively Big Between Regions

Besides obvious differences between urban and rural areas, there still exist serious differences between regions in China. Taking the year 2006 as an example, the expenditure per rural junior secondary school student in Beijing and Shanghai exceeded 10,000 Yuan, reaching 12,624 Yuan in Beijing. In central and western rural areas, the expenditure per junior secondary school student was just over 1200 Yuan. For example, the expenditure per rural junior secondary school student in Guizhou was only 1260 Yuan—one-tenth of that in Beijing. In 2006, the highest expenditure per rural primary school student was in Shanghai, having reached 9561 Yuan, while that of Henan was only 1068 Yuan—the former being nine times greater than the latter. Although the local input of educational expenditures is closely linked with local economic development level, the adjustment role of the central government cannot be ignored.

1.4.7 The Long-Term Physical Facilities Guarantee Mechanism for Rural Primary and Junior Secondary Schools Needs Further Improvement

In 2006, a total of 4.97 % of school buildings in primary schools in China were dilapidated; this percentage was 5.69 % in rural areas. The percentage of dilapidated school buildings in junior secondary schools in China was 3.25 %; in rural areas, this percentage was 3.72 %. The physical facilities of rural primary and junior secondary schools in central and western regions are poorer, with the percentage of dilapidated school buildings even reaching 10–15 %. To address this situation, the new mechanism should have the safety and protection of teachers and students as one of the main focuses.

1.4.8 Crowding-Out Effect of Multi-level Governments

With five levels in the governmental structure, China has complicated multi-level governmental relations, including not only relations between the central government and local governments, but also multi-level relations among provincial, municipal, county-level, and township governments from a local perspective. One of the keys for effective implementation of new mechanisms is to properly handle relations among multi-level governments. Particularly after the central government and provincial governments have taken more stringent measures for transfer payments, deeper research will be needed to guarantee the efforts made by county-level governments and prevent original education inputs by county-level governments from being crowed out. Problems have already emerged regarding a decreased ratio of educational budget inputs at county levels compared to total financial expenditures in some counties after the execution of new mechanism. Proper handling of the crowding-out effect from multi-level governments plays a key role in the success of new mechanisms. In the long term, these mechanism should be carried out in an earnest manner to guarantee compulsory education expenditures.

Chapter 2
Study on Non-personnel Expenditure Standards for Rural Compulsory Education

Non-personnel expenditures for primary and junior secondary school are expenditures that ensure regular operation, teaching activities, and logistic services. These expenditures are important for guaranteeing that the school can accomplish schooling and teaching tasks, improve education quality, and maintain regular operation. In the past, schools could not offer all of the required curricula because of insufficient expenditures and operations being at a very low level. After implementation of the new mechanisms, non-personnel expenditures for schools have been guaranteed and improved remarkably. However, these expenditures are still not adequate, as primary and junior secondary schools cannot supply high-quality nine-year compulsory education for every student. Therefore, to perfect the new mechanism, it is necessary to establish a scientific and reasonable per-student non-personnel expenditure standard for rural compulsory education, including the improvement of fund guarantee level for rural compulsory education. A study on the approaches to per-student non-personnel expenditure standards for compulsory education will also be conducive to improving budget management, which will make the allocation of educational resources more reasonable and more efficient.

According to the Notice about Further Reforming the Fund Guarantee Mechanism for Rural Compulsory Education and Compulsory Education Law, the central government and local governments should determine non-personnel expenditure standards for primary and junior secondary schools in rural areas. This study tries to provide reasonable and scientific approaches for governments to determine non-personnel expenditure standards for primary and junior secondary schools.

To date, there have been five approaches to determine non-personnel expenditure standards around the world, each of which has advantages and disadvantages. However, no consensus has been reached on how to determine non-personnel expenditure standards in China. This study introduces these five approaches and analyzes the advantages and disadvantages of each approach. Then, some approaches that are suitable for China will be used to calculate non-personnel expenditure standards for rural compulsory education.

Y. Du and Z. Sun, *Research on Compulsory Education Financing in China*,
New Frontiers of Educational Research, DOI 10.1007/978-3-662-47830-1_2

2.1 Non-personnel Expenditure Standards for Rural Compulsory Education: Concept, Status Quo, and the Approaches

Some issues should be considered before we calculate non-personnel expenditure standards for primary and junior secondary schools: concept, scope, principles, and approaches. The concept tells us what non-personnel expenditures are; the scope provides the coverage of non-personnel expenditures; and the principles and approaches allow us to understand the basis of procedures to calculate non-personnel expenditure standards.

2.1.1 The Definition of Non-personnel Expenditures for Primary and Junior Secondary School

Educational expenditures include regular expenditures and construction expenditures. Regular expenditures are composed of personnel expenditures and non-personnel expenditures. Personnel expenditures refer to expenses on teacher and staff salaries, welfare, and allowances, among others. Non-personnel expenditures refer to expenses related to school operation, teaching, and equipment, among others. Construction expenditure refers to expenses for constructing school buildings. Non-personnel expenditures for equipment valued higher than 500 Yuan and construction expenditures are *capital expenditures*. Non-personnel expenditures for other items and personnel expenditures are *recurrent expenditures*. Therefore, one part of non-personnel expenditures is capital expenditures, whereas the other part is recurrent expenditures. Different systems and regulations have different descriptions of non-personnel expenditures for primary and junior secondary schools. Also, there is no uniform standard to classify the items of non-personnel expenditures. Therefore, it is necessary to clarify the concept of non-personnel expenditures before we study the approaches to non-personnel expenditure standards.

Recent policies and regulations have provided the definition and scope of non-personnel expenditures. In 1997, the Ministry of Finance promulgated the Financial System for Primary and Junior Secondary School, which defined that non-personnel expenditures, according to functions and accounting purposes, refer to expenses for teaching activities, line of duty, equipment, repair and maintenance, and others, which are necessaries for a school's regular operation. In 1998, the Accounting System for Primary and Junior Secondary School clarified the items of non-personnel expenditures from an accounting perspective, stating that non-personnel expenditures cover expenses for line of duty, teaching activities, equipment, repair and maintenance, and others. In 2006, the Provisional Regulations for Management of Non-personnel Expenditure for Rural Primary and Junior Secondary School defined, based on their function and scope, non-personnel expenditures for rural primary and junior secondary schools as expenses for guaranteeing the regular operation, teaching activities, and logistic services, including management, teacher training, experiment and practice, afterschool student activities, water and electricity, heating, transportation, travel, post and telecommunication, equipment, books, magazines and newspapers, and repair and maintenance. Non-personnel expenditures cannot be used for personnel, construction, or payments for debts.

The Guidance on Preparing Budget for Primary and Junior Secondary School, edited by the Ministry of Education in 2006, provided the following description for non-personnel expenditures: non-personnel expenditures reflect the necessary expenses for an entire year for maintaining the regular operation of a school and meeting the basic demands for teaching, including current non-personnel expenditures and special non-personnel expenditures. The current non-personnel expenditures mainly reflect the expenses needed for regular school operation, printing, water and electricity, post and telecommunication, heating, transportation, travel, meeting, training, welfare, temporary staff, renting, repair and maintenance, special materials, and other items throughout the year. Special non-personnel expenditures include expenses for basic facilities, such as office equipment, instructional equipment, transportation tools, books, magazines and newspapers, and other items in the budgetary year.

Although the different definitions of non-personnel expenditures seem to be consistent in nature, they are not consistent in terms of the scope of non-personnel expenditures in implementation in different regions. For example, disagreements still exist on whether the following expenses should be in the scope of non-personnel expenditures, such as expenses for temporary staff (substitute teachers), school cafeterias, heating, water, and electricity for residences or dormitories of both teachers and students. We hold that, according to regulations issued by the central government and local governments, all of these expenses should be borne by primary and junior secondary schools. Therefore, they should be included in the scope of non-personnel expenditures.

Based on these understandings, we hold that non-personnel expenditures for primary and junior secondary schools are expenses related to the regular operation of the school, teaching activities, and logistic services in order to ensure that the school can accomplish teaching tasks and improve education quality. Non-personnel expenditures mainly cover teaching activities and school management, teacher training, experiments and practice, afterschool student activities, water and electricity, heating, transportation, travel, post and telecommunication, equipment and facilities, books, magazines and newspapers, and current repair and maintenance for buildings and equipment. For accounting purposes, non-personnel expenditures should cover expenses in the line of duty, teaching activities, equipment and books, repair and maintenance, and others. Line-of-duty expenses should include office supplies, teachers' books, temporary staff, electricity and water, post and telecommunication, heating, transportation, travel, meetings, property management, and rent payments. Teaching activity expenses should include special materials and printing. Equipment and book expenses covers office equipment, special equipment, transportation tools, books, magazines, and newspapers. Repair and maintenance expenses consist of expenses for the repair of buildings and equipment. Other expenses includes training, hospitality, and miscellaneous items.

2.1.2 *Status Quo of Non-personnel Expenditures for Primary and Junior Secondary Schools in China*

Since the 1980s, the Chinese government has carried out many programs to explore non-personnel expenditure standards for primary and junior secondary schools. In 1989, focusing on uneven development in different regions, the National Education Commission[1] proposed the establishment of a material consumption ration system for non-personnel expenditures for primary and junior secondary schools so as to meet the demands of social and economic development and educational development. Also, the National Education Commission issued the Material Consumption Ration for Non-personnel Expenditure for Primary and Junior Secondary Schools in 1992 (also referred to as 92's Ration). At the beginning of this century, the Ministry of Finance and Ministry of Education put forward further requirements on how to determine non-personnel expenditure standards, requiring all provinces and autonomous regions to seriously measure and reasonably determine non-personnel expenditure standards. Meanwhile, it also required that developed regions could refer to 92's Ration to determine the non-personnel expenditure standards, considering the cost of information technology education and rural basic education development. Underdeveloped regions could determine non-personnel expenditure standards to keep schools operating smoothly.

Since 2001, to improve non-personnel expenditure guarantee levels gradually, the central government has issued related policies successively. On the one hand, they require that all local authorities determine reasonable non-personnel expenditure standards for primary and junior secondary schools in rural areas, while on the other hand requiring governments at various levels to share the financial responsibility. In 2001, the Decision of the State Council on Reform and Development of Basic Education clarified that the provincial government should be responsible for determining non-personnel expenditure standards for rural primary and junior secondary schools according to actual spending and demand for non-personnel expenditures in order to reasonably input the funds needed for regular operation of rural primary and junior secondary schools. Mainly, non-personnel expenditures are derived from miscellaneous fees collected by schools. If miscellaneous fees cannot meet the demands for non-personnel expenditures, the gap should be financed by county and township governments.

[1]The National Educational Commission of the PRC was a governmental organ of the State Council in charge of education. It was renamed the Ministry of Education in 1998.

On December 24, 2005, the State Council promulgated the Notice on Further Reforming Fund Guarantee Mechanism for Rural Compulsory Education, requiring governments at different levels to improve non-personnel expenditure guarantee levels for primary and junior secondary schools in rural areas jointly. In this notice, the State Council also requires local governments to implement per-student appropriation standards of budgetary non-personnel expenditures for rural primary and junior secondary schools determined by each provincial (autonomous region or municipality) government. By 2008, per-student non-personnel expenditure for rural junior secondary and primary students in all regions should reach the per-student standard of non-personnel expenditures determined by each provincial (autonomous region or municipality) government before the autumn semester of 2005. In 2009, central government issued the national standard of non-personnel expenditures for primary and junior secondary school in rural areas. In this year, 50 % of the gap, which is caused by non-personnel expenditure standards determined by each province (autonomous region or municipality) being lower than the national standard, will be jointly supplied by the central government and local governments according to the share-mechanism for miscellaneous fee exemptions.

Article 43 of the revised Law of Compulsory Education enacted on September 1, 2006 clearly states that per-student non-personnel expenditure standards are to be jointly determined by the Ministry of Finance and Ministry of Education of the State Council and will be adjusted according to economic and social development. Per-student non-personnel expenditure standards and their adjustment should meet the basic demands of schooling and teaching. The Law of Compulsory Education incorporates non-personnel expenditure standards of compulsory education into the state law system. Provincial governments shall determine local per-student non-personnel expenditure standards, which must be higher than the national standard.

As a result of a series of policies, remarkable changes have happened in the amount and structure of non-personnel expenditures for Chinese compulsory education. Before further discussing non-personnel expenditure standards for primary and junior secondary schools in China, we first analyze the status quo of non-personnel expenditures for primary and junior secondary schools in China and sample provinces.

2.1.2.1 Status Quo of Non-personnel Expenditures for Primary and Junior Secondary Schools in China

1. **Remarkable Growth of Non-personnel Expenditures**

   The central government has issued series of policies to provide rural compulsory education with an important strategic position in social development. To input more funds into compulsory education, the central government requires that most annual increases of educational funds be directed to rural education. Governments at different levels must establish and implement a fund guarantee mechanism for rural compulsory education. As a result, non-personnel

Table 2.1 Changes in non-personnel expenditures per student at primary and junior secondary schools in China (2003–2006) (Yuan)

	Primary schools	Rural primary schools	Junior secondary schools	Rural junior secondary schools
2003	280	200	477	307
2004	342	259	548	380
2005	423	332	668	496
2006	499	401	783	601
Growth of 2006 compared with 2003 (%)[a]	66.0	86.8	52.9	82.4

Data source Statistic Yearbook of Chinese Education Expenditure 2003–2006 (excluding data of Hong Kong, Macau, and Taiwan)
[a]The growth rate here is calculated based on comparable prices

expenditures for rural primary and junior secondary schools have increased remarkably (refer to Table 2.1). In 2006, the national non-personnel expenditure per rural primary school student was 401 Yuan, up by 86.8 % compared with that of 2003, based on the comparable prices. Per-student non-personnel expenditures for western rural primary schools increased 1.39-fold. The non-personnel expenditure per rural junior secondary school student was 601 Yuan, up by 82.4 % and per-student non-personnel expenditures for western rural junior secondary schools increased 1.12-fold.

The per-student current non-personnel expenditures for Chinese primary and junior secondary schools have increased remarkably (see Table 2.2). In 2006, the per-student non-personnel expenditure for rural primary schools was 315 Yuan, up by 86.9 % from 2003, based on the comparable prices. For primary schools in western rural areas, the per-student non-personnel expenditure increased 1.4-fold (and 1.5-fold in Inner Mongolia, Chongqing, Shannxi, and Xinjiang). In rural junior secondary schools, the per-student non-personnel expenditure was 478 Yuan, up by 81 %. The per-student non-personnel expenditure for rural junior secondary schoosl in western China increased by at least 1.26-fold. In Chongqing, Sichuan, and Xinjiang, it increased 1.5-fold compared with 2003.

Table 2.2 Changes in current non-personnel expenditures per student at primary and junior secondary schools in China (2003–2006) (Yuan)

	Primary schools	Rural primary schools	Junior secondary schools	Rural junior secondary schools
2003	230	157	394	246
2004	279	199	450	299
2005	340	252	541	382
2006	407	315	643	478
Growth of 2006 compared with 2003 (%)	64.8	86.9	52.0	81.0

2. **The Rise of the Proportion of Non-personnel Expenditures in Regular Expenditures**
   The regular expenditures for primary and junior secondary schools are composed of personnel expenditures and non-personnel expenditures. The proportion of non-personnel expenditures in regular expenditures for rural primary schools increased to 22 % in 2006 from 19 % in 2003. The proportion for rural junior secondary schools increased from 26 % in 2003 to 28 % in 2006. The increase in the proportion of non-personnel expenditures in regular expenditures demonstrates that the series of policies to improve the fund guarantee mechanism for rural compulsory education has made great progress (see Table 2.3).

3. **Certain Differences of Per-Student Non-personnel Expenditures for Rural Compulsory Education**
   The growth in the amount and proportion of non-personnel expenditures of regular expenditures for rural primary and junior secondary school shows that physical facilities of rural primary and junior secondary schools are being improved. However, due to the different financial abilities of local governments, there is still a difference in non-personnel expenditure standards for rural compulsory education among provinces (see Fig. 2.1). In 2006, the national per-student non-personnel expenditure for rural primary schools was 315 Yuan. The per-student non-personnel expenditure for rural primary schools in Beijing was highest at 2227 Yuan—15 times higher than that of the lowest in Guizhou, which is 149 Yuan. Additionally, six provinces were higher than 500 Yuan and 14 provinces were lower than 300 Yuan.

In 2006, the national per-student non-personnel expenditure at rural junior secondary schools was 478 Yuan (see Fig. 2.2). It reached 3689 Yuan in Beijing, while it was just 252 Yuan in Guizhou—the former is 15 times higher than the latter. The per-student non-personnel expenditure for rural junior secondary schools was greater than 500 Yuan in 13 provinces; in Anhui and Guizhou, it is less than 300 Yuan.

Table 2.3 The proportion of non-personnel expenditures in regular expenditures for primary and junior secondary schools (2003–2006) (Yuan)

	Rural primary schools		Rural junior secondary schools	
	Personnel expenditures	Non-personnel expenditures	Personnel expenditures	Non-personnel expenditures
2003	81	19	74	26
2004	80	20	73	27
2005	78	22	72	28
2006	78	22	72	28

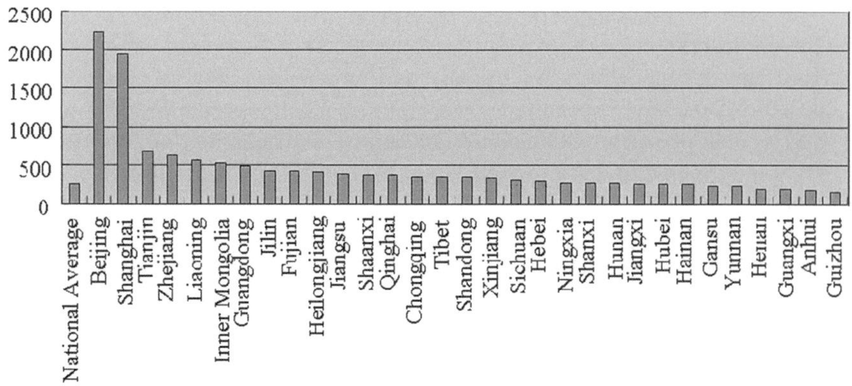

Fig. 2.1 Average per-student non-personnel expenditures for rural primary schools in 2006

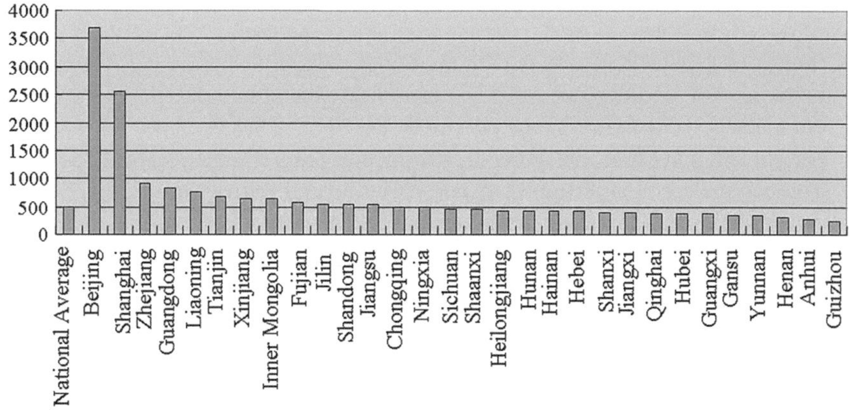

Fig. 2.2 Average per-student non-personnel expenditure for rural junior secondary schools in 2006. *Note* Excluding data of Hong Kong, Macau and Taiwan. *Note* Data are lacking for the Tibetan Autonomous Region

2.1.2.2 Non-personnel Expenditure Standards for Primary and Junior Secondary Schools in Four Sample Provinces

Based on the implementation of non-personnel expenditures in 12 sample counties of 4 sample provinces, data both at the macro and micro levels indicate that the implementation of the fund guarantee mechanism for rural compulsory education has improved the guarantee level for non-personnel expenditures. Most of the sample counties consider the scale of schools as an important factor to determine non-personnel expenditure standards and allocate non-personnel expenditures to primary and junior secondary schools. A higher standard for non-personnel expenditures is determined for small schools, which could promote the balanced development of schools within the same region. However, there are still some problems with non-personnel expenditure standards in sample provinces and counties.

1. **Differences of Non-personnel Expenditure Standards**
   According to policies issued by the central government, the provincial government determines the minimum non-personnel expenditure standard. The county government determines the local standard, but the local standard must be higher than the minimum non-personnel expenditure standard. Most of the county governments took the minimum non-personnel expenditure standard as the local standard. For this reason, a trivial difference or even no difference exists between counties in the same province, such as sample counties of Guangxi and Heilongjiang. However, local non-personnel expenditure standards are different in the sample counties of Hubei and Zhejiang. For example, in Zhejiang, the highest non-personnel expenditure standard for primary schools was 365 Yuan and the lowest was 242 Yuan; for junior secondary schools, the highest was 445 Yuan, which is 115 Yuan higher than the lowest. Meanwhile, at the provincial level, there still exist differences among minimum non-personnel expenditure standards (see Table 2.4). For example, the highest standard for township junior secondary schools is 470 Yuan per student in Heilongjiang and the lowest is 225 Yuan in Guangxi. In rural junior secondary schools, the highest is 330 Yuan per student in Zhejiang and the lowest is 195 Yuan in Guangxi.

Based on our analyses, we found that differences still exist in the non-personnel expenditure standards for primary and junior secondary schools among regions. In order to promote educational equity, it is urgent for the central government to determine a reasonable minimum national standard.]

2. **Differences in Non-personnel Expenditure Standards between Township Schools and Rural Schools**
   The differences in non-personnel expenditures not only exist among provinces, but also between township schools and rural schools (see Table 2.4). In Hubei and Guangxi, the minimum non-personnel expenditure standard for township

Table 2.4 The minimum non-personnel expenditure standard for primary and junior secondary schools determined by four provincial governments in 2007 (Yuan)

Province/autonomous region	Junior secondary schools		Primary schools	
	Rural	Township	Rural	Township
Heilongjiang	355	470	305	390
Zhejiang	330	330	230	230
Hubei	300	330	200	230
Guangxi Zhuang	195	225	140	170

Data source survey data

schools is 30 Yuan, higher than that for rural schools. In Heilongjiang, the minimum non-personnel expenditure standard for township primary schools is 85 Yuan, higher than that for rural primary school, and the difference for junior secondary schools between township and rural areas is 115 Yuan. However, Zhejiang supplies the same minimum standard for township schools and rural schools. To improve balanced development of education, the government should determine a higher non-personnel expenditure standard for rural schools.

3. **The Non-personnel Expenditure Shortage**
   Currently, the resources for non-personnel expenditures consist of both appropriation of miscellaneous fee exemptions and appropriation of budgetary non-personnel expenditures. Because these two types of appropriations are at very low levels, schools cannot get adequate non-personnel expenditures for their actual needs related to school operations. In addition, the government did not pay enough attention to special needs of boarding schools, such as additional water, electricity, and temporary staff. If the government ignores the changes and special needs of schools when determining non-personnel expenditure standards, school operations will be difficult because of the shortage of non-personnel expenditures.
4. **Lack of Methodology Support for the Determination of Non-personnel Expenditure Standards**
   In the survey, we found that the determination of non-personnel expenditure standards lacked methodology support. Most governments determined the standard according to their superior government and local financial ability, while few governments determined the standard according to the actual needs of primary and junior secondary school operations.
5. **Lack of Growth Mechanisms for Non-personnel Expenditure Standards**
   All of the sample provinces and counties have had education since 2002. With the reform and development of curriculum and teaching, the need for non-personnel expenditures for primary and junior secondary schools has been on the rise. In 2006, the central government issued the Notice on Resolutely Restraining Excessive Tuition and Fees Collection by Schools in Reform of Fund Guarantee Mechanism for Rural Compulsory Education, requiring primary and junior secondary schools to remove agency and service fees and incorporate these reasonable expenditures into the scope of non-personnel expenditures. This requires non-personnel expenditure standards to be adjusted with the continuous development and reform of education. However, in our survey, we found that only sample counties in Zhejiang had increased non-personnel expenditure standards. If the government does not increase the standards with all changes faced by compulsory education, schools will not improve the quality of education. To implement educational reforms successfully, a reasonable growth mechanism should be designed for non-personnel expenditure standards.

2.1.3 Principles to Determine Non-personnel Expenditure Standards for Primary and Junior Secondary Schools

2.1.3.1 The Non-personnel Expenditure Standard Should Match Educational Development

The development of educational objectives, content, teaching methods, and teaching techniques will bring new need for non-personnel expenditures. Meanwhile, the shift of compulsory educational strategies from popularization to quality requires more funds, especially for non-personnel expenditures. Therefore, the non-personnel expenditure standard should be adjusted in time to match educational development.

2.1.3.2 The Non-personnel Expenditure Standard Should Be Determined Based on Convergences and Variations of Schools

The mission of primary and junior secondary school is to ensure that quality education is available to every child, so most activities in schools are similar. However, the characteristics of schools are usually different, such as scale and facilities. In addition, the characteristics of the school districts differ by location, such as geography, climate, and local price. For example, schools in northern China, where it is much colder in winter, have to spend more of their non-personnel expenditures on heating. Because of the different characteristics of schools and school districts, schools will have different needs for non-personnel expenditures. Therefore, non-personnel expenditure standards should be determined according to the convergences and variation of different schools.

2.1.3.3 The Non-personnel Expenditure Standard Should Keep Stable and Be Increased Over Time

The precondition for non-personnel expenditures is that they should be adequate to meet a school's reasonable demands. If the government does not change the objectives, contents, and outcomes of compulsory education, the resources consumed by schools will be stable. Therefore, non-personnel expenditure standards should keep stable. However, they should be adjusted in a timely manner when the prices of those resources change. Otherwise, some educational activities will not be carried out.

2.1.4 The Approaches to Non-personnel Expenditure Standards for Primary and Junior Secondary Schools

At present, there is little domestic research on approaches to non-personnel expenditure standards for primary and junior secondary schools. The most frequently mentioned is the material consumption ration approach designed by the National Education Commission in (1992). Since 2000, the Ministry of Education has been requiring local governments to use this approach to determine non-personnel expenditure standards for compulsory education. Internationally, the determination of expenditure standards for primary and junior secondary schools is based on four approaches to adequate finance: the successful school/district approach, cost function approach, professional judgment approach, and evidence-based approach to provide adequate funds for schools to achieve high minimum outcomes. Fiscal adequacy encompasses not only fiscal inputs but also their linkage to education programs, student achievement, and school efficiency. The material consumption ration approach and the other four international approaches could provide methodology support for the determination of non-personnel expenditure standards.

2.1.4.1 Material Consumption Ration Approach

The steps of the material consumption ration approach are as follows:

1. Assume school scale, class scale, and physical facilities.
2. Design the necessary resources and quantity of these resources for assumed schools.
3. Multiply the quantity by price, respectively, to calculate the cost for each resource.
4. Sum up the total cost of these resources.
5. Divide the total cost by enrollments to calculate the per-student non-personnel expenditure.

A disadvantage of this approach is that it is hard to determine a uniform benchmark for school operations due to the great differences in local prices, school scales, and physical facilities. Moreover, even if the uniform benchmark is determined, it is still complicated and difficult to detail resources in practice. Therefore, this approach has not yet been applied universally. However, the approach focuses on the detailed needs of schools, so it has been taken as the basis to determine non-personnel expenditures in many areas.

2.1.4.2 Successful District/School Approach (Best Practice District/School Approach)

The successful district approach, which has been used in Illinois, Maryland, Mississippi, and Ohio, is to identify districts that have been successful in teaching its students proficiency standards and to set the adequacy level at the weighted average of the expenditures per pupil of those districts (Odden 2003). The successful districts do not include large city school districts, small rural school districts, and school districts at both extremes of the per pupil property wealth distribution in the state (Conley and Picus 2003). The key to using the successful school district approach is being able to determine the differences in how successful and unsuccessful schools spend their money (Picus 2004).

This approach is easy to explain to the public and makes intrinsic sense as a way to specify an adequate level of resources (Picus 2004). However, it is difficult to identify successful districts. When this approach was used in Ohio, only 8 of the state's 612 districts met the established criteria of successful schools, which analyzed both inputs and outcomes to determine successful schools. However, when only the criteria for outcomes were applied, 100 districts met the criteria (Augenblick et al. 2002). The spending of those successful districts is lower than the state average. The other disadvantage of this approach is that the adequate expenditure level typically identified is difficult to relate to the fiscal adequacy needs of big city and small rural districts, even with adjustments for pupil needs and geographic price differentials (Odden 2003).

2.1.4.3 Cost Function Approach

The economic cost function approach employs regression analysis with expenditure per pupil as the dependent variable; student and district characteristics, as well as performance levels desired, are the independent variables (Odden 2003). The equations in a cost function approach accommodate differences in pupil characteristics, district conditions, and educational prices across all districts in a state. Student characteristics include providing additional funds for children with disabilities, children from low-income families, or children who are English-language learners. District conditions taken into account include district size, population density, and number of schools and other factors outside of the control of a school district. Finally, the equations accommodate educational price differences—differences in the cost of the products and services needed to operate a school (Conley and Picus 2003).

Although this approach has a great deal of appeal among economists (Picus 2004), the complex statistical analyses required to make these cost function estimates can be difficult for policy makers and the general public to understand, which makes policy makers less inclined to accept the expenditure estimates that such models generate (Conley and Picus 2003).

2.1.4.4 Professional Judgment Approach

This professional judgment approach has been used most recently in Kansas, Maryland, Oregon, and Wyoming. This approach creates a group of educational experts who identify effective educational strategies for elementary, middle, and high schools, as well as for special needs students, then specify the educational resources required for each to ensure that most of the students in the school will be able to meet the state-established performance goals, attach a price to each ingredient, and finally sum everything up to obtain a total expenditure per pupil (Odden 2003).

A disadvantage is that, other than expert educational judgments, the strategies and ingredients have no clear link to actual performance levels (Odden 2003). The second disadvantage is that it depends on the judgments of educational professionals to identify strategies rather than building directly from research that demonstrates an actual linkage between educational strategy or program and student performance (Conley and Picus 2003). Other disadvantages stem from the potential subjectiveness of the process. For example, it is impossible to ensure that each team member has no conflict of interest that would lead him or her to make judgments that might influence their own circumstances (National Research Council 1999; Picus 2004). Furthermore, it provides little differentiation between strategies for the average school and strategies for schools with higher concentrations of at-risk students, second language learners, or other specialized populations (Conley and Picus 2003).

The advantages to the professional judgment approach are that it is easily explained to the public and the resulting estimates are based on the judgments of professional educators with experience in educating students (Picus 2004). The approach also makes it easy to adjust for local characteristics and issues, such as special student needs and geographic price variations (Odden 2003).

2.1.4.5 Evidence-Based Approach

The evidence-based approach depends on current educational research to identify the resources needed for a prototypical school to meet a state's student performance benchmarks, as developed by Allen Odden. This approach designs a set of elements that are required to deliver a high-quality, comprehensive, schoolwide instructional program, and it determines an adequate expenditure level by placing a price on each ingredient and aggregating to a total expenditure (e.g., Odden 2003). This approach may be used to identify adequate site, district, and state expenditure levels (Odden 2003).

This approach is more directly based on educational strategies that improve student performance and produce desired results, so it also helps schools to use funds most effectively (Odden 2003). However, research-based education strategies may not work in absolutely every situation (Picus 2004). Also, this approach did not include adequate funds to cover planning and preparation time for teachers and did not standardize costs across various designs, so it probably underestimated total costs somewhat (Conley and Picus 2003).

Based on the above analysis, five approaches are used comprehensively in this study. We use an item-specific integration approach and cost function approach to calculate the non-personnel expenditure standard. In the item-special integration approach, we mix the professional judgment approach, best practice school approach, evidence-based approach, and material consumption ration into one approach to calculate the non-personnel expenditure per student.

2.2 The Item-Specific Integration Approach to Non-personnel Expenditure Standards for Rural Compulsory Education

2.2.1 Introduction to the Approach

As shown in Picture 2.1, the education objective is the origin of the non-personnel expenditure demand. Since 2000, the central government has set up new objectives for compulsory education that primary and junior secondary schools should provide high-quality education for every student, which requires schools to improve management, reform teaching activities, and create a better educational environment. To achieve the educational objective, primary and junior secondary schools must be supplied with adequate non-personnel expenditures to get adequate physical resources. This study aims to determine reasonable non-personnel standards for primary and junior schools.

To ensure that every school achieves the required standards of school operation determined by the government, the government should provide adequate non-personnel expenditures for school. However, the government seems to be unclear on how to judge the adequacy of non-personnel expenditures. An approach is needed to clarify the real demand of non-personnel expenditure based on government requirements. A substantial method and procedure will be developed to calculate the non-personnel expenditure benchmarks, such as expenses for equipment, special materials, and books, which is the first step of the item-specific integration approach to calculate the minimum non-personnel standard without considering the differences of schools.

The item-specific integration approach calculates the standard for each item of non-personnel expenditure, based on the standards of school operation issued by government. The non-personnel expenditure for equipment, special materials, and books will be calculated according to the standards of school operation issued by the Ministry of Education; the non-personnel expenditure for training, labor union, and welfare will be calculated according to the required proportion of non-personnel expenditure ruled by policies; the non-personnel expenditure for the stable materials consumed by schools will be calculated according to 92's Ration;

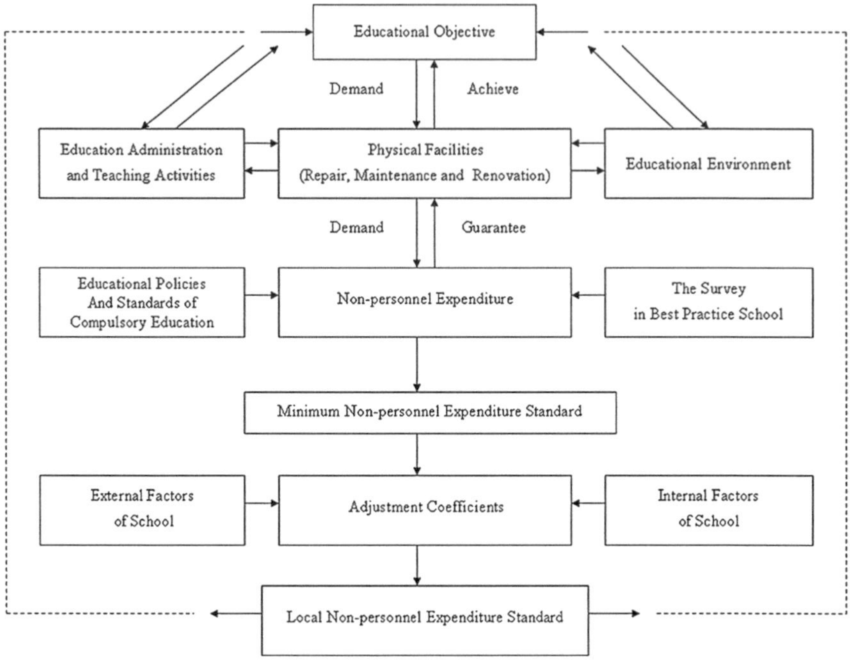

Picture 2.1 Flow chart of item-specific integration approach

and other non-personnel expenditures will be calculated by the professional judgment approach and best practice school approach. Finally, we sum the non-personnel expenditures for each item to get the total minimum non-personnel expenditure standard per student.

After getting the benchmark of non-personnel expenditures, we need to tackle the differences on the regional level, district level, and school level. Accordingly, the final step of the item-special integration approach is to calculate adjustment coefficients for differences, then multiply the minimum non-personnel expenditure with adjustment coefficients to acquire the adjusted standard suitable for the characteristics of schools and regions. The differences of schools include internal and external differences. Internal differences consist of school scale, class scale, boarding school or not, etc. External differences are comprised of geography, climate, local price, etc.

The main standards of school operation and policies issued by the government are as follows:

– Provisional Regulations on Non-personnel Expenditure for Rural Primary and Junior Secondary School issued by the Ministry of Education in 2006:

  The expenses for teachers' training will account for 5 % of the total non-personnel expenditure of the school, covering expenses for transportation, training materials, meals, and accommodation.

Table 2.5 Per-student floor area of school buildings for primary and junior secondary schools (unit: m^2)

School category	School scale	Recent index	Planned index
Primary schools[a]	4 classes	3.69	4.78
Primary schools	6 classes	4.84	7.02
	12 classes	4.34	5.98
	18 classes	4.02	5.47
Junior secondary schools	12 classes	6.01	10.25
	18 classes	5.78	9.72
	24 classes	5.63	9.41

[a]These primary schools only provide grade 1 to grade 3 primary educations to students

The allocation of non-personnel expenditures for rural primary and junior secondary schools will mainly be based on the enrollment of schools; full consideration will also be given to the actual operational situation of schools with different scales. The government should supply a higher per-student appropriation of non-personnel expenditures for poverty schools, small schools, and teaching points.

- School Buildings Standards for Rural Primary and Junior Secondary School issued by the Ministry of Education in 1996:

  Section Four of Chap. 4 states the per-student standard for floor areas of the school building, shown in Table 2.5.

- The Notice on the Regulations of Libraries at Primary and Junior Secondary School issued by the Ministry of Education in 2003 states that the books per student are as follows:

  40 books per student at junior secondary school I,[2] 25 books per student at junior secondary school II, 30 books per student at primary school I, and 15 books per student at primary school I. For newspapers, 80 kinds and 60 kinds are defined for junior secondary schools I and II, respectively; with 60 kinds and 40 kinds for primary school I and II, respectively. The annual increase for books should not be less than 1 % of the total books.

- Working Plan for Distance Education Projects Pilot for Rural Primary and Junior Secondary School:

  An average of about 16,000 Yuan will be invested in each satellite teaching station for rural primary schools. About 150,000 Yuan will be input into each rural junior secondary school to build a computer classroom.

- Material Consumption Ration of Non-personnel Expenditure for Primary and Junior Secondary School (1992):

[2]A primary/junior school I has at least 19 classes; a primary/junior school II has 18 or less classes.

92's Ration mainly covers resources consumed in teaching activities, administration and management, and student activities of primary and junior secondary schools. These resources should be paid by expenses for the line of duty and activities (refer to Appendix 2).

Moreover, the standards and policies also include Standards for Inspecting Nine-year Compulsory Education Popularization, Mathematics and Science Instruments and Equipment Benchmarks for Primary Schools, Mathematics and Science Instruments and Equipment Benchmarks for Junior Secondary School, Personnel Standard for Primary and Junior Secondary School, and other related regulations on expenses for training, labor unions, and welfare.

2.2.2 Calculation Process and Conclusions

2.2.2.1 Calculation Process

Based on the actual situation of rural compulsory education, benchmarks for school operation, best practice school data, and macro statistical data, we used this approach to calculate the average non-personnel expenditure per student in order to ensure that schools have adequate non-personnel expenditures to achieve the benchmarks of school operation issued by the government and to supply high-quality education to students.

1. **Assumed School Scale**
   In 2007, there were 8 classes in each rural primary school on average and 36 students in each class. Therefore, there were 291 students in each rural primary school. In each rural junior secondary school, there were 16 classes, 907 students in each school, and 57 students in each class on average (refer to Table 2.6). Compared with 92's Ration, which assumed the average school scale was 12 classes and 540 students, the scale of rural primary schools is obviously lower and that of rural junior secondary schools is much higher.

Table 2.6 School and class scale of rural primary and junior secondary schools in 2007

	Number of schools	Total enrollment	Number of classes	Average school size	Average number of classes in each school	Average class size
Rural primary schools	302,526	88,029,214	2,502,861	291	8	36
Rural junior secondary schools	51,515	46,733,133	832,741	907	16	57

Considering that the rural primary school scale in China is small, in this approach we assume the primary school scale is 8 classes and 300 students. Junior secondary schools still refer to the normative school scale assumed in 92's Ration—12 classes and 540 students.

2.2.2.2 Calculation of Major Items

Non-personnel expenditures include five parts: expense for line of duty, expense for activities, equipment, repair and maintenance and other. Major items in each part were calculated using suitable approaches. The processes and results of the calculations refer to Appendix 1 in detail. The following are the calculation processes of major items.

(a) **Expenses for Line of Duty**

- We used the material consumption ration approach to calculate office supplies. That is to say, expenses for office supplies determined in 92's Ration were multiplied by price indexes to get non-personnel expenditure standards. To get a precise standard, we multiplied the per student expenses for stationeries, hardware, and electric apparatus determined in 92's Ration with the accumulated price index for 1993 to 2006, respectively:

  Office supplies per primary student = [4.88 Yuan (stationeries) × 1.1 (price index)] + [2.49 Yuan (hardware and electric apparatus) × 1.18 (price index)] = 8.3 Yuan
  Office supplies per junior secondary student = [5.42 Yuan (stationeries) × 1.1 (price index)] + [2.49 Yuan (hardware and electric apparatus) × 1.18 (price index)] = 10.3 Yuan

- We used the best practice school approach to calculate non-personnel expenditure standards for water and electricity. According to the survey, a primary school student consumes an average of 10 tons of water and 30° of electricity, and 12 tons of water and 40° of electricity for a junior secondary school student. The water costs 1.3 Yuan per ton and electricity costs 0.6 Yuan per degree. The results of the calculation were as follows:

  Expenses for water and electricity per primary school student = [10 × 1.3] + [30 × 0.6] = 31 Yuan
  Expenses for water and electricity per junior secondary school student = [12 × 1.3] + [40 × 0.6] = 39.6 Yuan

(b) **Expenses for Teaching Activities**

- The non-personnel expenditure standard for special materials was calculated using the evidence-based approach. According to Mathematics and Science Instruments and Equipment Benchmarks for Primary and Junior

Secondary Schools, schools should be equipped with instruments that are valued less than 500 Yuan. If the lifespan of these instruments and equipment is 8 years, the depreciation rate will be 1/8 per year on average.

Expenses for special materials per primary school student are 14 Yuan.
Expenses for special materials per junior secondary student are 20 Yuan.

– We also used the evidence-based approach to calculate the non-personnel expenditure standard for newspapers. The books benchmark for primary and junior secondary schools II determined in the Notice on the Regulations of Libraries at Primary and Junior Secondary School stipulates that each primary school should buy 40 kinds of newspapers a year and spend 60 Yuan on each kind of newspaper on average. It also requires junior secondary schools to buy 60 kinds of newspapers in one year, each of which may cost 90 Yuan.

  Expenses for newspapers per primary school student = $[60 \times 40]/300 = 8$ Yuan
  Expenses for newspaper per junior secondary school student = $[90 \times 60]/540 = 10$ Yuan

(c) **Expenses for Equipment**

– We used the evidence-based approach to determine the non-personnel expenditure standard for equipment valued higher than 500 Yuan—instructional equipment that is necessary for primary and junior secondary schools to supply quality education to students. This equipment is also an important part of a school's fixed assets, which feature large-value, one-time investments and long-term usage. To share the cost to remedy investments, expenses for equipment could be calculated according to the state equipment benchmarks and life expectancy of the equipment.
  The calculation of special equipment expenses should be based on mathematics, science, music, sports, and art equipment benchmarks for primary schools and junior secondary schools, as determined by the Ministry of Education in 2006. We assume that 50 % of this equipment has a 5-year lifespan and the other 50 % has an 8-year lifespan.

  Expenses for special equipment per primary school student are 21.0 Yuan.
  Expenses for special equipment per junior secondary school student are 44.0 Yuan.

– Based on both the best practice school approach and professional judgment approach, we calculated the non-personnel expenditure standard for desks and chairs. According to the survey in best practice primary schools, one set of a double desk-and-chair costs 100 Yuan, or 50 Yuan per student. If we assume that there are 8 classes, 1 electrification classroom, 1 musical classroom, and 1 science experiment classroom in each primary school totaling 11 classes, the adjustment coefficient would be $11/8 = 1.375$.

According to the survey in best practice junior secondary schools, one set of a double desk-and-chair costs 120 Yuan, or 60 Yuan per student. If we assume that there are 12 classes, 1 electrification classroom, 1 musical classroom, 1 physics experiment classroom, 1 chemistry experiment classroom, and 1 biology experiment classroom in each junior secondary school totaling 17 classes, the adjustment coefficient would be 17/12 = 1.42. The depreciation is based on 8 years:

Expenses for desks and chairs per primary school student = [50/8] × 1.375 = 8.59 Yuan
Expenses for desks and chairs per junior secondary school student = [60/8] × 1.42 = 10.65 Yuan

(d) **Expenses for Repair and Maintenance**

- *Expenses for equipment repair and maintenance*: In 2007, national average value of instruments and equipment per rural primary school student was 238 Yuan and that of rural junior secondary school student was 375 Yuan. The expenses for repair and maintenance will account for 8 % of the original value:

  Expenses for equipment repair and maintenance per primary school student = 238 × 8 % = 19 Yuan
  Expenses for equipment repair and maintenance per junior secondary school student = 375 × 8 % = 30 Yuan

- *Expenses for building repair and maintenance*: In 2007, the national average school building floor area per primary school student was 5.6 m^2 and per junior secondary school student was 6.9 m^2, which are higher than the recent indicators but lower than the planned indicators of School Buildings Standards for rural primary and junior secondary school. The cost of building repair and maintenance is about 7 Yuan per m^2:

  Expenses for building repair and maintenance per primary school student = 5.6 × 7 = 39.2 Yuan
  Expenses for building repair and maintenance per junior secondary school student = 6.9 × 7 = 48.3 Yuan

- *Expenses for playground repair and maintenance*: According to the Standards for Inspecting Compulsory Education Popularization, each rural primary school will have a playground of 2000 m^2 with a 200-meter-long track and each rural junior secondary school will have a playground of 3000 m^2 with a 250-m-long track. The playground repair and maintenance costs 1 Yuan per m^2:

  Expenses for playground repair and maintenance per primary school student = 2000 × 1/300 = 6.7 Yuan
  Expenses for playground repair and maintenance per junior secondary school student = 3000 × 1/540 = 5.6 Yuan

(e) **Other Expenses**

- *Expenses for training*: According to Provisional Regulations on Non-personnel Expenditure Management for Rural Primary and Junior Secondary School, 5 % of the total annual non-personnel expenditure of schools will be spend on teacher training, including transportation, meals, training materials, and accommodation.

The cost of teacher and staff training at rural primary and junior secondary schools is comparatively high. If 3 % of total salaries is used for staff training in enterprises and we assume that the proportion of personnel expenditures in regular expenditure accounts for 70 %, the proportion of training expenses in total non-personnel expenditures will be increased to 7 %. Calculated by this proportion, training expenses per teacher at primary school and junior secondary schools are only 467.5 Yuan and 584.5 Yuan, respectively. In 2007, the ratio of students to teachers at primary schools and junior secondary schools were 18.7:1 and 16.7:1, respectively, in 2007. Accordingly, per student training expenses are 25 Yuan at primary schools and 35 Yuan at junior secondary schools.

According to the non-personnel expenditure standards for rural primary and junior secondary schools (refer to Appendix 1) calculated by above approaches, the total non-personnel expenditure per student at a primary school is 345 Yuan, which is 9.8 % higher than the national average of 2006; the total non-personnel expenditure per student at a junior secondary school is 495 Yuan, 3.5 % higher than the national average of 2006 (refer to Table 2.7). Meanwhile, the structure of non-personnel expenditures is becoming reasonable because the proportions of expenses for activities, equipment and books, and repair and maintenance in non-personnel expenditures have increased appropriately. The growth of the non-personnel expenditures for activities, equipment and books, and repair and maintenance will help schools to improve physical facilities and enhance education quality. The growth of training expenses shows that the quality of teachers and staff, which is a factor for schools to improve education quality, will be improved.

2.2.2.3 Adjustment Coefficients

The above per-student non-personnel expenditure standards of primary and junior secondary schools are 345 Yuan and 495 Yuan, respectively. These standards do not account for the differences between schools. Therefore, we will use adjustment coefficients to adjust the standards in order to calculate local standards. In an item-specific integration approach, we will focus our attention on the differences in school scale, class scale, boarding students, and others.

(a) **Adjustment Coefficients for School Scale and Class Scale**

92's Ration designed a normative prototype school with 12 classes, 540 total students, and 45 students in each class. According to the material consumption ration for different scale schools, the per-student non-personnel expenditure

Table 2.7 Our calculated non-personnel expenditure standards versus the national average of non-personnel expenditures per student in 2006

	Sum (Yuan)		Composition (%)	
	Rural primary school	Rural junior secondary school	Rural primary school	Rural junior secondary school
Calculation standard				
Total	345	495	100	100
Line of duty	104	139	30	28
Teaching activities	65	105	19	21
Equipment	56	88	16	18
Repair and maintenance	65	84	19	17
Others	56	80	16	16
Actual value of non-personnel expenditure per student in 2006				
Total	315	478	100	100
Line of duty	125	182	40	38
Teaching activities	47	71	15	15
Equipment	41	70	13	15
Repair and maintenance	56	88	18	18
Others	45	68	14	14

for schools with 12 classes is 1.14 times higher than that for the schools with 18 classes, among which expenses for the line of duty are 1.14 times, expenses for teaching activities are 10.9 times, expenses for equipment are 1.15 times, expenses for repair and maintenance are 1.15 times, and other expenses are 1.13 times.

92's Ration only considered differences of school scale, not differences of class scale. In the survey, we found that the smaller the class scale is, the higher the per-student non-personnel expenditure is. Also, 80 % of non-personnel expenditures will still keep stable as the number of classes decreases. Therefore, when we determine and calculate non-personnel expenditure standards, school scale and class scale should be taken into account. Adjustment coefficients should be set for small schools and schools with small class sizes to ensure that adequate non-personnel expenditure are supplied to these schools and that school operation and teaching activities are smooth. Therefore, we could use the adjustment coefficients shown in Table 2.8 to calculate non-personnel expenditure standards for primary schools with less than 300 students and junior secondary schools with less than 500 students.

(b) **Adjustment Coefficient for Boarding Students**

According to the survey, the non-personnel expenditure per boarding student is 150 Yuan higher than that per non-boarding student. The 150 Yuan mainly

Table 2.8 Adjustment coefficients for school scale and class scale

	Total	Line of duty	Activities	Equipment	Repair and maintenance	Others
18 classes						
A1. Composition of junior secondary schools in 2006	1	0.38	0.15	0.15	0.18	0.14
A2. Composition of primary schools in 2006	1	0.40	0.15	0.13	0.18	0.14
Less than 18 classes						
B1. The coefficient of junior secondary schools with 12 classes		1.14	1.09	1.15	1.15	1.13
B2. The coefficient of primary schools with 8 classes		1.14	1.09	1.15	1.15	1.13
Adjustment coefficient: $c = a \times b$						
C1 for junior secondary schools with 12 classes	1.135	0.433	0.164	0.173	0.207	0.158
C2 for primary schools with 8 classes	1.078	0.456	0.164	0.150	0.150	0.158
Small class scale						
D1. The coefficient of 12 classes in junior secondary schools	1.10		Calculation: $(45/40 - 1) \times 0.8 + 1 = 1.10$			
D2. The coefficient of 8 classes in primary schools	1.23		Calculation: $(45/35 - 1) \times 0.8 + 1 = 1.23$			
Adjustment coefficient: $\mathbf{e} = \mathbf{c} \times \mathbf{d}$						
E1 for junior secondary schools	1.25		25 % of non-personnel expenditure standard per student will be added when a student less than the ration.			
E2 for primary schools	1.29		29 % of non-personnel expenditure standard per student will be added when a student less than the ration.			

includes 40 Yuan for expenses for water and electricity, 20 Yuan for daily life expenses, 50 Yuan for a subsidy of teachers due to morning and evening self-study of students, 30–40 Yuan for expenses for repair of beds and other miscellaneous expenses. Deducting 40 Yuan that is collected to cover the accommodation of boarding students, 100 Yuan needs to be subsidized for each student.

2.2.3 *Conclusion*

According to the requirements for standards of compulsory education, an item-specific integration approach gives full consideration to internal and external factors influencing non-personnel expenditure demands. If the government sets up standards for compulsory education, then the government should provide adequate funds to ensure that schools achieve those standards. We used an evidence-based approach, material consumption ration approach, professional judgment approach, and best practice school approach to calculate non-personnel expenditure standards for rural primary and junior secondary schools. Based on our results, the per-student minimum non-personnel expenditure standard for rural primary schools should be 345 Yuan per year, which is 9.8 % higher than the 2006 national average; the standard for rural junior secondary schools should be 495 Yuan per student per year, which is 3.5 % higher than the 2006 national average. We adjusted the minimum standards according to differences between schools, such as climate and geological condition, school scale, class scale, boarding school or not, and so on.

Due to limitations of time and data, the non-personnel expenditure standards for rural primary and junior secondary schools calculated in this study do not cover all items, such as expenses for property management, renting, and transportation tools. However, these expenses are indispensable for schools. Although this means that the minimum standards calculated in this study are lower than actual needs, we still hope that item-specific integration provides methodology support for the government to determine reasonable non-personnel expenditure standards.

2.3 Cost Function Approach to Non-personnel Expenditure for Primary and Junior Secondary Schools

2.3.1 *Research Methods and Data*

2.3.1.1 Cost Function

The cost function approach refers to the fact that demands of educational funds are not only influenced by the features of students and schools but also by expected educational output level. Generally speaking, the higher the expected educational output is, the higher the demands for funds are. Therefore, educational outputs (student achievements) are determined by inputs (fund). Under the condition of considering the features of students and schools, the funds per student necessary for achieving certain achievements can be calculated, which could be used as non-personnel expenditure standards.

The basic form of the educational cost function is as follows:

$$E_{it} = h(S_{it}, F_{it}, P_{it}, Z_{it}, e_{it}, u_{it})$$

E_{it} represents the average educational expenses per student of a school in the *t* year; S_{it} is output; Z_{it} represents the features of students and schools; F_{it} represents the features of a student's family; P_{it} is the price vector of educational fund input factors; e_{it} represents the vectors that could not be observed; and u_{it} represents random errors.

The concrete form of cost function is a multiple regression equation. The dependent variable is educational expenses per student of the school and the independent variables measure output, features of students and schools, features of student families, and prices of educational fund input factors. The process to estimate educational fund demands is as follows:

1. Form the educational cost function E_{it} and multiple regression Eq.
2. Set down high minimum student achievement S^*_{it}.
3. Put the high minimum student achievement, the features of both students and schools, and prices into the regression model to estimate the fund input E^*_{it}. This fund input is necessary for schools to reach high minimum achievement.

We use the above model to estimate the funds needed by primary school and junior secondary schools, respectively.

2.3.1.2 Description of Variables

1. **The Actual Expenses of Non-personnel Expenditures Per Student of a School**
   In this study, the actual expenses of non-personnel expenditures per student are used as a dependent variable, which is calculated as follows: total annual expenses of non-personnel expenditure of the school/total annual enrollment of the school. Among samples used in this study (refer to introduction of samples), Guangxi has the lowest actual non-personnel expenses per student in the year (165.85 Yuan), while Zhejiang has the highest (519.48 Yuan), with the difference rate being 3.15. In junior secondary schools, Guangxi still has the lowest actual non-personnel expenses per student (218.59 Yuan) and Zhejiang has the highest one (722.49 Yuan), with the difference rate being 3.3. Comparing the current non-personnel expenditure standards, the actual non-personnel

expenditures of all provinces have reached the standards required in Notice on Provisional Regulations on Management of Non-personnel Expenditure for Rural Primary and Junior Secondary School. But considering the actual situation, the current level of non-personnel expenditure can only guarantee that schools operate at a relatively low level but is far from meeting the demands of school development.

2. **Student Achievement**
In this study, the indicators measuring the school achievements of students (educational output) refer to the standard cores of Chinese and mathematics. Because there are no standard examinations for Chinese and mathematics in practice, we converted the original scores of Chinese and mathematics to standard scores according to different provinces. The standard scores are independent of the difficulty of examinations and could show the rank of this school among schools of the same category in the province in terms of average scores. In this way, we could avoid the disadvantage of weak comparability due to the varying difficulties of examinations in different provinces. The conversion formula for standard scores is as follows:

$$\mathrm{stand\_exam}_{ijk} = 10 \times \frac{\mathrm{orig\_exam}_{ijk} - \mathrm{mean}_{ik}}{\mathrm{s}_{ik}} + 50$$

Here, i refers to the code of province, with $i = 1, 2, 3, 4$; j refers to the code of the school, with $j = 1, 2\ldots; \mathrm{n}_i$; k refers to the code of the subject, with $k = 1, 2$; $\mathrm{stand\_exam}_{ijk}$ refers to the standard score of subject k of school j in province i; $\mathrm{orig\_exam}_{ijk}$ refers to the original score of subject k of school j in province i; mean_{ik} refers to the average score of subject k of province i; and s_{ik} refers to the standard difference of subject k of province i.

3. **Teacher Salary Index**
The teacher salary index refers to price variables in factors of educational fund inputs. In practice, we introduce the teacher salary index into the model because teachers play an irreplaceable role in school and exert great impact on school outcomes. In addition, the proportion of non-personnel expenditures in rural compulsory education expenditures decreased from 28.3 % in 1993 to 25.4 % in 2004, partly reflecting that the proportion of personnel expenditure is on the rise. It also indicates that although total educational expenditures have been increased in rural areas, the expenditures may guarantee teachers' salaries at first and only guarantee that schools operate at a low level. The adequacy of non-personnel expenditures could not be guaranteed at all (3).
Currently, the labor market is experiencing increased liquidity and schools need to increase personnel expenditures to attract more high-quality teachers with advanced educational degrees, professional titles, and long-term teaching experiences. This will bring more pressure on the payment of non-personnel expenditures. Therefore, teachers' salaries exert important indirect impacts on the non-personnel expenditures per student.

This study tries to find a balanced relationship between adequate expense levels of non-personnel expenditures and student outputs. Other variables are all regarded as control variables, which should be the least influenced by the controllable factors of schools. To achieve this objective, this study does not consider the controllable factors of local education departments, such as educational degrees, professional titles, and years of teaching experience. The salary index of teachers designed by Taylor (2004) is used to replace the salaries of teachers.
The calculation principles are as follows: First, use OLS regression with the average salary of full-time teachers being the dependent variable and features of schools and local features being independent variables:

$$\text{salary} = \alpha_0 + \alpha_1 \times x_1 + \alpha_2 \times x_2 + \alpha_3 \times x_3 + \alpha_4 \times x_4 + \varepsilon.$$

Here, salary refers to average salary of teachers, x_1 refers to the proportion of teachers holding educational degrees above junior colleagues, x_2 refers to the proportion of senior teachers, x_3 refers to the proportion of teachers having more than 10 years of teaching experience, and x_4 refers to the average training times of teachers each year.
Secondly, calculate the salary index of teachers: $\text{salary\_index} = \text{salary} - \overline{\text{salary}}$. $\overline{\text{salary}}$ refers to the estimation after regression of the first step; thus, the teacher salary index could also be regarded as the residual value of the first step, including uncontrollable factors of schools and educational departments.

4. **School Scale**
Schools with different scales have different demands for non-personnel expenditures. By adding the variables of student number and its quadratic term, on one hand we could control the impacts of student scales; on the other hand, we could estimate expense levels for schools of different scales.
5. **Features of Schools**
School features in the model include the school building area per student, number of books per student, school type, ratio of students and teachers, proportion of boarding students, use of well water or not, and heating or not.

School building area per student Non-personnel expenditure includes expenses for property management and repair and maintenance. The larger the school building area per student is, the higher the expenses for property management and repair and maintenance and non-personnel expenditure per student are. This study introduces school building area per student to control the impacts of school building area on the expenses of non-personnel expenditures per student.

Books per student Expenses for books, magazines, and newspapers are an important component of non-personnel expenditures. The books possessed will exert an impact on the expenses of school funds. Therefore, this study introduces an indicator of books per student to control the difference of book availability at schools.

Variable of school types This variable is only used in the cost function model for primary schools. The sample primary schools include teaching points, village regular schools, and central primary schools. Table 2.3 shows that the proportion of village regular primary schools is the highest (over 50 %) and the proportion of teaching points is the lowest (less than 10 %). Under the county-centered educational administration system, the county government has taken the responsibility of governance and financing, and central primary schools play an administrative role. Therefore, central primary schools need more non-personnel expenditures. Additionally, central primary schools have higher-quality education and teaching points have lower quality. Therefore, this study introduces the variable of school type to control the impacts of school types.

Ratio of students and teachers In order to investigate the minimum guaranteed non-personnel expenditure necessary for achieving high minimum outcomes, the ratio of students and teachers will exert important impacts on teaching quality. For research purposes, this study introduces the variable of the ratio of students and teachers to control differences in student achievements due to different ratios of students and teachers.

Proportion of boarding students Undoubtedly, the longer boarding students stay at schools, the more water, electricity, and other resources are consumed. With the proportion of boarding students increasing, expenses for water, electricity, and equipment maintenance will also be increased. The adjustment of school distributions in recent years made it common for schools to abolish teaching points for centralized education; as a result, the number of boarding students is sharply increasing. Among the sample primary schools, Zhejiang has the highest proportion of boarding students at 20.37 %; in junior secondary schools, Guangxi has the highest proportion of boarding students at 72.68 %. Therefore, when the non-personnel expenditure standard is determined, full consideration should be given to the proportion of boarding students. This study introduces the proportion of boarding students to control its impacts on the non-personnel expenditures of schools.

Resources of water There are two major sources of water: well water and tap water. If schools use well water, expenses for electricity (for pumping) and personnel funds are only needed to acquire water instead of higher payments for the expense of tap water. The use of well water could decrease the expenses of non-personnel expenditures. Particularly for schools in southern China such as Guangxi, using well water will dramatically decrease the water expenses of schools. Therefore, this study introduces well water as a controllable variable to investigate relationships between non-personnel expenditures per student and school achievements of students under the preconditions of controlling water resources.

Heating or not This indicator is targeted for Heilongjiang, which is located in the frigid zone. Expenses for heating equipment, resources, and maintenance are needed, accounting for 30 % of non-personnel expenditures for primary schools in Heilongjiang. This study introduces the variable of heating (1 represents yes and 0 represents no heating) to control the impacts of heating expenses on non-personnel expenditures.

6. **School Courses**
   Under the precondition of other courses, the proportion of experiment courses will directly exert an impact on the demands for non-personnel expenditures. Therefore, the time of experiment courses is introduced into the model to measure this relationship. In the model for primary schools, it refers to the class time of natural experiment courses per week per class. In the model for junior secondary schools, it refers to the class time of physics, chemistry, and biology experiment courses per week.

2.3.1.3 Sample Introduction

In total, there are 411 schools in this study. After selection based on each index, only 365 schools were entered into the cost function model, among which 300 are primary schools and 65 are junior secondary schools. The regional distribution is shown in Table 2.9.

2.3.2 *Estimated Results*

Tables 2.10 and 2.11 provide estimated results of models for primary schools and junior secondary schools. The equation results for the cost function of primary schools and junior secondary schools also show similar results. The effectiveness of

Table 2.9 Sample distribution

	Guangxi				Hubei			
County	Guiping	Yongfu	Rong'an	Sum	Xiaochang	Wuexue	Chibi	Sum
Town number	4	4	3	11	4	7	4	15
Primary school number	63	22	37	122	39	36	23	98
Junior secondary school number	4	3	5	12	10	5	9	24
	Zhejiang				Heilongjiang			
County	Jiangshan	An'ji	Lin'an	Sum	Mishan	Tangyuan	Keshan	Sum
Town number	5	5	4	14	4	4	3	11
Primary school number	10	8	16	34	4	12	30	46
Junior secondary school number	5	3	6	14	4	6	5	15

Table 2.10 Regression of the education cost function for primary schools

	Coefficient	t-statistics
Constant term	−303.325*	−1.75
Performance of student		
Standard average score for mathematics	0.373*	1.13
Standard average score for Chinese course	4.606*	1.82
School scale		
Student number	−14.606*	−1.13
Square of student number	0.023*	1.82
Features of teachers		
Teacher's salary index	0.115**	6.4
School equipment		
School building area per student	−0.169	−0.16
Books of books per student	0.881**	4.1
Features of schools		
Kind of schools	36.873*	1.91
Ratio of students to teachers	−128.060	−0.65
Percentage of boarding students	0.952	1.38
Use of well water	−19.670	−0.97
Heating or not	30.332**	5.97
Courses		
Time of natural experiment classes	0.019	0.02

Note
*refers to being obvious at the level of 10 %
**refers to being obvious at the level of 5 %

model for junior secondary schools is not so obvious, which is probably the result of small sample numbers. Therefore, we focus our explanation on the results for the primary school model.

In Table 2.10, student achievements for Chinese and mathematics are in direct proportion with non-personnel expenditures per student. Under the same conditions, a 1-point increase in the Chinese score will lead to an increase of 4.6 Yuan for the per-student non-personnel expenditure. A1-point increase in the mathematics scores will result in an increase of 0.373 Yuan in the per-student non-personnel expenditure. This shows that a stable increase in non-personnel expenditures will increase student achievements. Educators in various areas acknowledge that a lack of per-student non-personnel expenditures and insufficient non-personnel expenditures will limit teaching activities. The non-personnel expenditure should be increased in order to ensure that schools achieve school outcomes benchmarks.

The variable coefficient of enrollment is negative, while its square is positive, showing that the relationship between school scale and per-student non-personnel expenditures are represented in the features of a U-curve with a critical value. When the number of students is less than the critical value, the per-student non-personnel

Table 2.11 Regression of the education cost function for junior secondary schools

	Coefficient	t-statistics
Constant terms	163.681**	3.24
Performance of student		
Standard average score of mathematics	2.253	0.71
Standard average score of Chinese course	1.515	−1.48
School scale		
Number of students	−0.267	−1.46
Square of student number	0.000	0.81
Features of teachers		
Teacher's salary index	0.047**	2.11
School facilities		
School building area per student	0.689	0.19
Books of books per student	−0.078	−0.04
Features of schools		
Ratio of students and teachers	78.597	2.14
Percentage of boarding students	−0.480	−0.36
Use of well water	−15.614	−0.45
Heating or not	4.002	0.03
Courses		
Time of physical experiments	2.527	1
Time of chemical experiments	1.771	0.18
Time of biological experiments	6.155	1.25

Note
*refers to being obvious at the level of 10 %
**refers to being obvious at the level of 5 %

expenditure will decrease with the increase of enrollments; when the number of students is more than the critical value, the per-student non-personnel expenditure will increase with the increase of enrollment. According to the result of the regression, the critical value is 1270. However, most sample primary schools in this study are on a small scale and the highest average enrollment of primary schools is 784.31 students of Zhejiang, far from this critical value. On one hand, it shows that the smaller the scale of a school is, the higher the per-student expenditure will be; on the other hand, the main reason for small average school scale is the existence of teaching points. Therefore, the adjustment of school distributions should be made so as to achieve a scaled economy by appropriately expanding school scales.

Under the control of other conditions, if schools use well water, the per-student non-personnel expenditure will decrease by 19 Yuan. If schools have heating equipment, the per-student non-personnel expenditure will dramatically increase by 30 Yuan. If schools are central primary schools, the per-student non-personnel expenditure will be 36 Yuan higher than village primary schools. Therefore, when the non-personnel expenditure standard is calculated, educational departments should give full consideration to extra cost needs related to the special conditions of schools; at the same time, schools should be encouraged to take full advantage of energy-saving resources to decrease the expenses of non-personnel expenditure. For example, primary and junior secondary schools in Heilongjiang must spend more non-personnel expenditures on heating because Heilongjiang is located in frigid-temperate zone. Guangxi is located in a subtropical zone and water consumption is higher than other regions, which will undoubtedly increase water expenses in non-personnel expenditures. If schools are located in regions with underground water resources, schools should be encouraged to reasonably use well water to achieve the goal of saving non-personnel expenditures. If schools are central primary schools, in order to ensure teaching quality and cover expenses for extra administration, governments should also increase the appropriation of non-personnel expenditures correspondingly.

The number of books per student also exerts an impact on per-student non-personnel expenditures. If other variables are unchanged, for a per-student increase of one book, the per-student non-personnel expenditure will be increased by 1 Yuan. The teacher salary index also affects non-personnel expenditures, indicating that staff expenditures should be considered in this approach.

Class hours per week of experiments also have a direct relationship with per-student non-personnel expenditures. The increase of natural experiments in primary schools does not increase the demands for non-personnel expenditures by much. The results show that an increase of one class hour of natural experiments will lead to less than 0.1 Yuan increase in per-student non-personnel expenditures. In junior secondary schools, this will have a great impact. If other indicators remain unchanged, an increase of one class hour of physics experiments per week will result in an increase of about 2 Yuan in per-student non-personnel expenditures; an increase of one class hour of chemical experiment a week will result in an increase of about 1.7 Yuan in per-student non-personnel expenditures; and an increase of one class hour of biological experiments per week will lead to an increase of about 6 Yuan in per-student non-personnel expenditures.

2.3.3 *Use Cost Function to Calculate Non-personnel Expenditures*

According to the results of above model, we acquire per-student non-personnel expenditures after inputting various variables into the model. In the process of calculation, the score standards should be determined first. Because there are not unified and authoritative score standards for students in compulsory education, we

Table 2.12 Estimation for adequate non-personnel expenditures for primary schools in four provinces (unit: Yuan)

			Guangxi	Hubei	Zhejiang	Heilongjiang
85 Points	Use of well water	Central primary schools	299	302	510	350
		Village primary schools	294	297	505	345
		Junior secondary schools	723	808	903	818
	Do not use well water	Central primary schools	338	341	549	389
		Village primary schools	303	306	514	354
		Junior secondary schools	738	823	918	834
90 Points	Use of well water	Central primary schools	357	361	569	409
		Village primary schools	323	326	534	374
		Junior secondary schools	742	826	922	837
	Do not use well water	Central primary schools	366	369	577	417
		Village primary schools	331	334	542	382
		Junior secondary schools	757	843	937	853

analyzed averaged scores of students from four sample provinces, which are around 80 points. For the purpose of improving educational output quality, this study set the output standards as 85 and 90 points of original scores, which will be put into a standard score conversion formula to calculate the standard scores. Other variables include the average value of the province. In this way, based on the two standards of scores, we calculated the per-student non-personnel expenditures for the primary and junior secondary schools in four provinces, as shown in Table 2.12.

From Table 2.12, we could find that if students achieve 85 points in Chinese and mathematics scores, under the condition of using well water, the per-student non-personnel expenditures for central primary schools and village primary schools in Guangxi are 299 Yuan and 294 Yuan; the per-student non-personnel expenditures for central primary schools and village primary schools in Hubei are 302 Yuan and 297 Yuan; the per-student non-personnel expenditures for central primary schools and village primary schools in Zhejiang are 510 Yuan and 505 Yuan; and the per-student non-personnel expenditures for central primary schools and village primary schools in Heilongjiang are 350 Yuan and 345 Yuan.

If students achieve 90 points in Chinese and mathematics scores, under the condition of using well water, the per-student non-personnel expenditures for central primary schools and village primary schools in Guangxi are 357 Yuan and 323 Yuan; the per-student non-personnel expenditures for central primary schools and village primary schools in Hubei are 361 Yuan and 326 Yuan; the per-student non-personnel expenditures for central primary schools and village primary schools in Zhejiang are 569 Yuan and 534 Yuan; and the per-student non-personnel expenditures for central primary schools and village primary schools in Heilongjiang are 409 Yuan and 374 Yuan.

2.3.4 Conclusion

In this session, we used the cost function approach to determine non-personnel expenditure standards. After setting certain educational output standards (student achievements) and considering the features of schools and students, we may use the cost function approach to calculate non-personnel expenditure standards for the outputs of different levels. The relationships between the various factors of the educational cost function model and the non-personnel expenditure standards are basically identical to actual conditions, indicating that this approach could provide methodology support for the determination of non-personnel expenditure standards.

When comparing actual expenses of non-personnel expenditures and the standard of non-personnel expenditures calculated in this study, we can see that there are still great gaps. The non-personnel expenditure standards calculated in this study are higher than the non-personnel expenditure standards implemented by sample provinces and the actual expenses of four provinces. Additionally, attention should be paid to the fact that actual non-personnel expenditure expenses of schools were used as dependent variables, which do not meet the demands of school development. Therefore, the non-personnel expenditure standards calculated in this study are relatively low and need to be improved and perfected with the support of more accurate data.

Appendix 1: Calculation of Non-personnel Expenditure Standards for Rural Compulsory Education

	Primary schools	Junior secondary schools	Approaches	Calculation
Total (Yuan)	344.6	494.3		Calculated on the basis of a primary school with 300 students and junior secondary school with 540 students
Non-personnel expenditure for Line of duty	103.7	138.5		
Office expenses1: office suppliers	8.3	10.3	Material consumption ration approach (office expenses of 92's Ration × price index)	Per primary student = 4.88 (stationeries) × 1.1 + 2.49 (hardware) × 1.18 = 8.3 Yuan
				Per junior secondary student = 5.42 (stationeries) × 1.1 + 2.49 (hardware) × 1.18 = 10.3 Yuan
Office expenses 2: teachers' books	4.0	8.0	Professional judgment approach, assuming 45 students per class	3 sets per class of primary school, four books each set, one book costs 15 Yuan and a set costs 60 Yuan
				Per student = 60 × 3/45 = 4 Yuan
				5 sets per class of primary school, four books in one set, one book costs 18 Yuan and a set costs 72 Yuan
				Per student = 72 × 5/45 = 8 Yuan
Temporary workers	16.0	17.8	Professional judgment approach	One worker per primary school and two per junior secondary school
				Average price of rural labor force is 400 Yuan per person per month
				Personnel expenditure for temporary workers per primary student = 400 Yuan × 12 months × 1 person/300 students = 16 Yuan
				Personnel expenditure for temporary workers per junior secondary student = 400 × 12 × 2/540 = 17.8 Yuan

(continued)

(continued)

	Primary schools	Junior secondary schools	Approaches	Calculation
Water and electricity	31.0	39.6	Best practice school approach and Professional judgment approach	11.15 tons of water and 31° of electricity per primary student consumed in best practice school; assuming that 10 tons of water and 31° of electricity consumed by each student, average water costs 1.3 Yuan per ton and electricity costs 0.6 Yuan per degree
				Per student expenses for water and electricity = 10 × 1.3 + 30 × 0.6 = 31 Yuan
				11.5 tons of water and 41° of electricity per junior secondary school student consumed in best practice school; assuming that12 tons of water and 40° of electricity consumed by each student, 1° of electricity costs 0.6 Yuan and 1 ton of water costs 1.3 Yuan
				Per student expenses for water and electricity = 12 × 1.3 + 40 × 0.6 = 39.6 Yuan
Post and telecommunication	8.8	9.2	Professional judgment approach	
# Expenses for communication by telephone	6.7	6.7		2 telephones per primary school and each telephone spends 100 Yuan per month and calculated by 10
				Per student expenses for telephone = 100 × 2 × 10/300 = 6.7 Yuan
				3 telephones per junior secondary school and each telephone spends 120 Yuan per month and calculated by 10
				Per student expenses for telephone = 120 × 3 × 10/540 = 6.7 Yua

(continued)

(continued)

	Primary schools	Junior secondary schools	Approaches	Calculation
Heating or cooling	117.6	144.9	The coldest region: best practice school approach and Professional judgment approach	Average 6 heating months and 0.06 tons of coal per m^2 consumed. The coal price is 350 Yuan per ton
				Rural primary school: in 2007, national average per-student floor area of school building was 5.6 m^2. Heating expenses per student = 0.06 × 5.6 × 350 = 117.6 Yuan
				Rural junior secondary school: in 2007, national average per student floor areas of school building was 6.9 m^2. Heating expenses per student = 0.06 × 6.9 × 350 = 144.9 Yuan
	41.2	50.7	Professional judgment approach	In northern China, heating period per year lasts 4 months and the energy consumed is half of the coldest region
				Per primary student = 117.6 × 0.5 × 0.7 = 41.2 Yuan
				Per junior secondary student = 144.9 × 0.5 × 0.7 = 50.7 Yuan
	10.6	13.0	Survey data and professional judgment approach	Other regions: one month for the coldest and one month of hottest and energy consumption is 0.3 times of the coldest region
				Per primary student = 117.6 Yuan × 0.3 × 0.3 = 10.6 Yuan
				Per junior secondary student = 144.9 × 0.3 × 0.3 = 13.0 Yuan
Property management				
Transportation	4.2	10.9	Best practice school approach	Average of best practice schools
Travel	12.0	16.0	Best practice schools approach	Average of best practice schools
Renting				

(continued)

(continued)

	Primary schools	Junior secondary schools	Approaches	Calculation
Meeting	3.0	5.0	Best practice schools approach	Average of best practice schools
Environmental sanitation	5.8	8.7	Material consumption ration approach (office expenses of 92's Ration × price index)	Based on 92's Ration, per student 2.8 Yuan for primary school and 4.2 Yuan for junior secondary school; price index is 1.6, and the standard is increased by 30 %
				Per primary school student = 2.8 × 1.6 × 1.3 = 5.8 Yuan
				Per junior secondary school student = 4.2 × 1.6 × 1.3 = 8.7 Yuan
Teaching activities	64.8	105.1		
Printing	3.2	8.4	Best practice schools approach	Average of best practice schools
Special materials expenses 1: Expenses for consumptive materials	4.0	12.0	Best practice schools approach	Average of best practice schools
Special materials expenses 2: teaching facilities (less than 500 Yuan)	14.0	20.0	Evidence-based approach	Evidence: "Mathematics and Science Instruments and Equipment Benchmarks" for primary and junior secondary schools; assuming 8-year depreciation for these facilities
Expenses for newspapers and materials	8.0	10.0	Evidence-based approach	Evidence: The Notice on the Regulations of Libraries at Primary and Junior Secondary School stating that primary school should buy 40 kinds of newspapers and each kind costs 60 Yuan averagely; junior secondary school should buy 60 kinds of newspapers and each kind costs 90 Yuan averagely
				Per primary school student = 60 × 40/300 = 8 Yuan
				Per junior secondary school student = 90 × 60/540 = 10 Yuan

(continued)

(continued)

	Primary schools	Junior secondary schools	Approaches	Calculation
Music, sports, and art activities	13.0	15.0	Evidence-based approach	Evidence: standards of musical, sports, and art equipment for primary school and junior secondary school determined by Ministry of Education
				Consumptive materials and equipment valued under 500 Yuan will be calculated by 8-year depreciation
Student activities	8.0	10.0	Professional judgment approach	For primary schools, four activities include National Day, Children's Day, school year, and community activities
				For junior secondary schools, above four activities and a sports game. Each activity cost 2 Yuan per Student
Teaching research	2.7	4.2	Professional judgment approach	Assuming that per primary school teacher expenses for teaching research is 50 Yuan a year and the national ratio of students to teachers at rural primary school is 18.7:1: per student = 50/18.7 = 2.7 Yuan
				Assuming that per primary school teacher expenses for teaching research is 70 Yuan a year and the national ratio of students and teachers at rural primary school is 16.7:1: per student = 70/16.7 = 4.2 Yuan
Other activities	5.2	10.5	Professional judgment approach	For primary school, the expenses for other activities account for 8 % of non-personnel expenditure for teaching activities;
				For junior secondary school, these expenses account for 1 %
Information technology	6.7	15.0	Evidence-based approach	Evidence: Working Plan for Distance education Projects Pilot for Rural Primary and Junior Secondary School. An average of about 16,000 Yuan will be invested in each

(continued)

(continued)

	Primary schools	Junior secondary schools	Approaches	Calculation
				satellite teaching station for rural primary schools. About 150,000 Yuan will be input into each rural junior secondary school to build computer classroom.
				Per primary school student = 16,000/300/8 = 6.7 Yuan
				Per junior secondary school student = 60,000/540/8 = 15 Yuan
Equipment	56.1	87.7		
Office equipment	19.0	21.0	Best practice school approach	Average of best practice schools
Special equipment	21.0	44.0	Evidence-based approach	Evidence: "Mathematics and Science Instruments and Equipment Benchmarks" for primary and junior secondary school, and standards of musical, sports and art equipment for primary school and junior secondary school determined by Ministry of Education
				This special equipment costs more than 500 Yuan. 50 % will be depreciated by 5 years and 50 % by 8 years.
Desks and chairs	8.59	10.65	Best practice school approach and Professional judgment approach	One set of double desk-and-chair for primary school costs 100 Yuan, or 50 Yuan per student. On the basis of average of 8 classes per school plus one electrification classroom, one musical classroom and one natural experiment classroom, totaling 11 classes. The adjustment coefficient is 11/8 = 1.375. Desks and chairs are depreciated by 8 years.
				Per student = 50/8 × 1.375 = 8.59 Yuan
				One set of double desk-and-chair for junior secondary school costs 120 Yuan, or 60 Yuan per student. On the basis of average of 12 classes per school plus one

(continued)

(continued)

	Primary schools	Junior secondary schools	Approaches	Calculation
				electrification classroom, one musical classroom and one physics experiment classroom, one chemical experiment classroom and one biological experiment classroom totaling 17 classes. The adjustment coefficient is 17/12 = 1.42. Desks and chairs are depreciated by 8 years.
				Per student = 60/8 × 1.42 = 10.65 Yuan
Transportation tools				
Books and others	7.5	12.0	Evidence-based approach	Evidence: The Notice on the Regulations of Libraries at Primary and Junior Secondary School issued by Ministry of Education, requiring updating per primary school student is 0.5 books and 0.8 books for junior secondary student. If 15 Yuan per book, the expenses per primary student = 15 × 0.5 = 7.5 Yuan and per junior secondary school student = 15 × 0.8 = 12 Yuan
Repair and maintenance	64.9	83.9		
Equipment repair and maintenance	19	30	Professional judgment approach	In 2007, the national average value of instruments and equipment of rural primary school student is 238 Yuan. If repair and maintenance expenses account for 8 % of the original value, per student expenses = 238 × 8 % = 19.04 Yuan
				In 2007, the national average value of instruments and equipment of rural junior secondary school student is 375 Yuan. If repair and maintenance expenses account for 8 % of the original value, per student expenses = 375 × 8 % = 30 Yuan

(continued)

(continued)

	Primary schools	Junior secondary schools	Approaches	Calculation
School building repair and maintenance	39.2	48.3	Professional judgment approach	In 2007, the national average floor areas of school building per rural primary school student is 5.6 m^2. Assuming 7 Yuan per m^2 for maintenance, the per student maintenance expenses = 5.6 × 7 = 39.2 Yuan
				In 2007, the national average school building per rural junior secondary school student is 6.9 m^2. Assuming 7 Yuan per m^2 for maintenance, the per student maintenance expenses = 6.9 × 7 = 48.3 Yuan
Playground repair and maintenance	6.7	5.6	Evidence-based approach	Evidence: Standards for Checking Nine-Year Compulsory Education Universal.
				Each primary school must have 200 meter-long tracks and 2000 m^2. Each junior secondary school must have 250 meter-long tracks and 3000 m^2
				We assume that the cost of repair and maintenance per m^2 is 1 Yuan.
				Per primary school student = 2000 × 1/300 = 6.7 Yuan
				Per junior secondary school student = 3000 × 1/540 = 5.6 Yuan
Other expenses	57	80		
Reception	7	10	Best practice school approach	Average of best practice schools, 2 % of total non-personnel expenditure
Training	25	35	Evidence-based approach	Evidence: Provisional Regulations on Non-personnel Expenditure Management for Rural Primary and Junior Secondary School. This regulation requires 5 % of total annual non-personnel expenditures of schools to be spent

(continued)

(continued)

	Primary schools	Junior secondary schools	Approaches	Calculation
				on teacher training, such as transportation, meals, training materials, and accommodation.
				In this study, spending on training accounts for 7 % of total non-personnel expenditures. So, training expenses per teacher at primary schools and junior secondary schools are only 467.5 Yuan and 584.5 Yuan, respectively. In 2007, the ratio of students to teachers at primary schools and junior secondary schools were 18.7:1 and 16.7:1, respectively. According to this, per student training expenses at primary school is 25 Yuan, and it is 35 Yuan at junior secondary school.
Labor union and welfare	18	25	Evidence-based approach	Evidence: related educational policies.
				2 % of total salaries should be spent on labor union and welfare.
				The proportion of expenses for labor union and welfare in total non-personnel expenditures. = 2 % × (7/3) = 5 %
Other expenses	7	10	Professional judgment approach	Other expenses about account for 2 % of total non-personnel expenditures.

Appendix 2: Material Consumption Ration Per Student Issued by National Education Commission in 1993

Category	Items	Primary school		Junior secondary school	
		Sum	Composition	Sum	Composition
	Sum (Yuan)	124.94	100	168.79	100
	Consumptive material	47.14	37.73	77.28	45.78
Line of duty	Subtotal	22.64	18.12	26.69	15.813
	Office suppliers	4.88	3.906	5.42	3.209
	Water, electricity, and fuel	9.42	7.537	11.32	6.707
	Fuel for vehicles	3.85	3.084	3.85	2.283
	Hardware	2.49	1.989	3.67	2.174
	Environmental sanitation	2.00	1.604	2.43	1.441
Activities	Subtotal	22.25	17.81	46.91	27.793
	Teaching facilities	8.71	6.973	10.84	6.425
	Electronic audio-visual teaching	2.32	1.859	3.15	1.869
	Natural experiment	0.71	0.569	–	–
	Physics experiment	–	–	0.68	0.402
	Chemistry experiment	–	–	11.74	6.953
	Biology experiment	–	–	2.86	1.697
	Sports facilities	7.94	6.359	7.61	4.509
	Health care	0.82	0.657	1.76	1.042
	Music and art	0.91	0.732	0.83	0.492
	Labor technical education	0.83	0.662	7.43	4.404
Contingency expenses		2.24	1.796	3.68	2.180
Others	Subtotal	77.80	62.27	91.51	54.214
	Building repair	22.22	17.786	22.22	13.166
	Equipment and instruments repair	45.78	36.638	45.78	27.121
	Equipment purchase	7.11	5.694	18.35	10.874
	Travel, post and telecommunication, and training	2.69	2.156	5.15	3.052
The background of school assumed		12 classes, 540 students, original value of equipment is 294,000 Yuan		12 classes, 540 students, original value of equipment is 294,000 Yuan	

References

Augenblick, J., Myers, J., Silverstein, J., et al. (2002). *Calculation of the cost of a suitable education in Kansas in 2000-2001 using two different analytic approaches*. Augenblick & Myers, Incorporated.

Conley, D. T., & Picus, L. O. (2003). Oregon's quality education model: Linking adequacy and outcomes. *Educational Policy, 17*, 586–612.

National Educational Commission. (1992). *Material consumption ration of non-personnel expenditure for primary and junior secondary school.*

National Research Council (US). Policy Division. Board on Sustainable Development (1999). *Our common journey: a transition toward sustainability*. National Academies Press.

Odden, A. (2003). *Equity and adequacy in school finance today*. www.edsource.org/pdf/sfwquityadequacy.pdf.

Picus, L. O. (2004). School finance adequacy: Implications for school principals. *NASSP Bulletin, 88*(640), 3.

Taylor, L. (2004). Adjusting for geographic variations in teacher compensation: Updating the Texas cost-of-education index. *A report prepared for the Texas Legislature Joint Committee on Public School Finance, The Texas School Finance Project*. Austin, TX. Available at http://www.capitol.state.tx.us/psf/reports.htm

Chapter 3
Progress and Countermeasures of Student Assistance Policy in Compulsory Education

A student assistance policy based on Two Exemptions and One Subsidy (TEOS) has taken shape in China's compulsory education. The TEOS policy refers to exempting low-income students from tuition and miscellaneous fees, supplies them with free textbooks, and provides living subsidies for boarding students from low-income families. In this chapter, we analyze the student assistance policy in compulsory education—its development, status quo, problems, and countermeasures. Special attention will be given to the policy core of student assistance, TEOS.

Since the Compulsory Education Law of the People's Republic of China was promulgated in 1986, the student assistance policy in compulsory education has experienced three development stages: the initial stage (1986–1996), the slowly developing stage (1997–2002), and the rapidly developing stage (2003–2008). The formation, development, and continuous improvement of TEOS, particularly the coverage and assistance, intensified quickly after 2005, achieving a remarkable twofold effect of scaling down the dropout rate and mitigating farmers' burden. However, after analyzing current implementation of TEOS, we have discovered some problems and provided some constructive suggestions. Particularly, we focus on the living subsidy for indigent boarding students, who face some special problems. To provide methodology support for determining a reasonable living subsidy standard, we conducted a study on boarding students' living costs by survey.

3.1 Formation and Development of Student Assistance Policy in Compulsory Education

When the economy develops at a low level, the school dropout rate due to poverty is a significant factor impeding compulsory education implementation and popularization. Along with the government's gradual recognition of significance for the establishment of a student assistance policy, a compulsory education student assistance policy has been implemented, with initial and rapid development processes.

Y. Du and Z. Sun, *Research on Compulsory Education Financing in China*,
New Frontiers of Educational Research, DOI 10.1007/978-3-662-47830-1_3

3.1.1 Initial Stage: 1986–1996

The student assistance policy in compulsory education underwent preliminary formation of the policy framework, but there were shortcomings, including indistinct responsibility, feeble operability, and few financial inputs, which had insignificant effects.

Regarding financial assistance to children in poverty, the Compulsory Education Law enacted in 1986 stated that "the State shall set up student assistance fund to help the indigent students go to school." The law thus expressed a positive stance of the government toward education financial assistance for children from low-income families, although the provisions were not concrete because they neither clarified at which level the government would take financial responsibility nor quantified the actual amount of assistance to indigent children.

Rules for Implementation of Compulsory Education Law, which was promulgated in 1992, explicitly stipulated the assistance target but diminished the assistance scope. As indicated in the following provisions, "miscellaneous fees should be exempted for those students in financial difficulty pursuant to degree of poverty" and "the poor students entitled for the assistance refer to those who study at junior secondary school or special education school from families in economic difficulty and the students learning at primary school or other boarding schools are from families under indigent circumstance in minority nationality residential areas, economically underdeveloped regions and remote regions." These provisions have excluded the assistance entitlement of indigent students at primary schools from localities other than the aforementioned areas.

The Rules detailed the responsibility of the government at each level, and the Rules were the important legal regulations for the decentralized finance and decentralized management systems. However, there were no detailed provisions regarding a student financial assistance policy, no poverty benchmark, no student subsidy criteria, and even no fund source set forth in those provisions; instead, the local governments were held responsible for funding all financial assistance: "The specific implementation method for education financial assistance policy shall be provided by provincial government."

Under the Notice on Improvement of Primary and Junior Secondary School Student Subsidy System, issued jointly by the National Education Committee and the Ministry of Finance in 1995, all local governments were required to improve and consolidate the subsidy system. The Notice required them "to implement multilevel management and funding pursuant to financial system and educational management system," but there was no provision for what financial responsibility the central government should undertake, nor explicit guidelines on how local governments at various levels share the funding responsibility.

Due to the ambiguity in the provisions and responsibility, not enough incentives were given to students from poor families for access to school. In 1996, compulsory education scholarships and subsidies from governments at all levels totaled 158 million Yuan, with 118 million for junior secondary school students and 40 million for primary school students.[1] Scholarships and subsidies granted to secondary school students were higher than those for primary school students. Over this period, there was a great deal of funds contributed by nongovernmental organizations (e.g., "Hope Projects," "Spring Buds Project") to assist a large number of indigent children and alleviate the impacts of poverty on their access to school, despite the limited financial assistance from the government owing to a financial shortage.

3.1.2 Slowly Developing Stage: 1997–2002

While approaching the deadline of the Two Basics objective in 2000, the student assistance policy experienced certain advancement in the later 1990s: the central government began assuming relevant responsibility and operability was significantly strengthened. However, coverage was still limited to the indigent students from poverty areas.

In October 1997, the National Education Committee[2] and the Ministry of Finance issued the Method of Implementation of Compulsory Education Subsidy in Poverty Regions. In addition, the central government started to provide direct grants to indigent children. It was also decided to provide 130 million Yuan for setting up the compulsory education student subsidy in national poverty regions in the Ninth Five-year Plan Period, which would subsidize tuition and miscellaneous fees and textbook expenses for indigent children in some national poverty alleviation counties. This method placed the responsibility on the central government; stipulated subsidy target criteria, subsidy standards, application and appraisal methods; and implemented organizations, fund allocation procedures, supervision, and audit requirements to strengthen the operability of the assistance policy. In addition, the method has changed the provisions that are relevant to primary school student assistance and prioritized primary school student assistance.

In May 2001, Decisions on Basic Education Reform and Development (hereinafter referred to as "Decision") pointed out that the governments at all levels should improve and implement primary and junior secondary school student subsidy systems by adopting approaches such as the reduction and exemption from miscellaneous fees and textbook expenses and subsidization for boarding expenses (TEOS) to mitigate the financial burden on families. A pilot program, which supplied free textbooks to primary and junior secondary school students from poor indigent families, commenced in 2001. This program built up the initial framework of TEOS in compulsory education.

[1] All data on nationwide educational expenditures quoted in this article are from China Educational Finance Statistical Yearbook published by China Statistics Press in previous years, unless otherwise specified.

[2] The National Education Committee was renamed as the Ministry of Education in 1998.

In order to implement the Decision, the Ministry of Education, Ministry of Finance, and the Poverty Alleviation Development Leadership Office under the State Council jointly issued the Notice on Implementation and Improvement of Primary and Junior Secondary School Indigent Students Subsidy System in September 2001, which restates that the central government would establish a special fund to provide assistance to indigent students for compulsory education and requires that local governments take primary financial responsibility for the student assistance under a decentralized management system and shared funding approach.

Since 2000, some local governments have conducted active exploration of financial assistance to indigent students in compulsory education. Yunnan Province started a "three exemptions" program for 120,000 primary school students in rural areas of 25 counties along the border to offer free textbooks, as well as exemptions from tuition, miscellaneous fees, and stationary charges. The cost of this program was covered by provincial governments. The expenditures of "three exemptions" were allocated to those counties by the provincial government at the standard of 150 Yuan per student. Counties were responsible for implementation.

Guangdong Province exempted children from families with per-capita income less than 1500 Yuan in rural areas from textbook expenses, tuition, and miscellaneous fees. This program was initiated in the autumn of 2001 and covered approximately 1 million students.

Ningbo in Zhejiang Province implemented the TEOS policy covering 131 primary schools and 21 junior secondary schools in the autumn of 2002. All students at these schools were exempted from miscellaneous fees and boarding expenses. Meanwhile, some of the students from families with economic difficulties received subsidies. Approximately 33,700 students at 152 primary and junior secondary schools, including more than 8000 boarding students, received the TEOS. In all, 5 % of primary and junior secondary school students benefited from the policy.

During this period, the progress of student assistance in compulsory education showed that the central government started to undertake financial responsibility and raised the TEOS policy. Local governments at all levels began exploration for the establishment of a local assistance policy. However, there was no complete design for a student assistance policy. The objective and sharing system for student assistance needed to be clarified. The subsidy standard and coverage of subsidy needed to be increased. In 2002, a total of 685 million Yuan, including scholarships and subsidies, was provided by governments at all levels. A total of 293 million Yuan was granted to junior secondary schools and 392 million Yuan to primary schools. Primary school students take priority in the allocation of assistance.

3.1.3 Rapidly Developing Stage: 2003–2008

Although the Chinese economy has grown rapidly, China is still facing some serious social problems. At the dawn of the twenty first century, income differences had been swiftly augmented and farmers' income growth was sluggish. Disadvantaged groups were in a difficult position. Public and civilians intensively called for social justice and equity. After the Sixteenth National Congress of CPC in October 2002, the new leadership took *people-oriented* as a governance concept and *harmonious society* as development thought. After this Congress, rural area development, farmer welfare, and other issues have received unprecedented attention. It was in this background that the student assistance policy was quickly promoted by gradual expansion, including assistance scope, extension of assistance strength, clarification of responsibilities of the government at different levels, and shared funding under certain proportions.

Assistance Scope Gradually Extended—In September 2003, the State Council issued the Decision on Further Strengthening Education in Rural Areas, which defined the assistance target as students in compulsory education from families with economic difficulties. In 2005, education fund guarantee mechanism reform was deepened and implemented to enable the scope of TEOS to not only encompass students from indigent families but to gradually benefit all students in rural compulsory education. In 2006, all students in rural western China were entitled to exemptions from tuition and miscellaneous fees. In 2007, exemptions from tuitions and miscellaneous fees were extended to the countryside in central and eastern China. Indigent students in compulsory education across the country were exempted from textbook fees in 2006, and all students in rural areas enjoyed free textbooks starting in the autumn semester of 2007. Additionally, the coverage of living subsidies for indigent boarding students has been further expanded, although the assistance target was largely concentrated on the boarding students from indigent families in rural regions.

Assistance Effort and Volume Escalated—In the spring of 2005, the central government increased the textbook allowance standard from the original 55, 100, and 60 Yuan per student for primary school students, junior secondary school students and special school[3] students to 70, 140, and 70 Yuan, respectively; these amounts were further raised to 90, 180, and 90 Yuan in 2008.

On November 28, 2007, the Notice on Regulating and Improving Fund Guarantee Mechanism for Rural Compulsory Education set forth the following provision: "As of autumn semester in 2007, free national curriculum textbooks will be provided to all students in compulsory education in rural areas and the funds required for implementation of this program shall be borne by central government. From spring semester in 2008, free local curriculum textbooks will be provided to all students in rural compulsory education, and the fund demanded would be afforded by local government." Then, the students were able to get not only free national curriculum textbooks but also free local curriculum textbooks.

There was no uniform standard for boarding subsidies; they varied from one region to another. The majority of provinces adopted a scheme of 1 Yuan per student per day, or less than 1 Yuan, in a boarding subsidy program. However,

[3]Special Schools provide 7-year special education to blindness or deaf-mute children.

commencing in the autumn semester of 2007, the baseline was increased to 2 Yuan per primary school student per day and 3 Yuan for junior secondary school students, as measured for 250 school days per school year.

Responsibility of Governments at All Levels Clarified and the Fund Contribution Shared Proportionally—The TEOS policy implementation gradually established a mechanism to clarify the financial responsibility of governments at all levels. The tuition and miscellaneous fees were borne by central and local governments at a ratio of 8:2 in western China and 6:4 in central China; the ratio in eastern China was to be determined in light of the practical financial conditions of the provinces. The expenditures for free textbooks in central and western China would be assumed by the central government and the expenditures in eastern China would be borne by local governments. In the autumn semester of 2007, the central government started to bear all funds for free national curriculum textbooks for students in rural areas in compulsory education. The living subsidy was borne by local governments and the allowance target, criteria, and method was decided by local governments. From the autumn semester of 2007, the central government set the baseline of 2 Yuan per primary school student per day and 3 Yuan for junior secondary school students. If the local governments of central and western China implemented boarding student living subsidies at the national baseline criteria, the central government assumed 50 % of the funding.

Remarkable effects were achieved in the establishment of an assistance policy for students in rural compulsory education during this period; most significantly, the policy increased the backfill of a large number of students to their classrooms or public schools. Take Guangxi and Hubei, for instance. In Guangxi, 219,000 students went back to school in 2006, including 132,000 students coming back to private schools (107,000 primary school students and 25,000 junior secondary school students), 61,000 children of migrant workers (46,000 primary school students and 15,000 junior secondary school students), and 26,000 dropouts (16,000 primary school students and 10,000 junior secondary school students). In Hubei, 38,600 students went back to school, including 5447 dropouts in 2007.

The second effect achieved in this period was the alleviation of farmers' burden. At a macro level, TEOS has relieved a huge financial burden from the farmers. In 2007, the funds for "two exemptions" reached 1.13 billion in Guangxi and 992 million in Hubei, funds for TEOS came to 382 million in Heilongjiang, and the funds for exemptions from tuition and miscellaneous fees, textbooks and exercise books, and boarding fee amounted to 652 million in Zhejiang. At a household level, an average family with a child in primary school in the Guangxi countryside could have their payment reduced by 400 Yuan each year under the TEOS scheme or 200 Yuan under "two exemptions." For the family of a junior secondary school student, about 500 Yuan could be saved under TEOS or 350 Yuan under "two exemptions." The TEOS policy has actually alleviated a great deal of the financial burden of indigent families.

3.2 Analysis of the TEOS Policy for the Current Situation

As shown in the previous analysis, the TEOS policy, as one component of new mechanism, had been implemented earlier but improved in the past two years, and it achieved outstanding results in both increasing the enrollment ratio and mitigating farmers' burden. How was this policy implemented? Is the ultimate result in compliance with the policy's objectives? In this section, we conducted a survey and compared data on the provincial, county, and family levels in four sample provinces.

3.2.1 Policy Analysis of Exemptions from Tuition and Miscellaneous Fees and Free Textbooks in the Current Situation

3.2.1.1 Progress of the Miscellaneous Fee Exemption and Free Textbook Policy at the Provincial Level

The policy of exemption from tuition and miscellaneous fees and free textbooks is mainly directed by the central government. Provincial governments have developed a corresponding implementation method in their responsibility range to positively promote the implementation of the policy. The progress of the "two exemptions" policy in the four sample provinces during 2006–2007 is indicated in Tables 3.1 and 3.2, based on the data collected from the provinces.

1. **Progress in Policy Exemptions from Tuition and Miscellaneous Fees and Textbook Costs in the Guangxi Zhuang Autonomous Region**
   Guangxi was the first location to established an educational fund guarantee mechanism in compulsory education among the four sample provinces/autonomous regions. In January 2006, the Guangxi Department of Finance and Department of Education established the Implementation Plan For Exemption of Rural Students During Compulsory Education from Their Tuition and Miscellaneous Fees and Subsidizing Non-personnel Expenditure for Primary and Junior Secondary Schools (Tentative), under which the standards for exemptions from miscellaneous fees were set out: 65 Yuan per primary school student per semester in rural areas, 80 Yuan per primary school student per semester in townships, 90 Yuan per junior secondary school student per semester in rural areas, and 105 Yuan per junior secondary school student per semester in townships. This plan also stipulated that 80 % of the exemptions are to be funded by the central government, with the remaining 20 % funded by the autonomous region. For exemptions from tuition and miscellaneous fees in the cities and townships where the policy was implemented in advance, the funds needed to come from the prefecture and county finance. In western China,

Table 3.1 Implementation status of exemptions from tuition and miscellaneous fees in the sample provinces

Province/autonomous region	Standard (Yuan/Year)	Financed by	Beneficiaries (10^4)		Ratio (%)	
			2006	2007	2006	2007
Guangxi	Primary school: rural area 130, township 160; Junior secondary school: rural area 180, township 210	Central government: 80 %; Autonomous Region: 20 %	632.54	626.36	92	93
Hubei	Primary school: rural area 170, township 200; Junior secondary school: rural area 270, township 300	Central government: others: 60 %; Provincial government: 40 %	185.6	581.7	27	89
Heilongjiang	Primary school: rural area 60, township 180; Junior secondary school: rural area 90, township 220	Central government: 60 %; Provincial government: 40 %	112	336	31	92
Zhejiang	Primary school: rural area 200, township 200; Junior secondary school: rural area 260, township 260	Central government: 0 %; Provincial government: 100, 70, 50, 30 and 20 % pursuant to economic development level in the areas; County government: 0, 30, 50, 70 and 80 % pursuant to economic development conditions in the areas	–	462.9	–	92

Table 3.2 The implementation of a free textbook policy in the sample provinces

Province (autonomous region)	Standard (Yuan/year)	Financed by	Beneficiaries (10^4)		Ratio (%)	
			2006	Spring 2007	2006	Spring 2007
Guangxi	Primary school: 70; Junior secondary school: 140	Central government: 100 %	132.63	133.23	19	20
Hubei	Primary school: 70; Junior secondary school: 140	Central government: 100 %	151	151	22	23
Heilongjiang	Primary school: 70; Junior secondary school: 140	Central government: 100 %	82	103	22	28
Zhejiang		Central government: 0 %; Provincial government: 70, 50 and 0 % pursuant to economic development conditions in the areas; County government: 30, 50 and 100 % pursuant to economic development conditions in the areas	–	83.3	–	16.6

expenditures for free textbooks were funded by the central government. The standards for free textbooks were 70 Yuan per primary school student and 140 Yuan per junior secondary school student per year in central and western China. In 2006, the miscellaneous fee exemptions totaled 993.86 million Yuan, where 909.3 million Yuan was funded by the central government, 179.14 million Yuan by the autonomous region, and 5.42 million Yuan by the prefecture and county governments. In all, 92 % of students in compulsory education[4] in the autonomous region received a total of 6.33 million Yuan in benefits from the exemption. The free textbooks were valued at 121.60 million Yuan, which were solely funded by the central government and supplied to 1.33 million students (19 %).

[4]In this chapter, "all students in compulsory education" means students in the rural areas covered by the Fund Guarantee Mechanism for rural compulsory education.

In 2007, more than 1 billion Yuan (1.008847 billion) of tuition and miscellaneous fees were exempted, of which 809.3 million Yuan was from the central government, 199.34 million Yuan was from the autonomous region, and 2.03 million Yuan was from the prefecture and counties. A total of 6.26 million students were exempted from tuition and miscellaneous fees and the coverage ratio reached 93 %—a higher percentage than 2006 because of the lower number of total students; the number of students who received the exemption was actually decreased by 60,000. In the spring of 2007, 60.8 million Yuan for free textbooks was provided by the central government to benefit 1.33 million students, covering 20 % of students.

2. **Progress of Policy Exemptions for Tuition and Miscellaneous Fees and Textbook Costs in Hubei Province**

To implement the Notice on Reforming the Fund Guarantee Mechanism for Rural Compulsory Education issued by the State Council, Hubei Province issued the Notice on Implementation of Fund Guarantee Mechanism for Rural Compulsory Education in July 2006 to point out the fulfillment of the TEOS objectives in the Province in 2007 and set forth specific provisions, under which the free textbooks were to be funded by the central government. In 2006, the expenditures for exemptions from tuition and miscellaneous fees were funded by local governments. However, since 2007, central and local governments jointly fund the expenditure at a ratio of 6:4. Provincial governments assume all responsibility for local governments. The province adopted the national uniform standard for free textbooks of 70 Yuan per primary school student and 140 Yuan per junior secondary school student per school year. The standard for exemptions from miscellaneous fees was set out: 170 Yuan per primary school student and 270 Yuan per junior secondary school student in rural areas and 200 Yuan per primary school student and 300 Yuan per junior secondary school student per school year.

In 2006, tuition and miscellaneous fee exemptions amounted to 31.216 million Yuan, of which 11.608 million Yuan went to primary schools and 19.608 million Yuan to junior secondary schools. A total of 1.856 million children received tuition and miscellaneous fee exemptions, accounting for 27 % of the aggregate number of students in rural compulsory education in the province. Among them, there were 1.084 million primary school students (28 % of primary school students) and 772,000 junior secondary school students (26 % of junior secondary school students). The free textbooks accounted for 15.171 million Yuan, of which 61.51 million Yuan was for primary schools and 90.2 million Yuan was for junior secondary schools. A total of 1.51 million students—22 % of all students—received free textbooks. Of these, 870,000 were primary school students (22 % of primary school students) and 640,000 were junior secondary school students (21 % of junior secondary school students).

From the spring of 2007, the province exempted all students in compulsory education in rural areas from their tuition and miscellaneous fees to cover 5.817 million students (89 % of students in rural and urban areas). The tuition and miscellaneous fees exempted came to 84.053 million Yuan—2.7 times of that in 2006. In the spring of 2007, 1.51 million students—23 % of all students—received free textbooks, which were valued at 75.65 million Yuan and funded by the central government.

3. **Progress on Policy Exemptions from Tuition and Miscellaneous Fees and Textbook Costs in Heilongjiang Province**

   To implement the Notice on Reforming the Fund Guarantee Mechanism for Rural Compulsory Education issued by the State Council, Heilongjiang Provincial Government issued the Notice on Implementation of Fund Guarantee Mechanism for Rural Compulsory Education in February 2007 to carry out exemptions from tuition and miscellaneous fees for rural students in compulsory education, supplying free textbooks to students from poor families and offering living subsidies to poor boarding students. Miscellaneous fee exemption standards were 60 Yuan per primary school student and 90 Yuan per junior secondary school student per school year in rural areas, whereas they were 180 Yuan per primary school student and 220 Yuan per junior secondary school student per school year in towns. The tuition and miscellaneous fees exemption was jointly funded by the central government and local finance at a ratio of 6:4, and the provincial government assumed all funding obligations for the local government. In urban areas, TEOS was initiated for students from families guaranteed by the minimum living standard guarantee system urban residents; that is, the free textbooks for students from such families would be funded by provincial governments, and exemptions from tuition and miscellaneous fees would be funded by the prefecture and county government. Children of migrant farmers in compulsory education received the same benefit.

   In 2006, the province actively implemented the TEOS policy, exempting 1.12 million students in rural areas from 87.51 million Yuan in tuition and miscellaneous fees and provided 820,000 indigent students in rural areas with free textbooks worth 83 million Yuan. A total of 31 % of all students benefited from tuition and miscellaneous fee exemptions and 22 % enjoyed free textbooks.

   In 2007, all rural students in compulsory education were exempted from tuition and miscellaneous fees. Tuition and miscellaneous fees totaling 186.56 million Yuan were exempted for 3.36 million students in Heilongjiang, which accounted for 92 % of students in rural compulsory education. In the spring of 2007, the number of students receiving free textbooks came to 1.03 million, accounting for 28 % of students in rural compulsory education. The free textbooks were valued at 76.19 million Yuan.

4. **Progress in Policy Exemptions from Tuition and Miscellaneous Fees and Textbook Costs in Zhejiang Province**

   In April 2006, Zhejiang Department of Education, Department of Finance, and Bureau of Price Administration jointly promulgated Notice on Implementation of Tuition and Miscellaneous Fees Exemption for Students in Compulsory Education in Zhejiang Province, which decided that the tuition and miscellaneous fees exemptions would be implemented from the autumn of 2006. In January 2007, the provincial government issued Notice on Implementation of Reforming the Fund Guarantee Mechanism for Rural Compulsory Education to stipulate the compulsory education funds guarantee mechanism in Zhejiang Province. According to the provision of these two documents, tuition and miscellaneous fees in compulsory education would be exempted and the program would be funded by provincial, prefecture, and county governments in various proportions for provincial contributions ranging from 20, 30, 50, 70, and 100 %. The count part fund of the prefecture and county government was determined by their financial ability. The tuition and miscellaneous fees exemption standards were 130 and 160 Yuan per student per school year for primary and junior secondary schools in rural areas, respectively, and 200 and 260 Yuan per student per school year in urban areas, respectively.

In addition, the province has set relevant financial assistance policies for students with various economic difficulties, including the students from families under the minimum living standard, disabled students, and students from other disadvantaged families. The province provides them with free textbooks, free exercise books, and free boarding. Furthermore, children from low-income families[5] and minority students are provided with free textbooks and exercise books. For the students whose families encounter temporary difficulties owing to disaster, specific exemption standards will be decided by the prefecture and county government and the assistance will be jointly contributed by provincial, prefecture, and county governments, with 70 % coming from the provincial government for 31 counties and cities and 50 % from the provincial government for the other 14 counties and cities. For the remaining regions, the prefecture and county government would take responsibility.

In 2006, all students in compulsory education were exempted from tuition and miscellaneous fees amounting to 1.105 billion Yuan, in which 460 million Yuan was contributed by the provincial government. The students, who were from families with per-capita incomes less than 1500 Yuan in rural areas and 3000 Yuan in urban areas, were supplied with free textbooks and exercise books.

In 2007, Zhejiang provided tuition and miscellaneous fee exemptions for 4.629 million students in compulsory education—reaching 92, or 96 % of students at primary schools and 85 % at junior secondary schools. The value of the exemptions came to 507.12 million. Meanwhile, there were 833,000 students provided with assistance, including free textbooks and exercise books; this number accounted for 16.6 % of students, specifically 17.2 % for junior secondary school students and 15.5 % for primary school students. The expenditures for free textbooks and exercise books amounted to 123.44 million Yuan.

---

[5]The lowest income criteria in 2007 were 2000 Yuan in per-capita income per year in rural areas and 4000 Yuan in towns and cities.

3.2.1.2 Progress in the Miscellaneous Fee Exemptions and Free Textbook Policy in Sample Counties

In this section, we further examine the tuition and miscellaneous fees exemptions and free textbook policies at the county and school level. The data at the county and school levels are from 12 sample counties within four sample provinces.

1. **Data Analysis at the County Level**
   Tables 3.3 and 3.4 reflect the basic information of the implementation of miscellaneous fee exemptions and free textbook policies in 12 sample counties, based on the data collected from these counties.

   (a) **Miscellaneous Fee Exception Policy**
   As shown in Table 3.3, the miscellaneous fee exemption policy was properly implemented in 12 counties. In 2006, six counties in Zhejiang and Guangxi provided tuition and miscellaneous fee exemptions for all students in rural compulsory education, while the exemption ratio in two poverty-stricken counties in Hubei and Heilongjiang Provinces was quite high; however, in non-poverty stricken counties, only a small number of students received the exemption. In 2007, the miscellaneous fee exemption achieved complete coverage in the 12 counties.

   (b) **Free Textbook Policy**
   As shown in Table 3.4, where results are consistent with the results at the provincial level, there was no remarkable change in the implementation of

Table 3.3 Miscellaneous fee exemption in the sample counties

Sample province	Sample county	2006 farmer per-capita income (Yuan)	Exemption from miscellaneous fee coverage (%)		Primary school student coverage (%)		Junior secondary school student coverage (%)	
			2006	2007	2006	2007	2006	2007
Guangxi	Rong'an	2022	100	100	100	100	100	100
	Guiping	2560	100	100	100	100	100	100
	Yongfu	3175	100	100	100	100	100	100
Hubei	Xiaochang	1906	46.0	100	52.2	100	39.6	100
	Wuxue	3401	12.5	100	12.8	100	12.2	100
	Chibi	3542	13.5	100	14.0	100	12.9	100
Heilongjiang	Tangyuan	1148	93.1	100	87.3	100	100	100
	Keshan	3490	25.5	100	24.0	100	27.8	100
	Mishan	4273	26.3	100	25.8	100	26.9	100
Zhejiang	Jiangshan	6177	100	100	100	100	100	100
	Lin'an	8011	100	100	100	100	100	100
	Ji'an	8031	99.9	96.4	98.8	96.4	100	96.4

Table 3.4 Free textbook policy implementation in the sample counties (county questionnaire)

Sample province	Sample county	Free textbook coverage (%)		Primary school student coverage (%)		Junior secondary school student coverage (%)	
		2006	2007	2006	2007	2006	2007
Guangxi	Rong'an	23.3	25.0	21.9	23.6	25.8	27.6
	Guiping	13.6	13.7	13.4	13.4	14.2	13.1
	Yongfu	15.8	15.9	16.8	16.8	14.5	14.1
Hubei	Xiaochang	46.0	41.4	52.2	31.1	39.6	63.7
	Wuxue	12.5	14.9	12.8	14.6	12.2	15.3
	Chibi	13.5	12.5	14.0	13.2	12.9	11.8
Heilongjiang	Tangyuan	50.0	50.5	45.2	44.5	60.9	62.9
	Keshan	28.1	27.7	26.5	28.4	30.6	26.6
	Mishan	29.0	29.4	29.3	30.4	28.8	28.2
Zhejiang	Jiangshan	1.8	–	1.6	–	2.4	–
	Lin'an	–	–	–	–	–	–
	Ji'an	–	–	–	–	–	–

the free textbook policy from spring 2006 to spring 2007, and majority of counties had less than 20 % of students receiving free textbooks. The main reason was that the quota for free textbooks allocated by the central government to provinces and counties did not change much, and the local governments did not input funds to increase the quota. In comparison with 2006, the percentage of students receiving free textbooks was slightly increased as a result of the reduction of total enrollment. We have not obtained the data relevant to free textbooks in Zhejiang for the provinces not covered under the free textbook policy by the central government. Therefore, no relevant data are provided in statistics as an independent item in its counties.

As revealed in Table 3.4, the free textbook quota distribution was made in favor of the poverty-stricken counties and cities in all sample provinces; hence, a much higher percentage of students received free textbooks in such counties. However, there was no provision set forth for the distribution of free textbooks between primary and junior secondary schools. The percentage of primary school students receiving free textbooks was high in some counties but low in others. The percentage in Heilongjiang was the highest, which is in compliance with the provincial data.

2. **Data Analysis at the School and Student Levels**
   We have analyzed the implementation of exemptions from tuition, miscellaneous fees, and textbook costs at the provincial and county levels. However, it is still not enough to examine whether the ultimate beneficiaries are the schools and the

students. Therefore, if we want to know about the two exemptions in detail, we also need to examine their implementation at school and student levels.

(a) **Miscellaneous Fee Exemption Policy**

Appendix 1 shows the miscellaneous fee exemption implementation in four sample provinces at the county level. The situation of the four sample provinces is described here.

In Guangxi, according to county-level data, three sample counties were all exempted from tuition and miscellaneous fees in 2006; however, the data collected from the schools in autumn 2006 indicated that two counties, Guiping and Rong'an, basically achieved exemptions from tuition and miscellaneous fees for all students, but Yongfu County showed fairly low exemption coverage.

In Hubei, in autumn 2006, Xiaochang County had over 40 % coverage for miscellaneous fee exemptions, the highest across Hubei Province. However, the coverage in Wuxue and Chibi counties was less than 20 %. These figures were roughly in compliance with the data from these counties.

In Zhejiang, the county-level data showed almost all tuition and miscellaneous fees exempted in 2006. In contrast to this conclusion, the school data gave merely 51 % coverage in Anji County in autumn 2006.

In Heilongjiang, the data from sample counties and schools were almost identical. For example, Tangyuan County exempted almost all tuition and miscellaneous fees, but the exemption coverage was less than 30 % in Mishan County and Keshan County.

(b) **Free Textbook Policy**

We examined the implementation of the free textbook policy from the spring semester of 2005 to the autumn semester of 2006 in four sample provinces at the school level. The implementation of the free textbook policy in primary schools is described here (see Appendix 2).

First, we grouped sample schools by province. We found a big difference in the proportion of students receiving free textbooks. The average coverage in Heilongjiang was the highest in each semester, with small fluctuations. Coverage was the lowest in Zhejiang, increasing from 4 to 9 %. As an eastern province, Zhejiang itself determined the scale and coverage of the free textbook policy; because it is developed province, the lowest coverage is reasonable. In 2005, the average coverage in Guangxi was higher than that in Hubei, but in 2006 the coverage was lower than that in Hubei. The reason is that the average coverage in Guangxi did not increase, but the average coverage increased from 16 to 30 % in Hubei. This phenomenon is not consistent with the objective of the policy. Based on the objective of this policy, the undeveloped areas and disadvantage groups should take priority, so the coverage and its increment in Guangxi should be the highest. This phenomenon shows that there are still some areas that are not clear or need improvement. When the central government assumed financial responsibility for the free textbook policy, the method for how the central government distributes expenditures for free textbooks to the provincial government should be more scientific and reasonable.

Second, if we grouped sample schools by county, we would see a different picture. Although the average coverage remained constant in Guangxi and Heilongjiang at the province level, the coverage at the county level showed different trends. There were some differences in the progress of the free textbook policy development among counties in each province. In Guangxi, the average coverage was reduced from 16 to 14 % in Guiping and from 25 to 22 % in Yongfu. However, in Rong'an within Guangxi, the average coverage increased from 28 to 30 %. In Heilongjiang, the average coverage in Tangyuan was the highest in these three sample counties in four semesters, which increased from 66 % in spring semester of 2005 to 74 % in the autumn semester of 2006. The average coverage in Mishan is higher than that in Keshan, but it reduced from 56 % in the spring semester of 2005 to 52 % in the autumn semester of 2006. The average coverage in Keshan was the lowest, and the highest coverage—34 %—occurred in the spring semester of 2006.

In Hubei, although the average coverage increased in three sample counties, the difference in the average coverage became larger. It increased fastest in Xiaochang, from 19 to 46 %. In Wuxue, it increased by 3 %, whereas it increased by 4 % in Chibi. There was no difference among the average coverage in three sample counties in the spring semester of 2005. However, the average coverage of Xiaochang was about two times more than that of Wuxue and Chibi in the autumn semester of 2006.

In Zhejiang, the progress of the free textbook policy development is very slow. Because Zhejiang is a developed province, the proportion of the poverty-stricken population is lower. The group targeted by the policy is very small and some poor students do not want to receive free textbooks, afraid of discrimination from their classmates. Until the autumn semester of 2006, there were 12 % of students receiving free textbooks in Jiangshan. Meanwhile, in Ji'an and Lin'an, there were just 6 and 4 % of students receiving free textbooks, respectively.

We find that there are some differences in the average coverage among sample counties within each sample province. Therefore, it is worth paying more attention to the method to allocate expenditures from the provincial government to the county government.

The implementation of the free textbook policy in junior secondary schools is the same as in primary schools, except for Tangyuan in Heilongjiang. Although the average coverage is highest in three sample counties within Heilongjiang, it reduced from 93 to 82 %. For more details, see Appendix 2.

Based on the analysis at the student level, we came to the same conclusion as from school data analysis. When we checked the implementation of the free textbook policy in four sample provinces at the student level (see Appendix 3) in the spring semester of 2007, there were still differences in free textbook policy coverage among the four sample provinces and among sample counties in each sample province. In all, 23 % of sample primary students and 29 % of sample junior secondary school students received free textbooks.

The average coverage of the free textbook policy for primary students was the highest in Heilongjiang and the lowest in Zhejiang. If considering sample students by county, the difference among counties can be shown:

- Guangxi: The average coverage is 12 % in Guiping, 20 % in Yongfu, and 29 % in Rong'an.
- Hubei: The average coverage is 39 % in Xiaochang, 14 % in Wuxue, and 9 % in Chibi.
- Zhejiang: The average coverage is 17 % in Jiangshan, 4 % in Ji'an, and 5 % in Lin'an.
- Heilongjiang: The average coverage is 50 % in Mishan, 88 % in Tangyuan, and 24 % in Keshan.

The average coverage for the free textbook policy for junior secondary school students is 23 % in Guangxi, 26 % in Hubei, 7 % in Zhejiang, and 68 % in Heilongjiang. The highest coverage occurs in Heilongjiang and the lowest is in Zhejiang. After grouping sample students by county, we found that the situation for the free textbook policy for junior secondary school students is the same as that for primary students, which shows great fluctuations in coverage for the policy among sample counties.

3.2.1.3 Household Survey in Rong'an County within Guangxi

The household survey in Rong'an County within Guangxi collected data for children and their family background from autumn 2005 to spring 2007. We selected five townships as samples—Yayao, Dajiang, Fushi, Tantou, and Dongqi—which were selected based on their economic development and farmer's income level.

From autumn 2005 to autumn 2006, there were about 28 % of students receiving free textbooks. In spring 2007, the percentage of students receiving free textbooks increased to 39 %. To further examine the free textbook policy, we grouped the sample students by township. The findings are described here.

Although the coverage of the free textbook policy increased in each sample township in the four provinces, the coverage levels were quite different from each other. Yayao is the most developed township both in economy and farmer's income, but the coverage in Yayao is the lowest. In Dongqi, although its economic development and farmer's income is the lowest, the coverage was not the highest. This seems to be inconsistent with the objective of the policy. In autumn 2005, the highest coverage was 35.78 %, which occurred in Tantou. In spring and autumn 2006, the highest coverage levels were 38.98 and 41.94 %, respectively, which were both in Fushi. In spring 2007, the coverage in Dajiang was the highest, reaching 60.87 %.

From autumn 2005 to autumn 2006, there was no great difference in the coverage of the free textbook policy in sample townships, excluding Yayao. However, in spring 2007, the coverage in Dajiang was much higher than that in other townships, with 20 % at least. As illustrated in these examples, although a township's economic development is one of factors in the method to allocate free textbooks from county government to township, other unobserved factors also determined the free textbook allocation. Before free textbooks are supplied for every student in rural compulsory education, it is interesting to examine the method of free textbook allocation in a county.

We not only examined the method to allocate free textbooks from county governments to townships, but also paid attention to the method to distribute the free textbooks from school to student. We aimed to find out the factors influencing free textbook distribution to students. We mainly focus on the student's individual factors and background of his or her family. The student's individual factors include gender and education information. The background of a student's family consists of economic capital, cultural capital, and social capital.

First, we examined whether a family's economic capital influenced children's receipt of free textbooks. We calculated the wealth index of the households, based on the information provided in the household survey. The method to assign the wealth index is as follows: if the family owns a color television, motorcycle, mobile phone, and telephone, we assigned 4 as the wealth index of the family. If the family possesses three of the four appliances, we assigned 3 as the wealth index of the family. Wealth index values of 2 and 1 were assigned similarly. The higher the wealth index is, the better economic condition of the family is. Table 3.5 describes the provision of free textbooks grouped by wealth index. Over 40 % of students

Table 3.5 Free textbook coverage for 6- to 16-year-olds in Rong'an County of Guangxi autonomous region (%)

	Autumn 2005	Spring 2006	Autumn 2006	Spring 2007
Total	28.31	28.57	28.37	38.84
Sample township				
Yayao	16.05	14.81	15.56	28.87
Dajiang	29.85	27.94	25.00	60.87
Fushi	31.03	38.98	41.94	35.82
Tantou	35.78	33.33	33.91	39.42
Dongqi	27.14	28.77	27.59	34.41
Wealth index				
0	20.69	31.03	29.41	29.03
1	31.88	32.86	32.05	41.56
2	32.12	32.14	33.55	44.81
3	23.16	22.68	21.15	33.93
4	27.27	23.21	22.58	33.93
Sample size	385	392	430	430

with wealth indexes of 1 and 2 received free textbooks; this group had the highest percentage of students receiving free textbooks. Over 30 % of students with wealth indexes of 3 and 4 received free textbooks. The problem seems to lie in the students with wealth indexes of zero, because the percentage of this group to receive free textbooks was relatively low.

Based on this analysis, we found that there were differences among the groups who received free textbooks. Second, in order to get a clearer picture of what factors determined the children who received free textbooks, we established a probit model in which the dependent variable is whether the student received free textbooks. The dependent variable is the pseudo-variable, where 1 represents that the student received free textbooks, and 0 represents that the student did not receive free textbooks. The explanatory variables are as follows:

Student gender: 1 for female and 0 for male
School type: 1 for junior secondary school and 0 for primary school
Household economic capital: measured by wealth index
Household cultural capital: measured by householder's education background, with 1 for having completed grade 9 and above, and 0 for under grade 9

Household social capital: measured by job of relatives or intimates. The greater the value is, the stronger the household social capital is. The types of relatives' jobs are strong social capital, and the types of intimates' jobs are weak social capital.

Table 3.6 shows the regression result. Comparing models 1, 2, and 3, we added a control variable of township to examine unobserved influences. However, whether the location of residence is controlled does not affect the regression results. In these models, we found the following:

Table 3.6 Probit model for measuring free textbooks for age 6–16 in Spring 2007 (*sample size* 361)

Explanatory variable	Model 1	Model 2	Model 3	Model 4	Model 5	Model 6
Student gender	0.0833	0.0904	0.0684	0.1151	0.1226	0.1024
School type	−0.1826	−0.1557	−0.1593	−0.1900	−0.1608	−0.1640
Household economic capital	−0.0258	−0.0406	−0.0685	−0.0694	−0.0635	−0.0943
Household cultural capital		−0.2570*	−0.2460*		−0.2526*	−0.2441*
Strong social capital		0.1127**			0.1142**	
Weak social capital			0.0940**			0.0991**
Township	No	No	No	Yes	Yes	Yes

**$p < 0.05$; *$p < 0.1$

1. Whether the student obtained free textbooks is not significantly associated with his or her family's economic status. This indicates that it is difficult to target the poorest students in practice when the coverage of free textbooks extends to 30 or 40 %.
2. Compared with a student whose parents had less than a ninth-grade education, a student whose parents completed grade 9 or above has fewer chances to receive free textbooks.
3. The stronger the social capital is, the greater is the chance for the student to get free textbooks. This illustrates that free textbook distribution is closely related to the social capital of a family.

3.2.1.4 Brief Summary

As shown, there are some differences in the implementation of the "two exemptions" among the four provinces. Heilongjiang had the lowest miscellaneous fee exemption standard in its primary and junior secondary schools in rural areas, whereas Zhejiang had the highest rural primary school exemption standard—triple that in Heilongjiang. Hubei had the highest junior secondary school exemption standard in rural areas, also tripling the standard adopted in Heilongjiang. However, the three provinces (autonomous region) have roughly the same approach for financial contributions to miscellaneous fee exemptions: the provincial government assumed the responsibility undertaken by the local governments at various levels. The miscellaneous fee exemption policy experienced rapid implementation. Up to 2007, the four provinces and region had provided exemptions from tuition and miscellaneous fees for all students in compulsory education in rural areas, and the coverage was over 92 % for all provinces and region.

The free textbook coverage did not change much over the two years, but the difference among four provinces and region was great. Guangxi, the most underdeveloped province that had the highest ratio of indigent students among the four provinces, had lower exemption coverage than Hubei (19 % in 2006 and 20 % in 2007 in Guangxi vs. 22 % in 2006 and 23 % in spring 2007 in Hubei) and Heilongjiang (22 % in 2006 and 28 % in spring 2007). The central government's method to allocate expenditures for free textbooks is unreasonable. The lowest free textbook coverage in Zhejiang might be because its population of indigent people is the smallest in the four provinces. From autumn 2007, the central government started to provide frees textbook for all students in rural compulsory education.

In the implementation of the student assistance policy, there are two problems that have not been resolved in practice. One is how to reasonably allocate expenditures from the central government to provincial governments and from provincial governments to county governments. The other is how to select poor students at the school level. The free textbook policy has covered all students in compulsory education in rural areas since autumn 2007 so this policy does not face these two problems. However, for other special policies to assist poor students, we still need to address these issues.

3.2.2 Current Situation of the Living Subsidy Policy for Indigent Boarding Students

The living subsidy for indigent boarding students is a very important part of TEOS. The objective of this policy is to alleviate the financial burden of families who send their children to school and to reduce the possibility of dropout due to poverty. At the initial stage, the living subsidy policy is in the weakest place within the TEOS policy. There are no clear provisions on the scale and standard of the subsidy, and all the financial responsibility lies with the local government, especially the county government. However, the situation changed dramatically in autumn 2007. The central government stipulated the minimum standard for the subsidy and also assumed 50 % of the expenditures, according to the minimum standard of the subsidy with encouragement of central government behavior. Some provincial governments also share a certain proportion of the expenditures for the subsidy. These behaviors reduced financial burden of county governments and made great progress for the subsidy policy. In this section, we analyze the implementation of this policy at provincial, county, school, and student levels.

3.2.2.1 Status Quo of the Living Subsidy Policy for Indigent Boarding Students at the Provincial Level

The living subsidy for indigent boarding students is an integral part of the compulsory education fund guarantee new mechanism implemented in 2006. Provincial governments stipulate relevant provisions to improve the living subsidy policy for indigent boarding student.

1. **Provisions and Implementation of Living Subsidy Policy for Indigent Boarding Students in Guangxi**
   In February 2006, the Department of Finance and Department of Education of Guangxi Zhuang Autonomous Region issued the Notice on Assuring Fund Guarantee Mechanism in Rural Compulsory Education and Strengthening Budget Management. Under the provisions of the Notice, the living subsidy for needy boarding students would be funded by the prefecture and county governments. The subsidy target, subsidy standard, and how to subsidize would be determined by prefecture and county governments.
   In 2006, the region-wide living subsidy amounted to 29.04 million Yuan, with 9.14 million contributed by the prefecture government and 19.9 million by the county government. There were 232,000 recipients, equal to 3.4 % of all students in compulsory education, in which 79,000 were primary school students (1.7 %) and 153,000 were junior secondary school students (6.7 %). In spring 2007, 339,200 indigent students were under the subsidy plan—5 % of all students in compulsory education in Guangxi.

2. **Provisions and Implementation of Living Subsidy Policy for Indigent Boarding Students in Hubei**
   In July 2006, Hubei issued the Notice on Implementation of Reforming Fund Guarantee Mechanism for Rural Compulsory Education. Similar to Guangxi, Hubei Provincial Government shifted the responsibility for the boarding student living subsidy to the county government. The governments at the prefecture and county level were required to establish the standard of living subsidies for the indigent boarding students.
   In 2006, approximately 763,000 indigent boarding students received living subsidies in the province, which is equivalent to 11 % of all students in rural compulsory education, including 75,000 primary school students (1.9 %) and 688,000 junior secondary school students (22.9 %). A total of 131.73 million Yuan of subsidy was granted.
   In spring 2007, 815,000 indigent boarding students received living subsidies, equivalent to 12.5 % of all students in compulsory education, where 85,000 were primary school students (2.3 %) and 730,000 were junior secondary school students (26.1 %).
3. **Provisions and Implementation of Living Subsidy Policy for Indigent Boarding Students in Heilongjiang**
   In February 2007, Heilongjiang Provincial Government issued the Notice on Implementation of Fund Guarantee Mechanism for Rural Compulsory Education. According to the Notice, all funds required for the living subsidy will be contributed by provincial and prefecture/county governments at a ratio of 7:3. The subsidy coverage is estimated to reach approximately 25 % and the standard will be 400 Yuan per student per year in 2009. In comparison with other provinces, Heilongjiang has developed the most explicit program with the highest portion of financial support from the provincial government.
   In 2006, Heilongjiang arranged 30.13 million Yuan of living subsidies for 124,000 boarding students from indigent families in rural areas; the coverage reached 3.4 %. In spring 2007, 30.13 million Yuan was allocated to 173,000 students—4.7 % of total students in compulsory education in the province—of which 43,000 were primary school students (2.0 %) and 130,000 were junior secondary school students (8.3 %). The subsidies totaled 43.37 million Yuan, with 24.255 million financed by the provincial government, 8.72 million by the prefecture government, and 10.395 million by the county government.
4. **Provisions and Implementation of Living Subsidy Policy for Indigent Boarding Students in Zhejiang**
   As a developed province in eastern China, Zhejiang did not accept the allowance fund under the new compulsory education mechanism policy from the central government, and its policies were somewhat different from that in central and western China. In January 2007, the province issued the Notice on Implementation of Fund Guarantee Mechanism for Compulsory Education to give various assistance policies to indigent students of different types. According to the Notice, students from families under the minimum living

standard, disabled students, and students from other disadvantaged families received boarding subsidies as well as free textbooks and exercise books. The government also provided the indigent students in compulsory education in rural areas with a free, nutritious meal; the lunch was offered to not only indigent boarding students but also to non-boarding students from poor families. In rural areas, any student with a family per-capita income less than 2000 Yuan was considered to be an indigent student. The subsidy fund contribution was shared by provincial, prefecture, and county governments—70 % from provincial governments in 31 counties and 50 % from provincial governments in 14 counties. In the remaining regions, the fund was supported by prefecture and county governments.

As indicated in above provisions, Zhejiang already had a student subsidy policy, but this policy was a little different from the national, as it was for free boarding and nutritious meals. A total of 5.8 % of students enjoyed the free meal in 2006; the coverage was increased to 7.6 % or 380,000 students in 2007. The expenditure for free boarding was 10.35 million Yuan in 2007, but no reliable information was available about the number of students who enjoyed the exemption.

Tables 3.7 and 3.8 indicate the progress of the living subsidy for indigent boarding student in four sample provinces based on survey data. Table 3.7 shows that Heilongjiang and Zhejiang provincial governments assumed the most financial responsibility for living subsidies for indigent boarding students. By contrast, in Guangxi and Hubei, all the financial responsibility was given to prefecture and county governments.

At the provincial level, we examined the implementation of the living subsidy for indigent boarding students from 2006 to spring 2007 (see Table 3.8). The number of recipients was the highest in Hubei and the lowest in Heilongjiang. The percentage of recipients among all students shows the same pattern. The proportion of recipients for total rural boarding students in Hubei was still the highest, but the proportion in Heilongjiang was higher than that of Guangxi. This indicates that the proportion of boarding students to total students in Heilongjiang is lower than that of Guangxi.

Comparing the policy implementation of 2006 with that of 2007, we find that the governments of the four provinces put more effort into this policy. All four

Table 3.7 Living subsidy policy for indigent boarding students in sample provinces

Province	Subsidy standard (Yuan/year)	Ratio of funding at various levels
Guangxi	None	100 % by county government
Hubei	None	100 % by county government
Heilongjiang	400	70 % by provincial government 30 %
Zhejiang[a]	None	70, 50, 0 % by provincial government 30, 50, 100 % by prefecture and county government

[a]Nutrition meal policy in Zhejiang Province

Table 3.8 Implementation of living subsidy policy for indigent boarding students in sample provinces

Province/region	Beneficiary (10^4)		Percent of all students (%)		Percent of all boarding students (%)		Percent of rural boarding students (%)[b]	
	2006	2007	2006	2007	2006	2007	2006	2007
Guangxi	23.2	33.9	3.4	5.0	11.38	16.54	11.70	16.99
Hubei	76.3	81.5	11.0	12.5	34.95	41.08	35.85	42.46
Heilongjiang	12.4	17.3	3.4	4.7	32.03	40.45	33.66	42.10
Zhejiang[a]	29.7	38.0	5.8	7.6	–	–	–	–

[a]Data for students receiving free meals in Zhejiang are based on the report by Liu Xiping, chief of Department of Education given at a conference

[b]Boarding students in rural area refers to the boarding students in townships and rural areas

indicators increased substantially. Recipients in Guangxi increased from 232,000 to 339,000—an increase of about 107,000, the biggest increase in absolute numbers. In 2007, the proportion of recipients in Hubei and Heilongjiang reached more than 40 %, which theoretically should cover most of the indigent boarding students. Of course, the percentage of boarding students that is indigent students depends on the poverty standard.

3.2.2.2 Implementation of Living Subsidy Policy for Indigent Boarding Students at the County Level and School Level

In this section, we examine the progress of the living subsidy policy for indigent boarding students at the county level. These analyses at the county level give a more detailed description of the living subsidy policy for indigent boarding students within each sample province.

1. **Data Analysis at the County Level**
   Unlike the miscellaneous fee exemption and free textbook policy, county governments are supposed to assume great financial responsibility under the boarding student subsidy policy and have more freedom in decision-making. Table 3.9 shows that big differences exist in the subsidy standard. Heilongjiang has a uniform standard in four sample provinces, which is the highest at 400 Yuan for per student per year. However, Guangxi and Hubei do not have a uniform subsidy standard in provinces. Different counties have different subsidy standards. In Hubei, the subsidy is completely assumed by the county government. In Guangxi, the county government assumes 60–70 % of expenditures for indigent boarding student living subsidies. In Heilongjiang, the county government assumes 30 % of financial responsibility for indigent boarding student living subsidies. The coverage of this policy is very low in most sample counties. Only Rong'an and Yongfu in Guangxi exceed 10 %. In addition, the coverage of the policy is not determined by economic development level.

Table 3.9 Implementation conditions for the living subsidy policy for indigent boarding students in the sample counties

Province	Sample County	2006 per farmer income (Yuan)	Per student subsidy standard (Yuan year)		CGFR (%)	Beneficiaries (student)		Coverage (%)	
			PS	JSS		2006	2007	2006	2007
Guangxi	Rong'an	2022	150	150	60	3465	3585	9.5	10.5
	Guiping	2560	220	220	67	500	1500	0.2	0.5
	Yongfu	3175	280	340	70	1591	3706	6.0	14.1
Hubei	Xiaochang	1906	80	80	100	–	6250	–	6.1
	Wuxue	3401	200	200	100	1500	2500	1.5	3.0
	Chibi	3542	300	300	100	–	1935	–	2.9
Heilongjiang	Tangyuan	1148	400	400	30	1073	1413	3.8	5.1
	Keshan	3490	400	400	30	614	614	1.4	1.5
	Mishan	4273	400	400	30	1031	1633	2.6	4.1
Zhejiang[a]	Jiangshan	6177	–	–	–	1105	–	1.9	–
	Lin'an	8011	–	–	–	–	–	–	–
	Ji'an	8031	–	–	–	846	827	1.9	1.8

[a]Only the number of students enjoying free meals was obtained; other data were not available

Note PS refers to primary school, JSS refers to junior secondary school, and CGFR refers to county government's financial responsibility

2. **Data Analysis at the School Level**
In Appendices 4 and 5, at the school level we examined the implementation of the indigent boarding student living subsidy in the four sample provinces from spring 2005 to autumn 2006. We found that if economic development and farmers' income level in a county is the lower, the proportions of the beneficiaries—both in total students and in total boarding students—are higher. After grouping the sample schools by province and by county, we found more details. Appendix 4 shows that the proportion of beneficiaries to total students first went up and then went down in Guangxi, Hubei, and Heilongjiang. The proportion in Zhejiang increased first, then decreased, and rose again. Guangxi started to implement the living subsidy policy for indigent boarding students at a higher level, but the progress of this policy development was slow. The proportion of beneficiaries to total students increased from 9.48 % in spring 2005 to 10.37 % in autumn 2006. Hubei began to implement the policy with a lower proportion of beneficiaries to total students, but the progress to develop the policy was fast. The proportion of beneficiaries to total students went up to 10.04 % in autumn 2006 from 2.54 % in spring 2005. This indicates that the proportion of beneficiaries to total students fluctuated because of inconsistent efforts by the county government. In Appendix 4, we also found that there is difference in the proportion of beneficiaries in total students among counties. The lower the economic development

level is, the higher the proportion is. This illustrates two points: (1) the lower the economic development level is, the more the policy demands are; and (2) the lower the economic development level is, the heavier the financial burden to implement the policy is. This makes a poverty-stricken county's finances worse. Therefore, we can come to two conclusions: the financial responsibility of implementing this policy should be transferred to a higher level of government; and a reasonable fund-sharing mechanism for indigent boarding student living subsidies should be established, in which the policy should be jointly funded by the central government and local governments.

In Appendix 5, we checked the implementation of the living subsidies for indigent boarding students in the four sample provinces from spring 2005 to autumn 2007, with the proportion of beneficiaries to total boarding students. In spring 2005, the proportion in Heilongjiang was the highest. In autumn 2007, the proportion in Hubei was the highest. From the descriptive statistics in Appendix 5, we found that the proportion of the beneficiaries to total boarding students fluctuated sharply. Another finding is that the lower economic development level is, the higher this proportion is.

There is a common characteristic between Appendices 4 and 5—the proportion of the beneficiaries to both total students and total boarding students fluctuated sharply in this period. Thus, because the financial responsibility of the living subsidy policy is taken by the local government, especially the county government, and there is no clear policy objective, the local government has more freedom to implement the policy. Local governments, especially county governments, determine whether to put more or less effort into the policy. Because of their financial limitations, local governments implement the policy in a limited fashion, not considering the real demand from the target group of the policy. Also, local officials' policy preference determines whether the objective of this policy can be realized or not.

To improve the living subsidies for indigent boarding students, it is crucial to set up a reasonable fund-sharing mechanism for the policy to increase transfer payments from higher level governments to county governments and guarantee the county government's adequate finance to implement the policy. Also, the central government or provincial government should design a scientific method to select indigent boarding students and stipulate the clear objective of the policy to release alleviate the financial burden of boarding students. With a financial guarantee and mandatory policy objective, the county government can implement this policy better and achieve more significant effects.

3.2.2.3 Analysis of Household Survey in Rong'an County of Guangxi

The household survey in Rong'an County within Guangxi collected data about students and their family background from autumn 2005 to spring 2007. We selected five townships as samples—Yayao, Dajiang, Fushi, Tantou and Dongqi—which were ordered by economic development and farmers' income level.

In autumn 2005, the proportion of beneficiaries to total boarding students was the highest in Tantou at 11.63 %; the proportion in Yayao was higher than that of others at 9.09 %; and the proportion in Dongqi was the lowest at 0 %, where the economic development and farmers' income level was the lowest. In spring 2006, Fushi's proportion of beneficiaries to total boarding students was the highest at 14.29 %; Tantou was higher than the others at 11.63 %; and the proportion of Dajiang was the lowest at 3.57 %. In autumn 2006, the proportion of beneficiaries to total boarding students was 13.33 % in Fushi, which was the highest; Tantou's proportion was 10.87 %, higher than that of others; and the proportion in Dajiang was 3.23 %, the lowest. This indicates that the method to allocate expenditures for living subsidies for indigent boarding student from the county governments to townships was not reasonable and scientific from autumn 2005 to autumn 2006. In spring of 2007, the lower economic development level was in each sample township, the higher the proportion of beneficiaries in total boarding students was. The proportion in Tantou was the highest, reaching 14 %. Yayao's proportion was the lowest, decreasing to 5.26 %. This shows that the method became more reasonable and scientific (Table 3.10).

We not only examined the method to allocate expenditures for the policy but also checked whether the beneficiaries were indigent boarding students or not. We identified whether a boarding student was an indigent student by his or her family's wealth index (the family's wealth index is the wealth index from the household survey analysis about the free textbook policy). We found that the proportion of those beneficiaries with a "0" for wealth index in total boarding students was the highest. The higher the wealth index was, the harder it was to identify indigent students. Therefore, the proportion of beneficiaries with a wealth index of 1 to 4

Table 3.10 Subsidy target percentage for boarding students aged 6–16 in Rong'an County, Guangxi

	Autumn 2005	Spring 2006	Autumn 2006	Spring 2007
Total	7.97	8.97	7.69	9.04
Township				
Yayao	9.09	8.89	8.16	5.26
Dajiang	3.57	3.57	3.23	6.06
Fushi	7.69	14.29	13.33	11.11
Tantou	11.63	11.63	10.87	14.00
Dongqi	0.00	6.67	3.57	10.00
Wealth index				
0	28.57	25.00	20.00	14.29
1	4.00	8.00	6.06	15.79
2	9.30	11.11	10.00	8.47
3	2.86	2.70	2.33	6.38
4	10.71	10.00	9.09	3.33
No. of samples	138	145	169	188

fluctuated among groups. However, from spring 2007, we found a good trend that the higher the wealth index of a boarding student's family is, the lower is the possibility that he or she received a living subsidy. This indicates that the method to distribute living subsidies to beneficiaries became more scientific.

To further examine the factors influencing whether indigent boarding students receive a living subsidy, we established a probit model in which the dependent variable is whether the student receives a living subsidy. The dependent variable is a pseudo-variable, where 1 represents that the student receives the living subsidy and 0 represents not. The explanatory variables are as follows:

Student gender: 1 for female and 0 for male
School type: 1 for junior secondary school and 0 for primary school
Household economic capital: measured by wealth index
Household cultural capital: measured by householder's education background, where 1 is for completing grade 9 and above and 0 is for less than a ninth-grade education

Household social capital: measured by job of relatives or intimates. The greater the value is, the stronger the household social capital is. The types of relatives' jobs indicate strong social capital, and the types of intimates' jobs indicate weak social capital.

Table 3.11 shows the regression results, which are as follows:

1. When the living subsidy policy coverage for indigent boarding student is small, it is easy to select out the poorest boarding students. Compared with the free textbook policy, whether a student can get the living subsidy is determined by his or her household wealth index.
2. There is a negative linear correlation between the student receiving a subsidy and his or her household wealth index. A primary school student is more likely to receive a living subsidy than a junior secondary school student, and a female student is more likely to receive it than a male student. This indicates that the beneficiaries of this policy are actually disadvantaged groups.
3. Compared with the free textbook policy, the implementation of the living subsidy policy for indigent boarding students does not have negative effects

Table 3.11 Probit model for measuring boarding subsidy for students aged 6–16 in Spring 2007 (*sample size* 159)

Explanatory variable	Model 1	Model 2	Model 3
Student gender	0.3582	0.4007	0.4427
School type	−0.3291	−0.2815	−0.2993
Household economic capital	-0.2772^{**}	-0.1854^{*}	-0.1917^{*}
Household cultural capital	–	−0.4175	−0.4235
Strong social capital	–	-0.2158^{*}	–
Weak social capital	–	–	−0.1079

$^{**}p < 0.05$; $^{*}p < 0.1$

from a student's household cultural capital and household social capital. However, after the coverage extend to 30–40 %, the implementation of the free textbook policy deviates from the target groups because of the negative factors, such as student's household cultural capital and household social capital. When the living subsidy policy for indigent boarding students further extends its coverage, it is crucial to design a scientific method to identify the real indigent boarding students.

3.3 Problems and Countermeasures of the TEOS Policy

Based on the analyses presented in this chapter, we have summarized the problems in the policy implementation process and give corresponding policy suggestions.

3.3.1 Problems and Countermeasures of the Miscellaneous Fee Exemption Policy

3.3.1.1 Problems

First, the miscellaneous fee exemption policy brings about a shortage of non-personnel expenditures. The reason is that the fiscal appropriation standards for the miscellaneous fee exemption are lower than the standards for miscellaneous fees.

Second, because there are some differences in the miscellaneous fee exemption standards among provinces and among counties in most provinces, the standards of miscellaneous fee exemption appropriation from the central government to provincial governments and from provincial governments to county governments are different among provinces and among counties. This approach of miscellaneous fee exemption appropriation leads to new inequities.

Third, the number of students in the appropriation formula is the statistic number from the previous year, so the fiscal appropriation does not meet the real demand. Finally, the free textbook policy does not cover private school students and children of migrant farmers.

3.3.1.2 Countermeasures

Considering the problems of implementing miscellaneous fee exemptions, there is much room to improve this policy.

First, the central government should set up a benchmark for non-personnel expenditures and provide an adjustment coefficient for non-personnel expenditures.

Miscellaneous fee exemptions are part of student assistance policies and can reduce the burden of students' families. Actually, in the past, miscellaneous fees were used as non-personnel expenditures in schools. In essence, a miscellaneous fee exemption means that the non-personnel expenditures of schools are no longer driven by miscellaneous fees but by the government. From this point of view, the miscellaneous fee exemption is just a temporary arrangement. In the end, the government should set a benchmark for non-personnel expenditures that is adequate to ensure school operation. Meanwhile, the government should also design adjustment coefficients for benchmarks of non-personnel expenditures, based on regional geographic variation, price variation, school and class scale variation, and others.

Second, miscellaneous fee exemptions should cover the students of non-profit private schools. In recent years, the miscellaneous fee exemption policy has covered all students in official compulsory education. To provide equal treatment to all children in rural areas, the miscellaneous fee exemption policy should also benefit students who attend private schools with education vouchers.

Third, the miscellaneous fee exemption policy should cover the children of migrant farmers. In the process of urbanization, many farmers migrate to urban areas. Their children also migrate to urban areas with them. In urban areas, these children are the disadvantaged group. They cannot benefit from miscellaneous fee exemptions due to the procedure and qualification certificate. The miscellaneous fee exemption policy must cover the children of migrant farmers to ensure these children's compulsory educational rights.

Fourth, it is crucial to check the real current enrollments in compulsory education for the number of students in the appropriation formula. Whether the appropriation for miscellaneous fee exemptions can meet the need of non-personnel expenditures of a school is determined by the number of students in the appropriation formula. We should find a reliable way to get the real enrollment in time.

3.3.2 Problems and Countermeasures of the Free Textbook Policy

3.3.2.1 Problems

First, the free textbook policy only covers textbooks for the national curriculum. Local curriculum textbooks and ancillary materials are still purchased by the students' families.

Second, the allocation of the free textbook fund has some problems at each level of government. Some provinces with a high percentage of poor students to total students get a low percentage of free textbook funds, while the coverage for free textbooks is higher in provinces with less indigent students. In some counties, free textbook support does not favor poor families because the method to select the poor students is not clear and objective.

Lastly, and the same problem as with the miscellaneous fee exemption policy, the policy does not give enough attention to migrant children and the indigent students of non-profit private schools.

3.3.2.2 Countermeasures

Considering the problems of implementing a free textbook policy, we suggest some ways to strengthen this policy.

First, the funding standard for free textbooks should be increased so that the free textbook policy can cover not only national curriculum textbooks but also local curriculum textbooks and ancillary materials. Before the end of this study, based on the same concern, the government improved the free textbook policy and stipulated that the provincial government would be in charge of providing free local curriculum textbooks. However, there are still some controversies on the ancillary materials, because it is difficult to give clear definitions on ancillary materials.

Second, in order to let migrant children and non-profit private school students enjoy free textbooks, government can borrow from international experience with education vouchers to design a voucher system for the migrant children and students at non-profit private schools.

Third, although the free textbook policy has covered all students in rural compulsory education since autumn 2007, we still need to attach importance to those problems in the allocation of free textbooks. The government should set up a relative information system and reasonable appropriation formula in order to improve the method to select poor students and the method to allocate funds.

3.3.3 Problems and Countermeasures of the Living Subsidy Policy for Indigent Boarding Students

3.3.3.1 Problems

Compared with the "two exemptions" policy, the progress of the "one subsidy" policy has much room for improvement.

First, there are no clear provisions on the coverage and subsidy standard—both the coverage and the standard are very low. For example, in Rong'an within Guangxi, the subsidy standard is 150 Yuan per year per student. However, a primary school student's living cost is about 123 Yuan per month. The 150 Yuan subsidy accounts for about one-tenth of the living cost. The indigent student will be in a difficult situation with such a low subsidy.

Second, the subsidy does not cover non-boarding indigent students. These poor students also are faced with a living cost burden, which may lead to them drop out of school.

Third, the assistance approach of the subsidy is unitary. The subsidy only provides cash to students or their parents. This approach cannot ensure that all of this cash is used for students' living costs.

Fourth, the method to select eligible students needs to be improved urgently. After this policy extends its coverage gradually, if the method is not perfect, the policy will deviate from its intended target groups.

3.3.3.2 Countermeasures

Considering the problems of implementing a free textbook policy, there exists much room to improve this policy.

First, local governments should set up scientific subsidy standards. Based on the boarding student's actual living costs, the government should set up a reasonable subsidy standard to ensure that the subsidy can guarantee the student's living.

Second, the government should design a clear method to select poor students in order to guarantee the objective of this policy. The subsidy should assist all targeted students selected by the scientific method. Based on this authentic method, we can get the number or the percentage of indigent students. Then, we can determine the need for funding of the indigent student subsidy.

Third, the subsidy should not only target poor boarding students but all poor students.

Fourth, it is crucial to design multiple approaches to assist poor students. Currently, the approach to assist the poor students is relatively unitary. Because the need for the subsidy is quite complex in practice, when we design the approach to assist poor students, we should take into account the complexity of providing multiple approaches for the subsidy. Taking Zhejiang as an example, the government provides a free lunch for poor students who need to take lunch at school.

3.4 Study on the Boarding Student Living Costs

With the implementation of a new policy for boarding student living subsidies, the subsidy standard increased to 2 Yuan per primary school student per day and 3 Yuan per junior secondary school student per day; the central government will take 50 % of the financial responsibility. Much progress has been made in living subsidies for indigent boarding students. However, we are still not sure that such a subsidy standard can cover all of a boarding student's living costs.

To set up a subsidy standard, we should get full information on boarding students' living costs. Thus, a study on boarding students' living costs is imperative. In general, the boarding students' cost is comprised of three parts: food, dormitory, and transportation expenses. The dormitory fee consists of rent, water, electricity, and other relevant fees the student submitted to the school. In this section, we estimate a boarding student's living costs by two sets of data: a sample school student survey and a household survey.

3.4.1 Study Based on Sample School Student Data

We sampled a class of students at grade 5 in sample primary schools and a class of students at grade 2 in sample secondary schools. However, the proportion of boarding students to sample students is small. In order to make this study representative, we selected sample students in four sample counties where the proportion of boarding students in sample students was higher: Yongfu of Guangxi, Wuxue of Hubei, Ji'an of Zhejiang, and Mishan of Heilongjiang. The descriptive statistic results are shown in Table 3.12. Both the average living cost per boarding student and its composition are presented.

The living cost for a primary school boarding student in Wuxue is 144 Yuan per month, which is the lowest. The living cost for a junior secondary school student in Wuxue is still the lowest, just reaching 176 Yuan per month. There are 10 months in one school year. Based on this, a primary school boarding student may pay at least 1440 Yuan for his or her living expenses and a junior secondary school student may spend 1760 Yuan on his or her living expenses in one school year. However, the new policy just supplies 2 Yuan per day or 500 Yuan per school year for a primary school indigent boarding student and 3 Yuan per day or 750 Yuan per school year for a junior secondary school indigent student. The living subsidy

Table 3.12 Living cost of boarding students in the four sample counties in Spring 2007

	Primary school				Junior secondary school			
	Total	Food	Dorm	Transport	Total	Food	Dorm	Transport
Yongfu (farmer's per-capital income in 2006: 3175 Yuan)								
Average (Yuan per month)	153	135	10	8	194	156	21	17
Composition (%)	100	88.24	6.54	5.23	100	80.41	10.82	8.76
Wuxue (farmer's per-capital income in 2006: 3401 Yuan)								
Average (Yuan per month)	144	138	5	1	176	143	7	26
Composition (%)	100	95.83	3.47	0.69	100	81.25	3.98	14.77
Mishan (farmer's per-capital income in 2006: 4273 Yuan)								
Average (Yuan per month)	166	127	25	14	210	162	25	23
Composition (%)	100	76.51	15.06	8.43	100	77.14	11.09	10.95
Ji'an (farmer's per-capital income in 2006: 8031 Yuan)								
Average (Yuan per month)	147	119	19	9	262	208	36	18
Composition (%)	100	80.95	12.93	6.12	100	79.39	13.74	6.87

supplied by the government does not satisfy the true living expenses for a boarding student. There is still a big gap between the standard of the subsidy and the true cost of living. The standard of the subsidy should be improved to a higher level.

In next few years, dorm fees will be exempted. However poor student still are faced with high living costs. These students' families also are faced with heavy financial burdens. The proportion of dorm costs to living costs is very low, however, whereas the proportion of food costs to living costs is the highest. Although the dorm is free, the standard of living subsidy implemented now is still not enough.

3.4.2 Study Based on Household Survey Data in Rong'an, Guangxi

Table 3.13 indicates that the primary school boarding student's monthly average living cost is 123 Yuan, of which 74 % is for food, 20 % for dorm, and 6 % for transportation. At junior secondary school, the boarding student's living cost averages 185 Yuan per month, consisting of 80 % for food, 12 % for dorm, and 8 % for transportation. The subsidy standard is 150 Yuan per year for both primary and junior secondary school boarding students from indigent families, which means that the yearly subsidy can roughly be a monthly living cost for a primary school

Table 3.13 Living cost of boarding students in Rong'an, Guangxi, in Spring 2007 (*Unit* Yuan per month)

	Primary school				Junior secondary school			
	Total	Food	Dorm	Transport	Total	Food	Dorm	Transport
	123	91	25	7	185	148	21	15
Township								
Yayao	188	113	62	12	273	214	42	17
Dajiang	176	143	8	26	196	158	20	17
Fushi	–	–	–	–	195	145	13	37
Tantou	76	67	8	0	93	80	9	4
Dongqi	88	85	3	0	115	104	7	5
Wealth index								
0	59	55	4	0	140	115	17	8
1	85	71	11	2	169	138	13	18
2	144	91	48	6	173	135	21	17
3	145	115	18	12	189	148	23	17
4	242	135	83	24	201	168	24	9
Whether boarding student receives the subsidy								
N	142	102	31	9	188	149	22	17
Y	61	53	7	1	155	114	26	15
Sample size	32	32	32	32	95	95	95	95

student, but not enough for a junior secondary school student to cover his or her monthly costs.

Table 3.13 also shows that the higher the economic development level in the township is, the higher the boarding student's living cost is. For instance, the average living cost in the most developed area, Yayao, is as more than twice that in the least developed areas of Tantou and Dongqi. In view of the relationship between the living cost and household economic condition, both primary school students and junior secondary school students have high living costs if their household wealth index is high. In addition, the living cost of the students receiving the subsidy is lower than the ones without the subsidy.

For primary school students, there is big difference in food, dorm, and transport expenses between the ones with the subsidy and the ones without. However, such a difference for junior secondary school students mainly presents only in food. We set up a multiple linear regression model for further analysis of the factors influencing the living cost of the boarding students. The dependent variables are monthly living costs of boarding students (unit: Yuan), such as total cost, food expenses, and transportation expenses. Explanatory variables are as follows:

Children gender: 1 for female and 0 for male
School type: 1 for junior secondary school and 0 for primary school
Household economic capital: measured by wealth index
Household cultural capital: measured by householder's education background, with 1 for grade 9 and above and 0 for under grade 9
Household social capital: measured by job of relatives. The bigger the value is, the stronger the household social capital is.

The distance from home to school: valued as 0 for a distance less than 1 km, 1 for a distance between 1 and 5 km, 2 for a distance between 5 and 10 km, 3 for a distance between 10 and 50 km, and 4 for a distance above 50 km.

The results of Table 3.14 show that the family's economic condition has a great influence on the total living cost and food expense, but no significant relationship

Table 3.14 Multiple linear regressions for living cost of boarding students at Rong'an, Guangxi, in spring 2007

Explanatory variable	Total cost		Food		Transport	
Children gender	36.27^{**}	29.24^{**}	28.97^{**}	27.95^{**}	4.18	3.15
School type	41.25^{**}	27.99^{*}	37.21^{**}	37.15^{**}	5.58^{**}	1.38
Household economic capital	15.95^{**}	10.06^{*}	11.18^{**}	9.49^{**}	−1.80	−1.34
Household cultural capital	2.12	13.99	13.21^{*}	16.54^{*}	−3.89	−3.99
Household social capital	11.28^{*}	−0.66	8.73^{**}	5.35	2.14^{**}	1.69^{*}
Distance from home to school	21.02	2.33	15.97^{**}	9.99	8.99^{**}	6.08^{*}
Township	None	Yes	None	Yes	None	Yes
Sample size	122	122	177	177	146	146

$^{**}p < 0.05$; $^{*}p < 0.1$

with the transportation fare. The food expense is higher for students from families with higher cultural background. The higher the household social capital is, the higher is the living cost for all items. The farther the travel distance from home to school is, the higher are the food and transport expenses. Additionally, all living cost items for junior secondary school students are higher than those of primary school students.

3.5 Conclusions

A TEOS-based student financial assistance policy in compulsory education has experienced its initial stage, a slowly developing stage, and a rapidly developing stage. The policy has presented more and more positive effects, along with continuous improvement and development of the TEOS policy. On one hand, the policy has increased the number of students returning to school and reduced dropouts due to poverty; on the other hand, it has remarkably diminished the burden of farmers. Based on the survey, we analyzed the status quo of implementation of the TEOS policy and perceived that further refinements and improvements are needed, although significant accomplishments have been achieved. After considering the drawbacks of the three assistance policies, we presented our suggestions.

Subsidy standards, coverage, and the fund sharing mechanism are the core features of the TEOS policy. The subsidy standard is a decisive factor for whether the individual need of a student can be met; the coverage is decisive as to whether the needs of the subsidy's target groups can be satisfied; and the fund sharing mechanism is decisive as to whether the finance source is ensured. A continuous increase in the subsidy standards and coverage emerged alongside the development process of the three policies.

From autumn 2007, the central government started funding 50 % of subsidy for indigent boarding students in central and western China. There is another characteristic of the three policies of TEOS: the central and local governments started sharing the funds, with the central government shouldering a large portion of the fund.

The miscellaneous fees are the main element constituting the non-personnel expenditures of schools. The study of non-personnel expenditure approaches in Chap. 2 can help to solve the miscellaneous fee exemption problem. The free textbook policy benefits all students in rural compulsory education. The improvement of its standard guarantees that the student can get both free national curriculum textbooks and free local curriculum textbooks. As for indigent boarding student living subsidies, after estimating the boarding students' living costs, we suggest that the standards for indigent boarding student living subsidies should be increased further. To provide every low-income student with an adequate subsidy, we also suggest that it is very important to design a clear standard of poverty and a perfect method to select eligible students.

Appendix 1: Percentage of Students Receiving Miscellaneous Fee Exemptions to Total Students (Based on Data from School Questionnaires, %)

		Primary school				Junior secondary school			
		2005		2006		2005		2006	
		Spr.	Aut.	Spr.	Aut.	Spr.	Aut.	Spr.	Aut.
Sample province									
Guangxi	Mean	25	31	81	92	20	20	77	79
	Median	20	19	94	100	16	18	89	100
Hubei	Mean	15	15	26	28	15	19	27	30
	Median	11	12	19	22	15	15	19	20
Zhejiang	Mean	5	15	25	80	3	27	29	91
	Median	2	4	8	99	2	4	11	100
Heilongjiang	Mean	39	36	51	38	35	51	42	54
	Median	28	26	46	30	43	46	45	45
Sample county									
Guiping	Mean	27	32	88	93	15	16	93	100
	Median	16	15	96	100	15	16	92	100
Yongfu	Mean	21	23	89	99	16	16	75	50
	Median	20	20	89	100	16	16	75	50
Rong'an	Mean	29	38	49	75	25	26	68	72
	Median	27	27	31	97	26	26	77	100
Xiaochang	Mean	20	19	37	43	15	22	35	40
	Median	16	16	32	43	15	20	44	49
Wuxue	Mean	10	11	13	13	17	18	24	26
	Median	9	9	13	13	18	18	18	18
Chibi	Mean	13	14	23	23	14	14	16	16
	Median	13	13	19	19	14	14	16	16
Jiangshan	Mean	8	10	12	64	5	34	34	100
	Median	5	8	10	95	5	17	19	100
Anji	Mean	1	3	3	99	3	3	4	51
	Median	1	3	1	100	3	3	4	51
Lin'an	Mean	1	27	72	86	1	34	87	100
	Median	1	2	93	100	1	2	87	100
Mishan	Mean	36	36	35	35	33	35	34	34
	Median	46	46	44	45	44	45	45	45
Tangyuan	Mean	75	72	73	70	4	68	51	100
	Median	99	99	97	98	4	100	51	100

(continued)

(continued)

		Primary school				Junior secondary school			
		2005		2006		2005		2006	
		Spr.	Aut.	Spr.	Aut.	Spr.	Aut.	Spr.	Aut.
Keshan	Mean	22	22	28	26	55	57	50	49
	Median	23	22	29	28	55	57	50	45
Total	Mean	23	25	45	58	18	28	42	59
	Median	17	17	29	49	15	16	33	51
No. of sample schools		209	231	159	207	39	43	43	46

Calculation method number of students exempted from tuition and miscellaneous fees is divided by all students enrolled in the year to get the percentage of exemption at the schools; then, the mean value and median are computed based on the school data

Appendix 2: Percentage of Students Receiving Free Textbooks to Total Students (Based on Data of School Questionnaires, %)

		Primary school				Junior secondary school			
		2005		2006		2005		2006	
		Spr.	Aut.	Spr.	Aut.	Spr.	Aut.	Spr.	Aut.
Sample province									
Guangxi	Mean	21	19	21	21	19	17	21	22
	Median	20	18	18	18	18	16	16	19
Hubei	Mean	16	16	27	30	14	18	27	30
	Median	11	12	19	22	14	14	19	20
Zhejiang	Mean	4	4	6	9	2	5	4	7
	Median	1	2	2	4	2	2	3	4
Heilongjiang	Mean	51	52	51	53	54	46	40	46
	Median	48	53	44	44	47	47	43	48
Sample county									
Guiping	Mean	16	15	14	14	16	15	16	16
	Median	15	15	15	14	16	16	16	15
Yongfu	Mean	23	20	22	22	19	15	16	17
	Median	22	20	20	21	18	16	16	16
Rong'an	Mean	28	25	29	30	22	23	30	31
	Median	27	26	29	31	22	23	31	31
Xiaochang	Mean	19	18	39	46	15	22	35	40
	Median	15	16	34	44	15	20	44	49
Wuxue	Mean	13	13	16	16	6	7	10	9
	Median	11	11	13	13	6	7	10	9

(continued)

(continued)

		Primary school				Junior secondary school			
		2005		2006		2005		2006	
		Spr.	Aut.	Spr.	Aut.	Spr.	Aut.	Spr.	Aut.
Chibi	Mean	13	14	18	17	13	13	14	15
	Median	12	12	17	18	12	13	13	13
Jiangshan	Mean	8	7	10	12	3	8	5	11
	Median	5	4	6	12	3	4	4	11
Anji	Mean	1	2	3	6	2	2	4	4
	Median	0	2	3	2	2	2	4	4
Lin'an	Mean	2	2	3	4	0	0	0	0
	Median	2	2	2	2	0	0	0	0
Mishan	Mean	56	59	52	52	47	39	38	38
	Median	53	55	52	51	47	47	46	46
Tangyuan	Mean	66	72	71	74	93	82	84	82
	Median	61	73	71	72	93	82	84	82
Keshan	Mean	28	27	34	32	24	25	27	24
	Median	29	27	34	35	24	25	37	24
Total	Mean	21	20	25	27	21	22	24	27
	Median	17	16	19	20	15	15	16	18
No. of schools		202	214	219	226	35	37	40	40

Calculation method number of student receiving free textbooks is divided by enrollment for the year to obtain the percentage of students receiving free textbooks; then, the mean value and median are calculated using data from the schools

Appendix 3: Percentage of Students Receiving Free Textbooks to Total Students in Spring 2007 (Based on Data of Student Questionnaires, %)

	Primary school	Junior secondary school
Sample province		
Guangxi	19	23
Hubei	20	26
Zhejiang	11	7
Heilongjiang	58	68
Sample county		
Guiping	12	16
Yongfu	20	28
Rong'an	29	28
Xiaochang	39	38

(continued)

(continued)

	Primary school	Junior secondary school
Wuxue	14	22
Chibi	9	16
Jiangshan	17	8
Anji	4	9
Lin'an	5	2
Mishan	50	46
Tangyuan	88	94
Keshan	24	65
Total	23	29
Sample number	4072	2706

Appendix 4: Percentage of Boarding Students Receiving Living Subsidies to Total Students (Based on Data of School Questionnaires, %)

		Spring 2005	Autumn 2005	Spring 2006	Autumn 2006
Sample province					
Guangxi	Mean	9.48	6.98	9.26	10.37
	Median	8.76	3.45	5.48	7.67
Hubei	Mean	2.54	0.85	8.73	10.04
	Median	2.86	0.21	4.5	6.68
Zhejiang	Mean	2.11	5.48	5.05	5.54
	Median	2.43	2.36	2.51	2.51
Heilongjiang	Mean	6.11	3.95	4.3	5.47
	Median	0.97	0.95	4.75	4.3
Sample county					
Guiping	Mean	–	0.57	0.59	0.71
	Median	–	0.56	0.56	0.71
Yongfu	Mean	10.05	5.94	8.9	10.09
	Median	10.53	5.26	8.97	7.84
Rong'an	Mean	9.28	8.55	11.72	12.47
	Median	6.01	5.6	9.96	10.75
Xiaochang	Mean	–	0	13.95	12.66
	Median	–	0	10.79	9.21
Wuxue	Mean	2.7	0.28	3.98	3.38
	Median	2.86	0.41	2.86	0.77

(continued)

(continued)

		Spring 2005	Autumn 2005	Spring 2006	Autumn 2006
Chibi	Mean	2.12	2.12	3.98	4.46
	Median	2.12	2.12	3.98	5.41
Jiangshan	Mean	2.34	8.28	7.93	8.83
	Median	2.5	5.04	3.93	2.53
Anji	Mean	1.34	1.9	2.52	2.52
	Median	1.34	2.3	2.64	2.64
Lin'an	Mean	2.94	2.94	1.42	1.89
	Median	2.94	2.94	1.42	1.32
Mishan	Mean	9.77	0.87	4.36	4.14
	Median	0.97	0.93	4.36	4.23
Tangyuan	Mean	4.5	7.24	4.74	9.2
	Median	4.04	6.75	4.75	7.11
Keshan	Mean	0	0	3.57	2.03
	Median	0	0	3.57	2.03
Total	Mean	6.5	5.33	7.78	8.55
	Median	2.86	2.27	4.38	4.95
The number of schools		39	47	65	73

Calculation method the number of boarding student receiving living subsidies is divided by enrollment in the current year to obtain the percentage at the schools; then, the mean value and median are calculated by using data from schools

Appendix 5: Percentage of Boarding Students Receiving Living Subsides to Total Boarding Students (Based on School Questionnaire, %)

		Spring 2005	Autumn 2005	Spring 2006	Autumn 2006	Spring 2007	Autumn 2007
Sample province							
Guangxi	Mean	35	26	29	28	32	18
	Median	34	20	32	20	33	23
Hubei	Mean	10	11	38	53	27	34
	Median	7	5	25	47	20	31
Zhejiang	Mean	3	7	8	9	13	17
	Median	3	3	3	3	3	11
Heilongjiang	Mean	44	31	15	22	14	18
	Median	38	3	16	16	16	18

(continued)

(continued)

		Spring 2005	Autumn 2005	Spring 2006	Autumn 2006	Spring 2007	Autumn 2007
Sample county							
Guiping	Mean	–	1	1	1	1	2
	Median	–	1	1	1	1	2
Yongfu	Mean	8	8	17	17	32	23
	Median	0	0	16	12	36	23
Rong'an	Mean	46	42	46	49	42	31
	Median	35	31	38	39	35	31
Xiaochang	Mean	–	0	61	58	33	30
	Median	–	0	62	56	29	31
Wuxue	Mean	6	5	15	47	19	85
	Median	5	5	6	47	10	85
Chibi	Mean	29	29	42	32	27	31
	Median	29	29	42	32	20	30
Jiangshan	Mean	3	11	12	16	23	31
	Median	3	10	13	21	29	32
Anji	Mean	2	2	4	4	4	5
	Median	2	2	3	3	3	3
Lin'an	Mean	7	7	3	4	6	13
	Median	7	7	3	3	6	13
Mishan	Mean	35	2	7	13	14	18
	Median	2	2	7	13	14	18
Tangyuan	Mean	73	73	23	40	–	–
	Median	73	73	23	24	–	–
Keshan	Mean	–	–	16	–	16	–
	Median	–	–	16	–	16	–
Total	Mean	23	19	27	29	26	24
	Median	8	5	16	20	21	21
Number of sample schools		26	33	53	56	60	36

Method The number of boarding students receiving living subsidies is divided by enrollment for the year to obtain the percentage at the schools; then, the mean value and median are calculated using data from schools

Chapter 4
Study of Equity in Compulsory Education Finance

An individual's understanding and pursuit of educational equity is based on his or her specific background. Equity in education finance mainly refers to three topics:

1. Whether the distribution of an education resource is equitable
2. What factors influence equity in the distribution of the education resource and the trends of the equity, especially the influence of reforms in education financing
3. What policymakers focus on in equity-oriented education financing policy

When the government is the provider of compulsory education, institutions are the important factor influencing the distribution of an education resource, such as educational policies and an education financing system.

Tax-fee reform in rural areas is an important turning point for compulsory education. China's decentralized compulsory education system was not created with tax-share reform, which was a centralized finance reform in 1994. After tax-fee reform, the central government started to take on more and more financial responsibility for rural compulsory education.

From 1994 to 2000, the inequity of compulsory education was increasing gradually. From 1988 to 1996, the regional differences in educational expenditures grew (Du 2000). From 1997 to 2000, the intra-provincial inequity of educational expenditures per student was higher than that of inter-provinces, and the inequity of per student educational expenditures was going up slowly (Tsang and Ding 2005). Per student educational expenditures in rural areas were lower than those in urban areas; they were also lower in poverty-stricken areas than in non-poverty-stricken areas (Wang 2003). The big difference of per student educational expenditure existed between rural areas and urban areas (Tsang and Ding 2005). Financial neutrality is an important condition to achieve equity; however, it did not exist because there was a close relationship between local financial ability and local educational expenditures (Wang 2001, 2003).

After the tax-fee reform of 1999, the central government began to give more attention to developing rural areas, such as by reducing farmers' burdens, increasing farmers' incomes, and developing rural education. To enhance rural compulsory education, the central government implemented a series of key compulsory education projects (see Chap. 1), implemented the Fund Guarantee

Y. Du and Z. Sun, *Research on Compulsory Education Financing in China*,
New Frontiers of Educational Research, DOI 10.1007/978-3-662-47830-1_4

Mechanism for Rural Compulsory Education in 2006, and decided to direct most educational expenditure into rural areas in 2003. The impacts from these projects and institutions include the following:

1. The students in rural areas or poverty-stricken counties may receive more educational resources than before. The difference between rural areas and urban areas or between poverty stricken and non-poverty-stricken counties is decreasing gradually. This refers to vertical equity—that is to say, the disadvantaged groups should receive more educational resources.
2. The relationship between educational resources received by students and local financial ability is decreasing because the central government has begun to focus on enhancing compulsory education in poor areas and rural areas. This is a question of financial neutrality. Financial equity argues that children should not receive different education because of their backgrounds, including family wealth and community wealth.
3. If the inequity between rural and urban areas or between poverty-stricken and non-poverty-stricken counties is decreasing, horizontal equity may be increased. Horizontal equity focuses on whether the government provides the same education for every child.

These three impacts are the objectives of the financial policies for compulsory education in the twenty-first century. How do these three impacts happen? We need use data to measure the equity or inequity. Based on the results of the measurements, we also can design some better financial policies or institutions for compulsory education. However, before we measure the equity or inequity, we must resolve three questions: How do we measure the education or educational resources received by students? Where are the data from? Finally, what are the methods to measure the equity or inequity?

4.1 The Method to Measure the Education or Educational Resources Received by Students

It is difficult to measure education or educational resources. We must quantify the education or educational resources. In this study, we use educational revenue and educational expenditures to reflect the education and educational resources received by students. Under educational finance, we focus on the equity of educational revenue or expenditure distribution. We direct our attention to the fund input, but not outcomes.

The other difficulty is how to accurately measure the educational revenue or expenditure every student receives. For example, we cannot know the difference of educational revenue received by student A and student B in the same school. However, we can suppose that every student in the same school receives the same education, the same educational resources, or the same fund input. That is to say,

Table 4.1 The indexes and specific indicators of fund input

Index	Specific indicator (Yuan per year)
Education revenue	Per-student average education revenue (excluding fiscal appropriation for construction)
	Per-student average fiscal appropriation
	Per-student average non-fiscal appropriation
Regular expenditure	Per-student average regular expenditure
	Per-student average budgetary regular expenditure
	Per-student average non-personnel expenditure
	Per-student average current non-personnel expenditure
Teacher's salary	Per-teacher average salary
Physical facilities	Per-student average floor space of schoolhouses (m^2)
	Per-student average special equipment value
	Per-student average books (book)

we may use the per student average fund input of a school instead of the fund input each student receives. In this study, we use the per student average fund input and expenditure of a county to measure the education or educational resources every student receives. In this way, the intra-difference will be ignored. The detailed indexes of fund input are shown in Table 4.1.

As shown in Table 4.1, we do not want to measure the equity of the construction expenditure. Why? Construction expenditure is used for building the schoolhouse. If the schoolhouses are in good condition, this school will spend much less on building the schoolhouse. Also, the government will supply less fiscal appropriation for this school for construction expenditures. Oppositely, a school with schoolhouses in poor condition will need much more funding for constructing the schoolhouse and will receive more fiscal appropriations from the government. This still brings about a new inequity, but this inequity is reasonable.

4.2 The Data Source

It is crucial to have accurate data to conduct this study. We gained the needed data from three provinces and one region. These three provinces and one region provide statistics for educational revenue and expenditures for the project team, which is the basis of national statistics of educational revenue and expenditure.

4.3 The Method to Measure the Equity

For easy depiction, we use x to represent an education resource (such as per-student educational expenditure), i to stand for individual or analysis unit (such as student, schools, county), and w to represent the endowment or background variables (such as revenue). We hereby give the meanings of these measurement methods. For technical details, please refer to Appendix.

4.3.1 Horizontal Equity

The method of horizontal equity measurement focuses on the differences of education resources distribution among groups or individuals. Horizontal equity takes absolute equity as its pursuit. Absolute equity means that different groups or individuals should be provided with the same education, especially fund inputs. There are a handful of indexes developed by the scholars to measure horizontal equity. These indexes and their characteristics are shown in Table 4.2. Those characteristics may explain the equity or inequity from various perspectives. In this study, we only chose the Gini coefficient and Theil coefficient measure and describe the degree of the horizontal equity.

The Gini coefficient is often used because it is able to be decomposed based on revenue sources and time. The former tells us what source takes the most important role in the Gini coefficient; the latter may tell us what causes the change in the Gini coefficient. These are a concern of ours and policy makers as they are helpful to design a better financial policy for compulsory education.

The Theil coefficient can let us know where the total difference is from—the intra-group difference or the inter-group difference. For example, 60 % of the total

Table 4.2 The indexes of horizontal equity and their characteristics

Method	Characteristics
Range ratio	The ratio of maximum to minimum; impossible to measure the difference in observation unit used between the maximum and minimum values
Quantile difference	May measure the differences of various values at distribution points
Relative mean deviation	Has no sensitivity to the transfer from lower to higher levels along the same side of the mean value
Mcloone index	Used for analysis of differences below the median
Verstegen index	Used for analysis of differences above the median
Coefficient of variation	Has strong sensitivity to any x transfer taking place horizontally but is not influenced by inflation
Logarithm standard deviation	Is more sensitive to the x changes on the lower levels and thus highlights the differences of x at lower level
Gini coefficient	The most direct measurement of x difference, gives consideration to the difference of x between each two i, and is not disturbed by inflation
GE index and Theil coefficient	The GE index, from the low to high value of parameters, changes from more sensitive to the differences on the low level to the differences on the high level
Atkinson index	Has a monotonic transformation relationship with GE index

difference is from the inter-group difference. Policy makers and decision makers should try to eliminate the inter-group difference in order to reduce the total difference.

In the measurement of horizontal equity, a problem is whether the criteria to judge the inequity are reasonable and acceptable. Odden and Picus (2000) gave a judgment criteria based on the experience in the United States: the Gini coefficient should be equal to or less than 0.05.

4.3.2 *Financial Neutrality*

Methods for measuring financial neutrality are based on the relationships between x (dependent variable, fund input) and w (independent variable, individual background). The basic assumption is as follows: the closer the relationship between them is, the higher the inequity is. In education finance, regression analysis is generally used to measure such a relationship. The specific measuring methods are divided into four categories: correlation coefficient, slope, elasticity, and adjusted relationship measurement. These methods may be classified into 11 types of specific techniques (see Appendix).

In this report, the correlation coefficient and elasticity analysis are mainly employed to measure financial neutrality. The correlation coefficient, whose value is from 0 to 1, is usually used to measure the relationship between x and w; here, 0 indicates the highest degree of financial neutrality. The higher the correlation coefficient is, the lower the financial neutrality is. Elasticity is the coefficient of w from the simple regression of x on w. If the coefficient of w is significant and greater than 0, we can say that financial neutrality does not exist. According to the experience of some countries, if the correlation coefficient is less than 0.5 and the elasticity or the coefficient of w is less than 0.1, the education finance system in a region satisfies the financial neutrality criteria (Odden and Picus 2000).

In this study, financial neutrality means that all the governments should provide the same education for every child, whether they are located in rich or poor areas with good or bad financial ability. In other words, the education a child receives should not be determined by the local economy, local treasury, or local government's financial ability. Based on much research, we use per capital gross domestic product (GDP) to stand for the local economy and local treasury and use per capital fiscal revenue to reflect the financial ability.

4.3.3 *Vertical Equity*

Before we measure the degree of vertical equity, we must answer three questions:

1. How do we define different backgrounds?
2. How does the government provide different education or fund inputs for groups with different backgrounds? In educational finance, this means how a varied

treatment is performed for groups with different backgrounds in education resource distribution.
3. Do we have any method to measure vertical equity?

In this study, we define the different background as rural and urban areas. The children and their schools in rural areas are disadvantaged groups, and we think that the government should input more funds into rural areas than urban areas. Namely, the government should provide a better education or more education resources for those disadvantaged groups. However, what excess of disadvantaged over advantaged groups is reasonable? We cannot answer this question. However, we hope to see that the difference between rural and urban areas decreases gradually in the twenty-first century.

The next step is to measure the difference between the two groups. In this study, we mainly adopt three methods examine the differences between rural and urban areas: the absolute difference of the two groups, the ratio of per-student education resources, and the comparison of growth rate of per-student education resources.

4.4 The Analysis of Horizontal Equity: Gini Coefficient

In this chapter, we analyze the equity or inequity of education resource distribution in four sample provinces from 2001 to 2006. We grouped the students by county. Although we should use the per student average education resources to measure horizontal equity, the unit of the statistics of educational revenue and expenditure is not consistent in this period. From 2002 to 2003, the unit is the township. After 2003, the unit becomes the school. To make the results of our analysis comparable, we need to use the same unit to compute the Gini coefficient and Theil coefficient for each year. Therefore, we selected the county as the analysis unit.

The perfect Gini or Theil coefficient should be computed with education resources received by each student. This is the true method to measure the equity or inequity of education resources among every student. However, we cannot know how many education resources a student receives. Therefore, we use the per-student average education resources of the analysis unit to compute the inequity.

There are two approaches to compute the equity, weighted with the number of students or not. What is the difference between the weighted and unweighted coefficients? Take the Gini coefficient as an example. We suppose there are two counties, A and B. There are 100 students in County A, and the per student average expenditure is 100 Yuan. There are 1000 students and 1000 Yuan per student average expenditure for County B. The unweighted Gini coefficient is 0.409 and the weighted one is 0.081. The former is the measurement of the difference between analysis units; the latter is the measurement of both the difference between analysis units and the difference between every student. However, the weighted coefficient truly ignores the changes of intra-analysis unit equity; we define that every student receives the same education resources in the intra-analysis unit. Although the weighted Gini has some shortcomings, it is much closer to the perfect Gini than the unweighted one (Milanovic 2007). So, we use the weighted Gini or Theil coefficient to measure the equity in this study.

4.4.1 The Gini Coefficient for Education Revenue and Its Decomposition

4.4.1.1 Gini Coefficient for Education Revenue

The Gini coefficient of per primary student average education revenue shows that the inequity of Guangxi and Hubei was increasing, but the equity of Zhejiang and Heilongjiang fluctuated with a decreasing trend in the period of 2001–2006. Contrastively, the Gini coefficient of Zhejiang and Heilongjiang is steadier than that of Guangxi and Hubei. In total, in each year of these 6 years, the Gini coefficient of Hubei was the highest, followed in order by Guangxi, Heilongjiang, and Zhejiang.

The inequity in junior secondary schools is different from that of primary schools. The Gini coefficient for a junior secondary school student in Heilongjiang is a steadier one. The inequity in Heilongjiang is the steadiest, although its inequity is always the highest. As for Hubei and Guangxi, the inequity was increasing from 2001 to 2006, which is the same as for primary school. In opposition, Zhejiang was making efforts to reduce the inequity. From 2001 to 2004, the Gini coefficient of Guangxi was the lowest, but Zhejiang's has become the lowest since 2005.

If we compare Fig. 4.1 with Fig. 4.2, there are some interesting findings. Firstly, in Heilongjiang, the inequity in junior secondary school is much higher than that in primary school. Also, the difference between junior secondary school and primary school is expanding: in 2006, we can see that the inequity of the former increased and the latter decreased. Secondly, although the inequity of junior secondary school

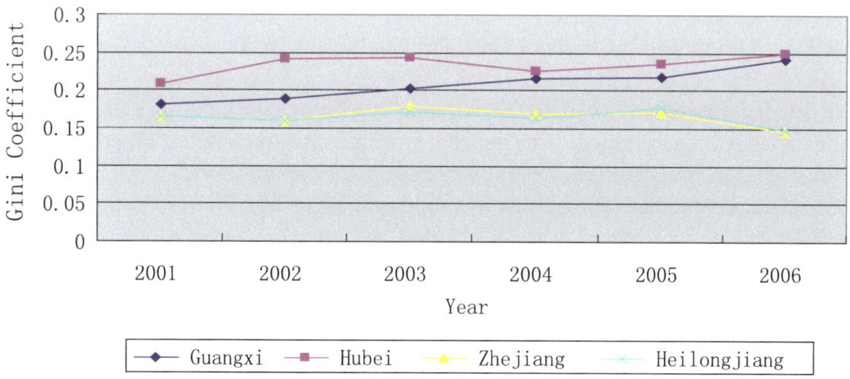

Fig. 4.1 Gini coefficient for education revenue per primary school student

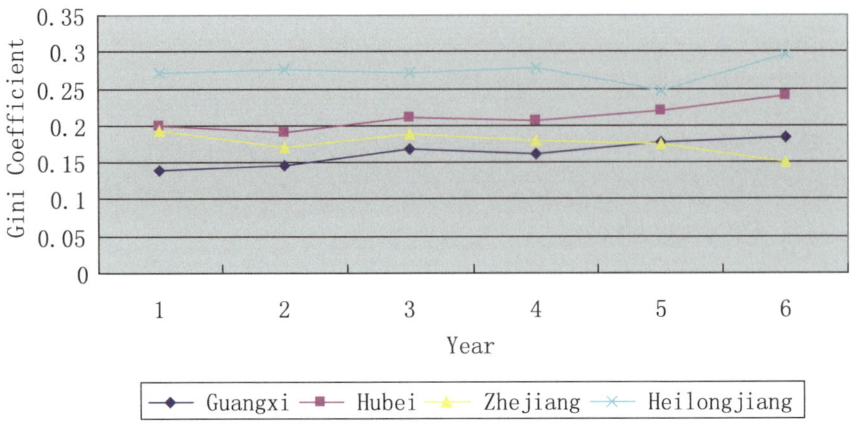

Fig. 4.2 Gini coefficient for education revenue per junior secondary school student

is lower than that of primary school in Guangxi, the difference of both keeps steady when they are increasing at a similar pace. Thirdly, in Zhejiang, the Gini coefficient of the education revenue per junior secondary school student is higher than that for a primary school student in 2001. As shown in Figs. 4.1 and 4.2, the difference of both Gini coefficients was decreasing, and even became the same in 2006. Fourthly, as for the inequity of primary school and junior secondary schools in Hubei, the difference of both was decreasing in the period of 2001–2006, and it became the same in 2006. From 2001 to 2004, the pace of the former was faster than that of the latter; however, from 2004, the pace of the latter was faster.

Do these findings illustrate that the government's decisions determine the trend of education revenue inequity? Theoretically, the government is the key provider of compulsory education. Therefore, we can use fiscal appropriation to reflect fund inputs from the government. Therefore, if we want to answer the question, we must decompose the Gini coefficient by fund input or education revenue sources.

4.4.1.2 The Decomposition of the Gini Coefficient by Revenue Source

We divided the sources of education revenue into fiscal appropriation and non-fiscal appropriation. To examine whether the government's preference determines the equity of education revenue, we computed the fiscal appropriation contribution ratio to the Gini coefficient. The results are shown in Figs. 4.3 and 4.4.

From these two figures, we can see that the contribution ratio of fiscal appropriation became higher gradually in the period of 2001–2006. In 2006, the contribution ratio increased to 80 % at least. Therefore, we can say that the inequity of education revenue is determined by the preference choice of the government. If the government does not reform the formula of fiscal appropriation, the inequity will

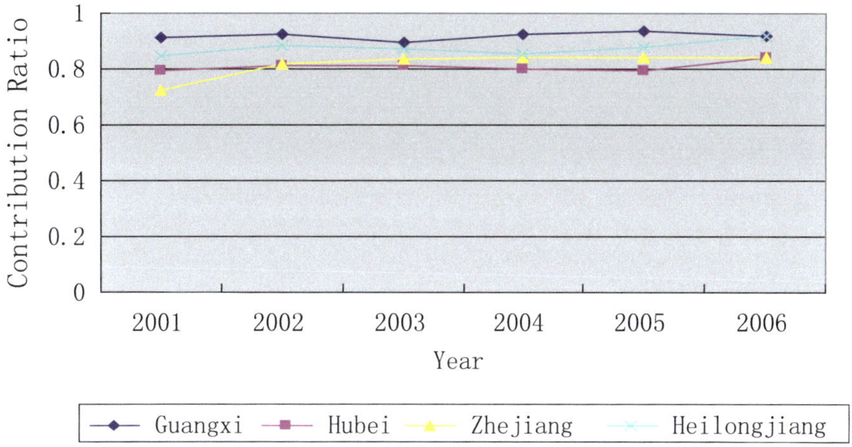

Fig. 4.3 The contribution ratio from the fiscal appropriation to the Gini coefficient of education revenue per primary school student

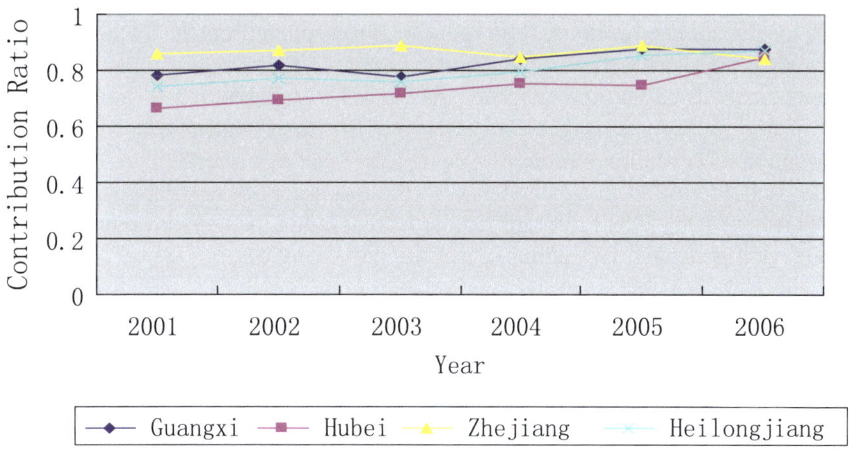

Fig. 4.4 The contribution ratio from fiscal appropriation to the Gini coefficient of education revenue per junior secondary school student

increase with fiscal input increase, such as in the junior secondary schools of Guangxi and Hubei. If the formula of fiscal appropriation results in more equity, the inequity will be reduced with fiscal input increases, as in the junior secondary school of Zhejiang. You also may find irregular fluctuation in Figs. 4.1 and 4.2. The reason may be that the formula of fiscal appropriation is changed irregularly. Therefore, we think that it is crucial for achieving the equity to design an equity formula to allocate or distribute fiscal appropriations (Fig. 4.5).

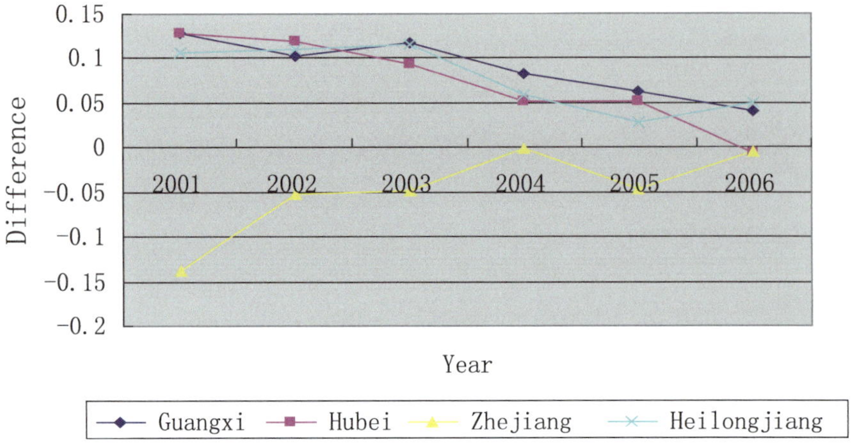

Fig. 4.5 The difference between both contribution ratios (primary school and junior secondary school)

We have measured the equity of education revenue, but education revenue is not equal to education expenditure. If the education revenue reflects the financial ability to employ physical facilities and human resources for education, the education expenditure will be the true education provided for students. If we want to know how many education resources were received by each student and whether the distribution of education resources is equity, we must measure the Gini coefficient of per student education expenditures. In the next section, we compute the Gini coefficient of per student average regular expenditures, budgetary regular expenditures, non-personnel expenditures, and teachers' salaries.

4.4.2 The Gini Coefficient for Regular Expenditures

4.4.2.1 Gini Coefficient for Regular Expenditures and Budgetary Regular Expenditures

Figure 4.6 shows us the Gini coefficients of average regular expenditures per primary school student for the four provinces, which are between 0.14 and 0.25. The Gini coefficient of Guangxi and Hubei is increasing, which indicates that the inequity of these two provinces was expanding. However, the inequities of Zhejiang and Heilongjiang do not have significant changes with small decreases. Although the equity is improving, we do find that the inequity expands at a slow pace or even does not expand with a small decrease. Zhejiang has the highest equity, followed by Heilongjiang, Guangxi, and Hubei in order.

From Fig. 4.7, we can see that the Gini coefficient of average regular expenditure per junior secondary school student in the four provinces increased at a very slow

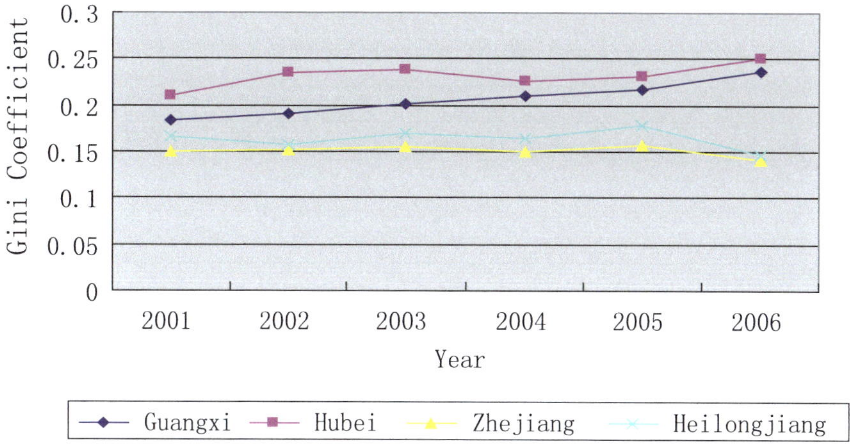

Fig. 4.6 Gini coefficient for average regular expenditures per primary school student

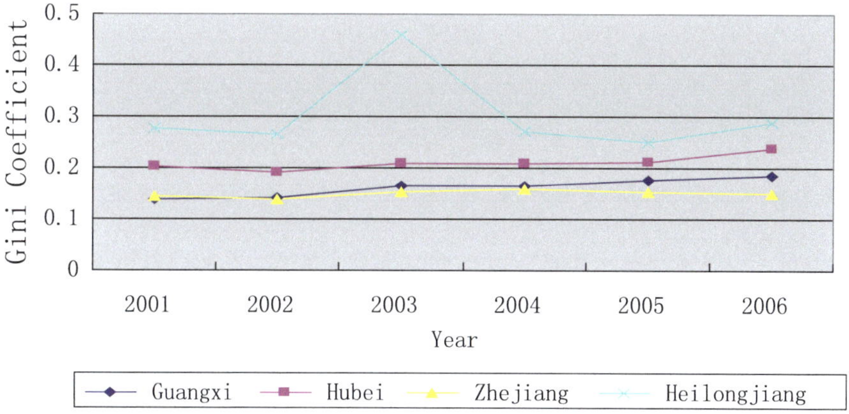

Fig. 4.7 Gini coefficient for average regular expenditures per junior secondary school student

pace. In 2003, Heilongjiang had Gini coefficient singularity, which reached 0.458. We hope to find out the reason in the next analysis. Zhejiang still has the best equity, followed by Guangxi, Hubei, and Heilongjiang. Perhaps we can conclude that the equity of education resource distribution is not only different between each province, but also between primary schools and junior secondary schools within a single province. Therefore, the equity or inequity is determined by the formula of fund input designed by the government (Figs. 4.8 and 4.9).

We also computed the Gini coefficient for average budgetary regular expenditure per student in order to compare it to the Gini coefficient of per student average regular expenditure. When the former is the same as or similar to the latter, the inequity of non-budgetary regular expenditures does not expand or reduce the total inequity. If the former is higher than the latter, the inequity of non-budgetary

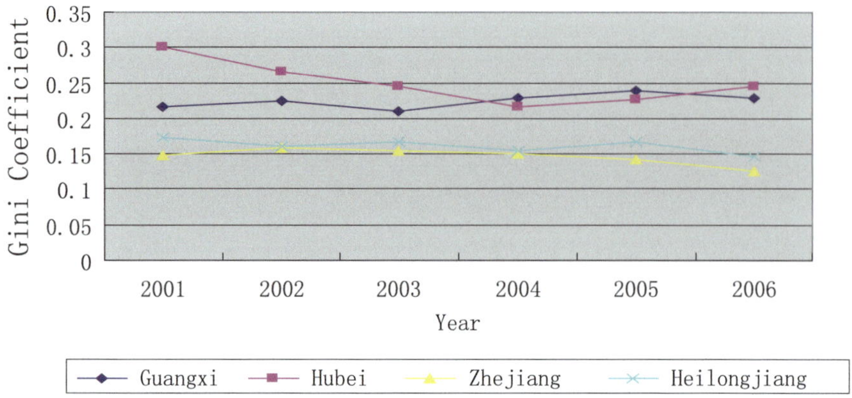

Fig. 4.8 Gini coefficient for average budgetary regular expenditures per primary school student

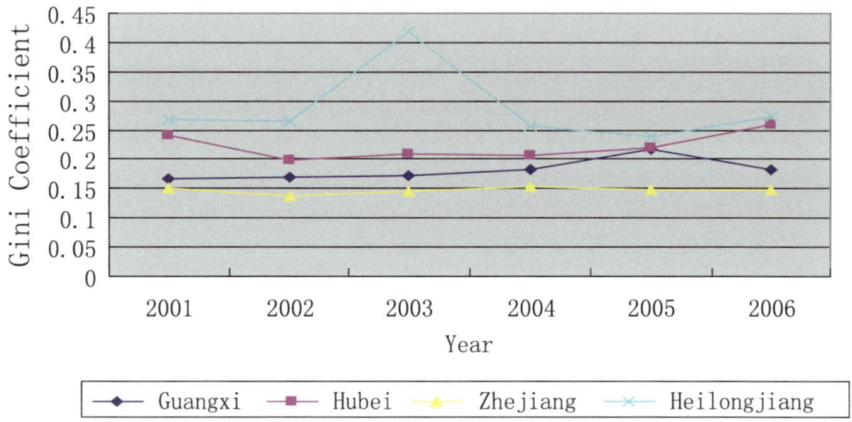

Fig. 4.9 Gini coefficient for average budgetary regular expenditures per junior secondary school student

regular expenditure eliminates the inequity of the former. This indicates that the groups who receive less budgetary regular expenditures will be provided with more non-budgetary regular expenditures. When the former is lower than the latter, we can say that the inequity of non-budgetary regular expenditures expands the total inequity.

At a primary school in Guangxi, the trends for budgetary regular expenditures and non-budgetary regular expenditures are opposite. The Gini coefficient trend for regular expenditures was going up from 2001 to 2006. However, the Gini coefficient trend for budgetary regular expenditures was going down—greater than that of regular expenditure. Until 2006, the Gini coefficients of both were very close. This illustrates that the inequity of non-budgetary regular expenditures reduces the inequity of budgetary regular expenditures during the period of 2001–2005.

The primary school in Hubei and junior secondary school in Guangxi showed the same characteristic. However, for other provinces and education stages in most years, non-budgetary regular expenditures expanded the total inequity. Therefore, we can conclude that the equity method to distribute non-budgetary regular expenditures may improve the equity.

4.4.2.2 The Gini Coefficient for Teacher's Salary

As a component of regular expenditures, the equity in personnel expenditures has always been an issue of public concern. If we compute the Gini coefficient of per student average teacher's salary, the Gini coefficient will reflect the teacher resource received by every student. However, the central government has determined the ratio of teachers to students for primary and junior secondary schools since 2001. Although teacher resources per student may be different in each school in a county, the ratio may be similar among counties. Therefore, for the Gini coefficient of per teacher average salary, we compute that the weight for the number of teachers not only reflects the teacher resources that students received, but also tells us the inequity of the per teacher average salary among counties.

Figures 4.10 and 4.11 present the changes in the Gini coefficient of average salary for primary schools and junior secondary schools in four provinces. For the primary schools, the inequity for teacher's salary from 2001 to 2003 in Guangxi and Hubei decreased, and then presented an upward trend after 2003. The inequity of Zhejiang and Heilongjiang in 2005 was higher than that of 2001, while a conspicuous decrease was shown in 2006. For the junior secondary schools, the inequity has been increasing at a very slow pace since 2001 in four provinces, while Heilongjiang and Zhejiang had a small decrease in 2006.

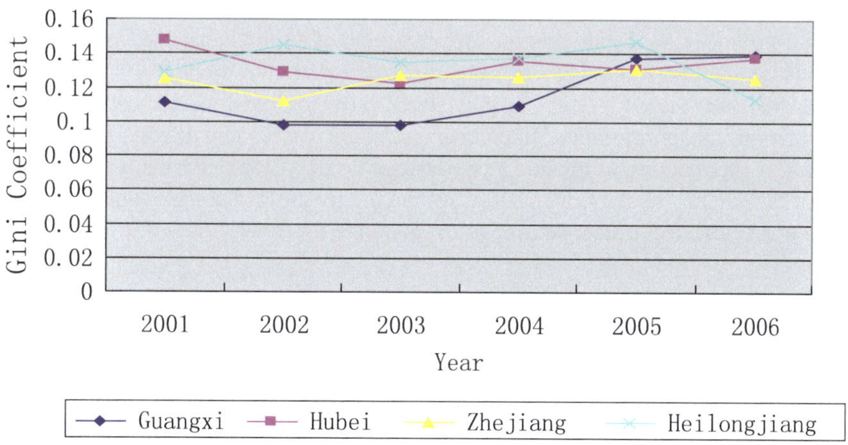

Fig. 4.10 Gini coefficient for average salary of a primary school teacher

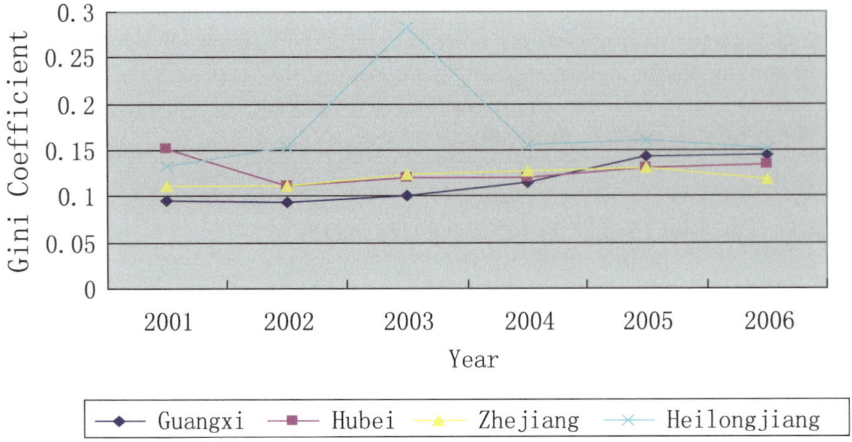

Fig. 4.11 Gini coefficient for average salary of a junior secondary school teacher

The Gini coefficient for teacher's salary has three remarkable characteristics (refer to Figs. 4.10 and 4.11). First, the degree of inequity in teacher's salary was rather low, with a small Gini coefficient ranging from 0.09 to 0.16 for primary school and 0.09–0.16 for junior secondary school. The possible reason for this result is that the teacher's salary was given priority among all kinds of education expenditures. Also, many county governments take the teacher's salary guarantee as the most crucial mission in education. In addition, all the local standards for the teachers' basic salaries were highly consistent. Secondly, although the difference for average salary was smaller, the overall trend for the inequity was going up. Thirdly, the intra-provincial difference of teacher's salary inequity narrowed gradually, which may have resulted from a county-centered system policy aiming to guarantee a teacher's salary carried out from 2001.

After comparing the inequity of a teacher's salary and budgetary teacher's salary in four provinces, we found that the inequity trend of the budgetary teacher's salary in Guangxi, Hubei, and Heilongjiang coincides with the teacher's salary. This shows that the teacher's salary in these three provinces was mainly dependent on budgetary fiscal appropriation. In comparison, there was no remarkable similarity in Zhejiang. The inequity of the budgetary teacher's salary was persistently lower than that of the teacher's salary, which tells us that the teachers of some counties receive more non-budgetary salary than others (Table 4.3).

4.4.2.3 The Gini Coefficient for Non-personnel Expenditures

Non-personnel expenditures are the main and important fund resources to ensure school operation and employ physical facilities. In the long term, the shortage of non-personnel expenditure is the biggest obstacle faced in education development;

Table 4.3 Gini coefficients for budgetary teacher's salary

	Province	2001	2002	2003	2004	2005	2006
Primary school	Guangxi	0.113	0.108	0.105	0.118	0.134	0.133
	Hubei	0.199	0.141	0.107	0.124	0.122	0.125
	Zhejiang	0.111	0.103	0.101	0.097	0.103	0.110
	Heilongjiang	0.128	0.142	0.131	0.136	0.140	0.111
Junior secondary school	Guangxi	0.103	0.108	0.097	0.111	0.135	0.135
	Hubei	0.191	0.121	0.105	0.109	0.122	0.127
	Zhejiang	0.128	0.104	0.102	0.107	0.109	0.107
	Heilongjiang	0.131	0.144	0.272	0.149	0.146	0.142

this is mainly caused by inequity of education resource distribution. In recent years, one focus of education financing reform is to design a guarantee mechanism for non-personnel expenditures. After the implementation of a new mechanism, we hope to see the inequity of non-personnel expenditures reduced.

As shown in Fig. 4.12, the Gini coefficient of the average non-personnel expenditure per primary school student in four provinces ranged from 0.25 to 0.31, which was higher than that of regular expenditure and teacher's salary. The trend of inequity went up in 2001 and 2002. After 2002, although there were fluctuations over the years, the overall trend of inequity was going down. However, in 2006, the inequity trend of Hubei increased.

As shown in Fig. 4.13, the inequity of average non-personnel expenditure per junior secondary school student was lower than that for primary schools in Guangxi and Hubei in the period of 2001–2006. In Zhejiang, the inequity in junior secondary schools from 2001 to 2003 was lower than that of primary schools, but higher after 2004. Moreover, the inequity in Heilongjiang was persistently higher than that of

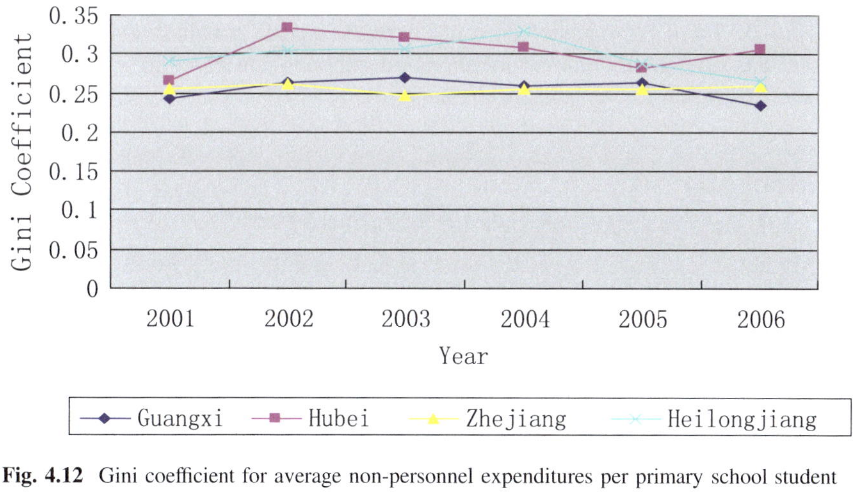

Fig. 4.12 Gini coefficient for average non-personnel expenditures per primary school student

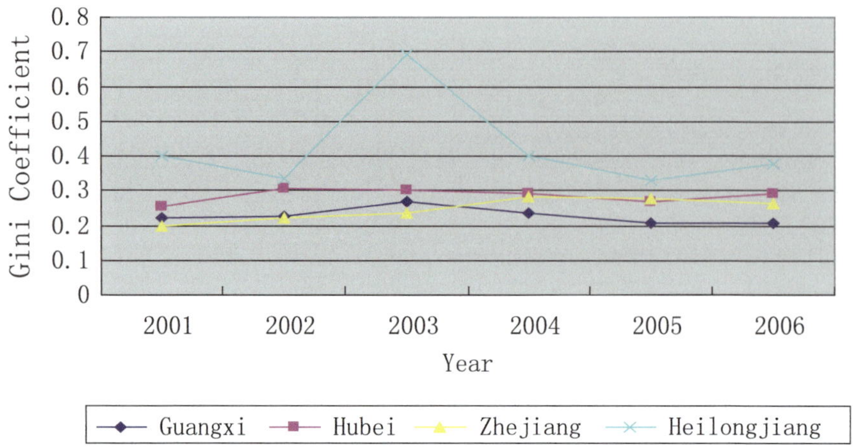

Fig. 4.13 Gini coefficient for average non-personnel expenditures per junior secondary school student

primary schools from 2001 to 2006. Heilongjiang and Hubei were ranked at the top for inequity, and the inequity of these two provinces continued to increase from 2005 to 2006. The inequity in Guangxi displayed a downward trend in these 6 years, and it was the lowest among the four provinces as of 2004.

Although the inequity of non-personnel expenditures increased in some years, it decreased, kept a steady trend, or increased at a slow pace. This is the outcome we hope to achieve with compulsory education financing reforms.

In these four provinces, we find that the inequity for regular expenditures, teacher's salary, and non-personnel expenditures decreased or kept steady based on the above analysis. This is a positive phenomenon, but what does it tell us? If the formula of appropriation does not change and this formula is not a fair one, the inequity will expand with the increase of per student average expenditure (see Sect. 4.6.2). When the inequity does not expand, we can conclude that the government has revised the unfair formula of appropriation in order to improve the equity of education resource distribution.

4.4.3 The Gini Coefficient for Physical Facilities

Physical facilities can be represented by capital equipment value and books, which are the accumulative stock of education resources. If the government inputs more funds into schools with poor physical facilities to improve the per student average capital equipment and books, the Gini coefficient of these two resources may be reduced. We can say that the government has made efforts to improve the equity. When the government provides the same fund input for the schools in poor and

Table 4.4 Gini coefficient of per student capital equipment value and books per student

	Per student capital equipment value						Per student books					
Year	2001	2002	2003	2004	2005	2006	2001	2002	2003	2004	2005	2006
Primary school												
Guangxi	0.450	0.350	0.391	0.388	0.325	0.289	0.168	0.169	0.203	0.180	0.163	0.179
Hubei	0.284	0.349	0.358	0.303	0.324	0.315	0.198	0.211	0.202	0.190	0.195	0.203
Zhejiang	0.289	0.282	0.268	0.263	0.274	0.279	0.198	0.206	0.189	0.186	0.175	0.170
Heilongjiang	0.461	0.382	0.416	0.404	0.418	0.390	0.227	0.231	0.253	0.266	0.288	0.274
Junior secondary school												
Guangxi	0.339	0.378	0.270	0.265	0.346	0.247	0.172	0.171	0.19	0.177	0.169	0.168
Hubei	0.256	0.298	0.295	0.311	0.308	0.304	0.194	0.204	0.182	0.176	0.199	0.206
Zhejiang	0.300	0.268	0.257	0.256	0.247	0.256	0.205	0.186	0.187	0.169	0.154	0.165
Heilongjiang	0.455	0.344	0.692	0.406	0.412	0.374	0.268	0.261	0.562	0.252	0.256	0.251

good facilities, or even more fund inputs for good schools, the inequity of these two resources may grow.

The inequity of per student average capital equipment for primary schools and junior secondary schools was generally decreasing with some fluctuation in the four provinces, excluding the junior secondary schools of Hubei. Although Hubei's inequity of capital equipment value was going up until 2004, the inequity decreased to 0.304 from 0.311 since 2005. The inequity of Heilongjiang is the highest, and Zhejiang's is the lowest.

The inequity of the average books per primary school student in Zhejiang, Heilongjiang, and Guangxi was generally decreasing with little fluctuation from 2001 to 2006. However, Hubei's inequity from 2002 to 2006 is higher than that of 2001, although the inequity has been reduced gradually since 2002. For junior secondary schools, the inequity of Guangxi and Zhejiang shows regular changes, but Hubei and Heilongjiang do not. Another thing attracting our attention is that Heilongjiang's inequity of per student average books is much higher than others, and Zhejiang's is still the lowest (Table 4.4).

4.5 The Analysis of Horizontal Equity: Theil Coefficient

4.5.1 Theil Coefficients for Regular Expenditures and Physical Facilities

In Guangxi, the Theil coefficient for regular expenditures for primary and junior secondary schools increased gradually from 2001 to 2006. The Theil coefficients for budgetary regular expenditure, teacher's salary, non-personnel expenditure, capital equipment, and books show irregular changes. However, we were glad to see that the Theil coefficients of 2006 were lower than those of 2005, except for books.

In Hubei, the Theil coefficient for regular expenditures for primary and junior secondary schools has an upward trend with fluctuations. The Theil coefficients of other resources are all changed irregularly. However, the Theil coefficients of 2006 are all higher than that of 2005, excluding that of capital equipment for junior secondary schools.

In Zhejiang, the Theil coefficient showed the steadiest changes. For regular expenditures, the Theil coefficient for junior secondary schools had a small and steady increase, but primary schools showed a decreasing trend. The Theil coefficients of other resources changed irregularly. Only the Theil coefficients for capital equipment and books for junior secondary schools and non-personnel expenditures for primary schools were higher in 2006 than in 2005.

In Heilongjiang, the Theil coefficient for regular expenditures in junior secondary schools is much higher than that for primary schools in each year. However, there is not a regular development trend. The Theil coefficients for other resources

Table 4.5 Theil coefficients for regular expenditures and physical facilities of Guangxi

	Year	RE	BRE	TS	NPE	CE	BO
Junior secondary school	2001	0.032	0.046	0.015	0.079	0.195	0.050
	2002	0.035	0.050	0.017	0.091	0.372	0.050
	2003	0.048	0.048	0.019	0.122	0.130	0.060
	2004	0.046	0.053	0.023	0.091	0.117	0.052
	2005	0.052	0.075	0.036	0.076	0.406	0.045
	2006	0.055	0.054	0.034	0.085	0.098	0.044
Primary school	2001	0.058	0.076	0.020	0.103	0.374	0.052
	2002	0.064	0.089	0.017	0.125	0.223	0.049
	2003	0.070	0.073	0.016	0.126	0.291	0.080
	2004	0.074	0.084	0.020	0.118	0.286	0.056
	2005	0.078	0.090	0.032	0.127	0.201	0.045
	2006	0.088	0.081	0.031	0.096	0.152	0.051

RE regular expenditure; *BRE* budgetary regular expenditure; *TS* teacher's salary; *NPE* non-personnel expenditure; *CE* capital equipment; *BO* books

have the same characteristics. The Theil coefficient for each primary school resource in 2006 was lower than for 2005. For junior secondary schools, the Theil coefficients for budgetary regular expenditure and non-personnel expenditure were higher than those for 2005.

Among the four provinces, the Theil coefficient for each resource has different characteristics. However, if we compare the Theil coefficient to the Gini coefficient we computed, we find they have similar characteristics. That is, both the Theil coefficient and Gini coefficient show the same inequity trend. However, the importance of the Theil coefficient is that it can be decomposed by inter-group and intra-group. This may be helpful to determine the source of the inequity. In the next section, we decompose the Theil coefficient by intra-county and inter-county at first. Secondly, we break up the Theil coefficient into inter-rural/urban inequity, as well as intra-rural inequity and intra-urban inequity. The decomposition may tell us how to reduce and even eliminate the inequity (Tables 4.5, 4.6, 4.7 and 4.8).

4.5.2 *The Decomposition of the Theil Coefficient: Intra-county and Inter-county*

In this section, we present the contribution ratio of intra-county and inter-county inequity to total inequity. If the contribution ratio of intra-county inequity is higher than that of inter-county inequity, the government should reduce intra-county inequity in order to reduce or eliminate the total inequity. We only decomposed the Theil coefficients of Guangxi, Hubei, and Zhejiang from 2004 to 2006, because these three provinces use the school as the unit of the education revenue and expenditure statistic; Heilongjiang still takes the county as the unit.

Table 4.6 Theil coefficients for regular expenditures and physical facilities of Hubei

	Year	RE	BRE	TS	NPE	CE	BO
Junior secondary School	2001	0.083	0.108	0.039	0.110	0.114	0.065
	2002	0.073	0.068	0.021	0.167	0.151	0.068
	2003	0.088	0.077	0.025	0.161	0.151	0.052
	2004	0.087	0.080	0.024	0.146	0.192	0.049
	2005	0.087	0.086	0.029	0.127	0.164	0.064
	2006	0.100	0.114	0.031	0.151	0.182	0.066
Primary school	2001	0.087	0.156	0.035	0.119	0.136	0.063
	2002	0.104	0.121	0.027	0.199	0.276	0.071
	2003	0.108	0.104	0.026	0.181	0.230	0.067
	2004	0.090	0.078	0.030	0.178	0.165	0.057
	2005	0.092	0.082	0.029	0.152	0.203	0.059
	2006	0.106	0.096	0.033	0.174	0.179	0.064

RE regular expenditure; *BRE* budgetary regular expenditure; *TS* teacher's salary; *NPE* non-personnel expenditure; *CE* capital equipment; *BO* books

Table 4.7 Theil coefficients for regular expenditures and physical facilities of Zhejiang

	Year	RE	BRE	TS	NPE	CE	BO
Junior secondary school	2001	0.032	0.037	0.020	0.060	0.157	0.068
	2002	0.032	0.031	0.021	0.076	0.115	0.056
	2003	0.040	0.034	0.025	0.095	0.105	0.056
	2004	0.041	0.037	0.026	0.131	0.104	0.046
	2005	0.041	0.036	0.028	0.128	0.101	0.038
	2006	0.040	0.035	0.022	0.115	0.111	0.043
Primary school	2001	0.041	0.035	0.025	0.116	0.139	0.066
	2002	0.042	0.041	0.020	0.126	0.126	0.068
	2003	0.042	0.038	0.026	0.104	0.127	0.058
	2004	0.038	0.036	0.025	0.107	0.115	0.055
	2005	0.042	0.033	0.028	0.108	0.136	0.050
	2006	0.036	0.027	0.025	0.116	0.135	0.046

RE regular expenditure; *BRE* budgetary regular expenditure; *TS* teacher's salary; *NPE* non-personnel expenditure; *CE* capital equipment; *BO* books

In Guangxi, the contribution ratio of inter-county inequity to regular expenditure and budgetary regular expenditure inequity is higher than 50 %. The contribution ratio of inter-county inequity to teacher's salary inequity is greater than 67.2 %. However, the inequity of non-personnel expenditure from intra-county inequity is gradually becoming higher, at least higher than 50 %. As for capital equipment and books, the contribution ratio from inter-county inequity is much higher.

In Hubei, the contribution of inter-county inequity to budgetary regular expenditure and teacher's salary is much higher. The capital equipment and books

Table 4.8 Theil coefficients for regular expenditures and physical facilities of Heilongjiang

	Year	RE	BRE	TS	NPE	CE	BO
Junior secondary School	2001	0.132	0.118	0.031	0.299	0.375	0.117
	2002	0.121	0.117	0.037	0.203	0.195	0.113
	2003	0.074	0.057	0.024	0.167	0.124	0.145
	2004	0.135	0.118	0.046	0.306	0.292	0.101
	2005	0.109	0.097	0.043	0.184	0.289	0.105
	2006	0.139	0.127	0.040	0.273	0.240	0.103
Primary school	2001	0.048	0.052	0.026	0.164	0.364	0.087
	2002	0.041	0.042	0.034	0.161	0.258	0.092
	2003	0.049	0.046	0.034	0.177	0.295	0.102
	2004	0.047	0.041	0.039	0.197	0.291	0.112
	2005	0.054	0.047	0.037	0.143	0.299	0.131
	2006	0.036	0.037	0.023	0.116	0.264	0.119

RE regular expenditure; *BRE* budgetary regular expenditure; *TS* teacher's salary; *NPE* non-personnel expenditure; *CE* capital equipment; *BO* books

inequity is mainly from intra-county inequity. The inequity of regular expenditure for primary schools mainly is derived from inter-county inequity. However, this inequity for junior secondary schools was from inter-county inequity in 2004, but was from intra-county inequity after 2004. The inequity of non-personnel expenditure has the same characteristics.

In Zhejiang, inter-county inequity's contribution to regular expenditure for primary and junior secondary schools was going down. In 2006, intra-county inequity exceeded inter-county inequity. The inequity of budgetary regular expenditure, non-personnel expenditure, capital equipment, and books mainly derived from intra-county inequity. However, the teacher's salary inequity is still mainly from inter-county inequity.

Based on the above analyses, the inequity of these three provinces may reflect the same two characteristics. Firstly, the teacher's salary inequity is mainly caused by inter-county inequity. The Gini coefficient and Theil coefficient may be used to reflect the inequity of teacher's salary, but not per student average teacher resources. Suppose that one teacher teaches a student all the time. If this teacher works in county A, he or she may be paid 2000 Yuan as the salary. However, if the teacher works in county B, he or she may be paid a higher or a lower salary. Although the teacher receives a different salary, the students receive the same teacher resource. Secondly, the inequity of capital equipment and books is mainly derived from intra-county inequity.

In terms of policy intervention, if the intra-county inequity is playing an important role in a dominating inequity, the county government shall be responsible for reducing or eliminating inequity. If the inter-county inequity takes an important role, the central and provincial governments should take the main responsibility (Tables 4.9, 4.10 and 4.11).

Table 4.9 Theil coefficient decomposition of intra-county and inter-county differences in Guangxi

	Difference	Contribution ratio (%): primary schools			Contribution ratio (%): junior secondary schools		
		2004	2005	2006	2004	2005	2006
RE	Intra-county	30.3	33.8	29.8	47.5	45.5	41.1
	Inter-county	69.7	66.2	70.2	52.5	54.5	58.9
BRE	Intra-county	28.6	32.9	32.1	45.8	42.4	44.8
	Inter-county	71.4	67.1	67.9	54.2	57.6	55.2
NPE	Intra-county	50.9	56.4	53.5	55.6	70.7	58.7
	Inter-county	49.1	43.6	46.5	44.4	29.3	41.3
TS	Intra-county	22.9	23.1	25.8	32.8	19.2	20.5
	Inter-county	77.1	76.9	74.2	67.2	80.8	79.5
CE	Intra-county	51.0	62.2	64.9	64.9	53.9	74.5
	Inter-county	49.0	37.8	35.1	35.1	46.1	25.5
BO	Intra-county	58.5	73.4	69.2	61.2	75.4	70.5
	Inter-county	41.5	26.6	30.8	38.8	24.6	29.5

RE regular expenditure; *BRE* budgetary regular expenditure; *TS* teacher's salary; *NPE* non-personnel expenditure; *CE* capital equipment; *BO* books

Table 4.10 Theil coefficient decomposition of intra-county and inter-county differences in Hubei

	Difference	Contribution ratio (%): primary schools			Contribution ratio (%): junior secondary schools		
		2004	2005	2006	2004	2005	2006
RE	Intra-county	33.8	40.5	38.3	33.8	65.1	65.1
	Inter-county	66.2	59.5	61.7	66.2	34.9	34.9
BRE	Intra-county	39	45.8	44.8	38.1	41.4	39.6
	Inter-county	61	54.2	55.2	61.9	58.6	60.4
NPE	Intra-county	49.4	54.6	55.1	45.8	51.1	46.3
	Inter-county	50.6	45.4	44.9	54.2	48.9	53.7
TS	Intra-county	29.3	36	36.1	37.9	40.7	38.1
	Inter-county	70.7	64	63.9	62.1	59.3	61.9
CE	Intra-county	63.4	64.3	65.9	56.9	65.5	61.0
	Inter-county	36.6	35.7	34.1	43.1	34.5	39.0
BO	Intra-county	59.8	69.0	71.8	65.6	64.5	67.2
	Inter-county	40.2	31.0	28.2	34.4	35.5	32.8

RE regular expenditure; *BRE* budgetary regular expenditure; *TS* teacher's salary; *NPE* non-personnel expenditure; *CE* capital equipment; *BO* books

In Zhejiang, the inequity of every resource for both primary and junior secondary schools shows the same characteristics. From 2001 to 2003, the intra-urban inequity contributed to total inequity at a very high ratio; however, after 2004, the inequity of every resource was mainly derived from intra-rural inequity. The inter-rural/urban inequity still contributes a small ratio.

Table 4.11 Theil coefficient decomposition of intra-county and inter-county differences in Zhejiang

	Difference	Contribution ratio (%): primary schools			Contribution ratio (%): junior secondary schools		
		2004	2005	2006	2004	2005	2006
RE	Intra-county	49.5	50.1	55.8	45.7	49.4	52.7
	Inter-county	50.5	49.9	44.2	54.3	50.6	47.3
BRE	Intra-county	55.6	60.2	63.3	52.5	56.1	51.0
	Inter-county	44.4	39.8	36.7	47.5	43.9	49.0
NPE	Intra-county	66.8	69.1	67.5	59.8	64.6	63.5
	Inter-county	33.2	30.9	32.5	40.2	35.4	36.5
TS	Intra-county	26.7	26.2	30.1	26.5	30.0	35.7
	Inter-county	73.3	73.8	69.9	73.5	70.0	64.3
	Inter-county	20.8	19.0	18.3	28.5	25.5	25.4
CE	Intra-county	68.5	69.2	65.0	66.9	68.3	65.7
	Inter-county	31.5	30.8	35.0	33.1	31.7	34.3
BO	Intra-county	59.0	66.1	67.5	64.6	71.7	71.4
	Inter-county	41.0	33.9	32.5	35.4	28.3	28.6

RE regular expenditure; *BRE* budgetary regular expenditure; *TS* teacher's salary; *NPE* non-personnel expenditure; *CE* capital equipment; *BO* books

In Heilongjiang, the inequity of each resource for primary schools is contributed mostly by intra-rural inequity. However, for junior secondary schools, the inequity of regular expenditure, non-personnel expenditure, teacher's salary, and capital equipment is mainly caused by intra-urban inequity. However, budgetary regular expenditure and books inequity mostly comes from intra-rural inequity. The contribution ratio of inter-rural/urban inequity is very small.

In these four provinces, the inter-rural/urban inequity of Heilongjiang is the lowest, and that of Hubei is the highest. Compared with intra-inequity, inter-inequity is much lower. Although this seems like a positive finding, it does not illustrate that the difference of education resources input into rural and urban areas is very small. We just know that intra-inequity contributed a higher ratio than inter-inequity. Therefore, it is necessary to compute the difference between rural and urban areas, as shown in Sect. 4.7 (Tables 4.12, 4.13, 4.14 and 4.15).

4.6 Financial Neutrality: The Relationship of Inter-county and Intra-county Inequity with GDP and Recurrent Fiscal Revenue

Financial neutrality means that all the governments should provide the same education for every child, whether they live in a rich or poor area. Students may live in different counties, but they should be provided with the same education. That is to

Table 4.12 Decomposition of the Theil coefficient of the urban and rural group differences in Guangxi

	Difference	Primary schools						Junior secondary schools					
		2001	2002	2003	2004	2005	2006	2001	2002	2003	2004	2005	2006
RE	Inter-urban/rural	17.1	14.8	19.1	16.9	13.2	9.7	8.3	4.6	4.9	6.1	15.7	7.0
	Intra-urban areas	13.2	16.1	20.6	20.7	24.0	20.0	48.1	50.3	49.7	60.6	26.0	34.7
	Intra-rural areas	69.7	69.1	60.3	62.3	62.9	70.3	43.7	45.1	45.4	33.2	58.3	58.2
BRE	Inter-urban/rural	12.3	11.8	12.9	11.5	7.2	5.6	4.6	2.7	1.9	1.9	8.3	3.0
	Intra-urban areas	10.0	12.9	14.3	16.8	20.9	17.7	40.3	41.9	48.4	57.5	27.6	31.5
	Intra-rural areas	77.7	75.3	72.8	71.6	71.9	76.7	55.1	55.4	49.7	40.5	64.2	65.5
NPE	Inter-urban/rural	13.1	10.1	15.7	18.1	18.7	7.3	6.2	1.3	3.6	7.1	8.6	1.9
	Intra-urban areas	20.8	20.1	29.3	32.6	38.5	30.1	38.1	36.3	39.3	58.7	25.8	31.5
	Intra-rural areas	66.1	69.8	55.0	49.2	42.8	62.6	55.7	62.4	57.2	34.2	65.6	66.6
TS	Inter-urban/rural	0.2	1.2	1.0	1.2	8.4	6.4	0.9	3.9	0.6	3.3	15.7	10.2
	Intra-urban areas	13.6	29.0	39.9	31.9	29.2	34.3	34.6	54.0	65.4	59.0	39.3	43.0
	Intra-rural areas	86.2	69.9	59.0	66.9	62.4	59.3	64.5	42.1	33.9	37.8	45.0	46.8
CE	Inter-urban/rural	11.7	19.1	21.1	13.8	19.1	13.2	1.8	0.0	1.9	2.4	7.1	1.8
	Intra-urban areas	45.7	30.1	39.9	37.2	36.2	32.9	38.6	16.8	45.5	54.9	66.5	31.7
	Intra-rural areas	42.6	50.9	39.0	49.0	44.7	53.9	59.6	83.2	52.6	42.7	26.4	66.6
BO	Inter-urban/rural	12.2	12.2	9.3	9.7	6.3	7.5	0.2	0.6	1.2	0.1	0.7	0.4
	Intra-urban areas	35.7	26.1	29.1	24.0	22.9	22.8	26.6	38.6	43.1	45.4	32.3	27.9
	Intra-rural areas	52.1	61.7	61.6	66.3	70.8	69.7	73.2	60.8	55.7	54.5	67.0	71.7

RE regular expenditure; *BRE* budgetary regular expenditure; *TS* teacher's salary; *NPE* non-personnel expenditure; *CE* capital equipment; *BO* books

Table 4.13 Decomposition of Theil coefficient of the urban and rural group differences in Hubei

	Difference	Primary schools						Junior secondary schools					
		2001	2002	2003	2004	2005	2006	2001	2002	2003	2004	2005	2006
RE	Inter-urban/rural	33.7	37.2	33.9	24.4	18.6	16.7	24.1	21.6	25.7	19.6	14.1	12.7
	Intra-urban areas	39.1	31.8	30.7	33.3	35.0	36.2	52.0	53.5	48.1	43.7	49.9	50.2
	Intra-rural areas	27.2	31.0	35.3	42.4	46.4	47.1	23.9	24.9	26.3	36.6	36.1	37.2
BRE	Inter-urban/rural	24.0	24.0	19.6	11.5	7.7	7.1	20.3	12.0	11.9	11.0	5.0	5.7
	Intra-urban areas	35.5	32.3	32.0	31.7	31.1	34.9	53.2	52.1	47.2	43.9	49.0	49.8
	Intra-rural areas	40.5	43.7	48.4	56.8	61.2	58.0	26.4	36.0	40.9	45.1	46.0	44.6
NPE	Inter-urban/rural	25.1	33.5	23.9	18.8	12.7	12.4	11.6	16.1	14.6	6.8	8.6	7.1
	Intra-urban areas	38.0	32.0	30.3	43.6	45.0	42.8	52.4	51.3	44.2	42.5	45.3	45.3
	Intra-rural areas	36.9	34.6	45.8	37.6	42.2	44.8	36.1	32.7	41.1	50.7	46.1	47.6
TS	Inter-urban/rural	16.6	18.5	26.3	13.0	18.0	22.2	20.1	10.6	19.5	13.6	14.1	15.0
	Intra-urban areas	31.1	32.6	36.7	29.6	36.5	31.6	52.0	46.2	45.5	37.7	40.4	40.7
	Intra-rural areas	52.3	48.8	37.0	57.4	45.4	46.2	27.9	43.2	35.0	48.7	45.5	44.3
CE	Inter-urban/rural	18.7	17.1	19.2	22.1	17.8	13.7	2.6	6.8	9.8	12.1	10.3	12.0
	Intra-urban areas	30.9	50.8	29.8	31.1	34.0	31.3	44.9	57.0	31.7	41.6	38.9	41.9
	Intra-rural areas	50.5	32.1	50.9	46.9	48.2	55.0	52.5	36.2	58.5	46.3	50.8	46.1
BO	Inter-urban/rural	5.0	1.8	2.5	0.8	1.1	0.3	2.1	2.6	5.9	1.8	1.1	0.1
	Intra-urban areas	26.1	26.2	27.3	22.3	23.8	23.9	38.0	33.2	36.5	29.8	35.4	35.6
	Intra-rural areas	68.8	72.0	70.3	76.9	75.2	75.8	59.8	64.2	57.6	68.5	63.5	64.2

RE regular expenditure; *BRE* budgetary regular expenditure; *TS* teacher's salary; *NPE* non-personnel expenditure; *CE* capital equipment; *BO* books

Table 4.14 Decomposition of Theil coefficient of the urban and rural group differences in Zhejiang

	Difference	Primary schools						Junior secondary schools					
		2001	2002	2003	2004	2005	2006	2001	2002	2003	2004	2005	2006
RE	Inter-urban/rural	15.8	6.9	3.8	3.8	5.5	3.7	12.9	9.3	2.2	10.3	8.2	7.3
	Intra-urban areas	59.2	77.3	77.8	42.6	45.0	44.1	67.1	72.5	81.4	39.4	45.5	44.7
	Intra-rural areas	25.0	15.8	18.4	53.6	49.5	52.2	19.9	18.2	16.4	50.3	46.3	48.1
BRE	Inter-urban/rural	9.2	3.2	1.1	0.3	1.1	0.3	10.2	1.5	1.1	2.3	2.5	1.0
	Intra-urban areas	53.8	64.3	70.5	42.2	38.4	41.9	68.8	50.8	77.4	42.8	39.5	39.7
	Intra-rural areas	36.9	32.4	28.3	57.5	60.4	57.8	21.0	47.7	21.4	54.9	58.0	59.4
NPE	Inter-urban/rural	19.7	7.9	4.2	1.7	4.3	3.1	11.1	4.1	0.7	5.0	3.9	3.9
	Intra-urban areas	62.7	79.2	76.6	44.5	47.3	47.3	57.8	76.9	79.5	47.2	43.1	46.6
	Intra-rural areas	17.6	12.9	19.2	53.8	48.4	49.6	31.1	18.9	19.8	47.9	53.0	49.5
TS	Inter-urban/rural	11.3	4.9	4.0	6.4	6.6	7.2	12.8	5.1	2.8	5.0	7.7	7.3
	Intra-urban areas	63.2	67.7	71.4	32.2	34.3	31.5	71.2	67.5	74.8	34.8	36.8	34.4
	Intra-rural areas	25.5	27.3	24.6	61.4	59.1	61.4	16.0	27.4	22.4	60.2	55.6	58.3
CE	Inter-urban/rural	13.6	10.4	6.2	9.3	12.6	12.0	2.6	5.5	3.0	5.8	7.9	5.6
	Intra-urban areas	61.6	68.1	79.1	48.0	51.6	41.6	56.9	76.3	79.4	44.0	38.0	41.6
	Intra-rural areas	24.8	21.5	14.7	42.7	35.8	46.4	40.6	18.1	17.6	50.2	54.1	52.8
BO	Inter-urban/rural	6.7	4.5	6.2	3.1	2.4	1.3	0.4	1.0	1.2	0.0	0.4	0.2
	Intra-urban areas	59.9	72.1	71.6	40.5	32.5	38.4	68.2	68.6	74.3	37.0	32.3	35.8
	Intra-rural areas	33.4	23.4	22.2	56.3	65.1	60.3	31.3	30.5	24.5	63.0	67.3	64.0

RE regular expenditure; *BRE* budgetary regular expenditure; *TS* teacher's salary; *NPE* non-personnel expenditure; *CE* capital equipment; *BO* books

Table 4.15 Decomposition of Theil coefficient of the urban and rural group differences in Heilongjiang

	Difference	Primary schools						Junior secondary schools					
		2001	2002	2003	2004	2005	2006	2001	2002	2003	2004	2005	2006
RE	Inter-urban/rural	4.7	4.3	2.3	0.2	0.0	2.7	26.2	32.9	28.2	24.5	17.3	17.4
	Intra-urban areas	37.4	43.2	48.2	49.5	43.8	53.2	35.0	36.3	44.2	43.4	43.3	40.0
	Intra-rural areas	57.8	52.5	49.5	50.3	56.2	44.1	38.8	30.8	27.6	32.1	39.4	42.6
BRE	Inter-urban/rural	2.2	0.6	0.0	1.1	1.5	7.1	23.3	26.5	21.2	18.4	9.9	10.4
	Intra-urban areas	32.4	41.0	44.4	43.6	41.5	49.0	26.1	33.4	35.2	40.3	43.5	37.9
	Intra-rural areas	65.4	58.4	55.6	55.3	57.0	43.9	50.6	40.1	43.6	41.3	46.6	51.7
NPE	Inter-urban/rural	10.1	6.2	4.5	5.7	8.7	4.4	16.9	18.9	22.3	15.3	11.4	11.6
	Intra-urban areas	44.0	35.6	33.8	42.1	39.9	43.6	51.8	44.7	55.5	48.8	41.5	50.1
	Intra-rural areas	45.9	58.2	61.7	52.2	51.5	52.0	31.3	36.5	22.2	36.0	47.2	38.2
TS	Inter-urban/rural	5.4	5.8	7.3	3.7	5.0	0.0	10.5	12.9	8.3	10.6	7.1	2.8
	Intra-urban areas	37.3	41.6	45.6	54.8	37.4	56.1	39.2	43.7	54.5	59.1	62.1	57.6
	Intra-rural areas	57.3	52.6	47.2	41.5	57.6	43.9	50.3	43.5	37.2	30.2	30.8	39.7
CE	Inter-urban/rural	15.7	20.1	6.2	12.5	12.5	17.0	13.3	20.8	24.1	21.8	16.4	12.4
	Intra-urban areas	40.2	33.1	24.7	32.4	39.6	37.6	53.5	48.4	44.2	42.8	49.9	45.5
	Intra-rural areas	44.1	46.8	69.1	55.1	47.9	45.4	33.3	30.8	31.6	35.4	33.7	42.1
BO	Inter-urban/rural	0.8	1.2	0.0	0.1	2.5	0.8	2.6	4.5	8.0	1.4	1.7	0.0
	Intra-urban areas	45.8	50.8	37.5	33.5	30.4	29.4	42.5	47.3	82.6	48.4	46.4	48.8
	Intra-rural areas	53.4	48.0	62.5	66.4	67.1	69.8	54.9	48.2	9.4	50.2	51.9	51.1

RE regular expenditure; *BRE* budgetary regular expenditure; *TS* teacher's salary; *NPE* non-personnel expenditure; *CE* capital equipment; *BO* books

say, although the counties have good or poor economics and financial ability, students should not receive different educations because of the county's development level of economics and financial ability. However, when we decomposed the Theil coefficient for inter-county and intra-county, the inequity derived from both inter-county inequity and intra-county inequity. Therefore, we want to know whether the inter-county inequity of regular expenditures is affected by local economics and financial ability. Do the local economics and financial ability affect intra-county inequity? If the formula of fiscal appropriation is not changed, does the inequity of regular expenditure increase or decrease with an increase of per student average regular expenditure?

4.6.1 The Relationship of Inter-county Inequity with Per Capita GDP and Per Capita General Fiscal Revenue

GDP is usually used to measure the development level of economics. In this study, we use per capita GDP instead of economics, and we use per capita recurrent fiscal revenue to represent the financial ability of the county government. According to Odden and Picus (2000), if the correlation coefficient is less than 0.5 and the elasticity (the coefficient of *w*) is less than 0.1, the education finance system in a region satisfies the financial neutrality criteria. Therefore, we compute the correlation coefficient and elasticity to measure whether financial neutrality exists. We also can say whether the transfer payment from central and provincial governments eliminates the inequity of fund inputs caused by local economics and financial ability.

4.6.1.1 Relationship of Per Student Regular Expenditure with Per Capita GDP

According to the criteria of the correlation coefficient being less than 0.5 and elasticity less than 0.1, Guangxi in 2005 and Hubei in 2005 and 2006 did not achieve financial neutrality. In other years, the four provinces are under the rule of financial neutrality. Although most of correlation coefficients in Table 4.16 are less than 0.5, we also wish the coefficient of *w* to not be significantly higher than 0.1. However, as shown in Table 4.17, most of the *w* values for per capita recurrent fiscal revenue are higher than 0.1. Therefore, if per capita GDP is increased by 1 Yuan, the per student average regular expenditure will be increased by 0.101 Yuan at least or 0.358 Yuan at most. Local economic development level still has some significant influence on per student average regular expenditure.

The *w* value for Guangxi and Hubei increased until 2003, then fluctuated. The *w* value for Zhejiang constantly increased. Heilongjiang's *w* value increased until

Table 4.16 The correlation coefficient of per student average regular expenditure with per capita GDP

	Province	2001	2002	2003	2004	2005	2006
Primary schools	Guangxi	0.23	0.231	0.264	0.492	0.534	0.331
	Hubei	0.126	0.224	0.334	0.239	0.591	0.589
	Zhejiang	0.027	−0.033	−0.058	0.113	0.181	0.384
	Heilongjiang	0.02	0.163	0.276	0.355	0.183	0.301
Junior secondary schools	Guangxi	0.408	0.433	0.362	0.411	0.521	0.17
	Hubei	0.082	0.232	0.186	0.209	0.595	0.612
	Zhejiang	0.223	0.215	0.218	0.321	0.281	0.417
	Heilongjiang	0.025	0.052	0.161	0.308	0.001	0.265

Table 4.17 The elasticity of per student average regular expenditure with per capita GDP

	Province	2001	2002	2003	2004	2005	2006
Primary schools	Guangxi	0.229^{***}	0.343^{***}	0.353^{***}	0.333^{***}	0.353^{***}	0.097
	Hubei	0.07	0.122^{*}	0.274^{***}	0.135^{**}	0.358^{***}	0.298^{***}
	Zhejiang	0.082	0.04	0.034	0.081	0.11^{**}	0.203^{***}
	Heilongjiang	0.007	0.091^{*}	0.196^{***}	0.166^{***}	0.101^{**}	0.111^{***}
Junior secondary schools	Guangxi	0.196^{***}	0.265^{***}	0.332^{***}	0.243^{***}	0.254^{***}	0.038
	Hubei	0.047	0.168^{***}	0.173^{**}	0.115^{**}	0.351^{***}	0.298^{***}
	Zhejiang	0.188^{**}	0.144^{***}	0.176^{***}	0.198^{***}	0.206^{***}	0.256^{***}
	Heilongjiang	0.01	0.056	0.123	0.207^{**}	0.012	0.119

Note The other control variables of all models include the logarithm of number of students, while the Ordinary Least Squares (OLS) model of data for three provinces includes year and province variables
*, **, and *** represent significance levels of 10, 5, and 1 %

2004, then decreased in 2005, and increased again in 2006. In each province, the *w* value of both primary schools and junior secondary schools presents the same change trend.

4.6.1.2 Relationships of Per Student Regular Expenditures with Per Capita Recurrent Fiscal Revenue

When the county government takes responsibility for financing compulsory education, its financial ability determines the amount of funds inputted into compulsory education more directly than the economics development level. Therefore, the inter-county inequity of per student average fund input is determined by inter-county differences in financial ability. However, since the rural tax-fee reform and county-centered system was implemented from 2001, central and provincial governments started to provide more and more transfer payments for county governments. Thus, the inter-county inequity of per student average fund input may be reduced or even eliminated.

The financial ability of the county government only has a very small influence to fund inputs for compulsory education. We used recurrent fiscal revenue to represent the financial ability, which does not include any transfer payments from central, provincial, and municipality governments. Like the criterion developed by Odden and Picus, the correlation coefficient of the per student average regular expenditure with per capita recurrent fiscal revenue should be less than 0.5 and the elasticity of regular expenditure with recurrent fiscal revenue should be less than 0.1 at the same time.

Primary schools not achieving financial neutrality included Guangxi in 2005; Hubei in 2006; Zhejiang in 2002, 2005, and 2006; and Heilongjiang of 2003. Junior secondary schools exceeding the rule for financial neutrality included Guangxi in 2002 and 2003, Hubei in 2006, and Zhejiang in 2001 and 2002. Although the correlation coefficient in most years is lower than 0.5, the elasticity is significantly higher than 0.1, except for primary schools in Heilongjiang in 2006. In 2001, if per capita recurrent fiscal revenue increased by 1 Yuan, per student average regular expenditure increased by 0.414 Yuan at most or 0.213 Yuan at least. In 2006, under the same conditions, per student average regular expenditure increased by 0.32 Yuan at most or 0.098 Yuan at least. This demonstrates that local financial ability still has an important influence on regular expenditure.

Based on the analysis of the relationship between per student average regular expenditure and per capita GDP and recurrent fiscal revenue, we found that financial neutrality did not happen every year. However, under the absolute financial neutrality, the correlation coefficient may not be equivalent to 0, but the elasticity must be 0. According to this, the government at the higher level of county must make more of an effort to achieve financial neutrality (Tables 4.18 and 4.19).

Table 4.18 Correlation coefficient of per student average regular expenditure with per capita recurrent fiscal revenue

	Province	2001	2002	2003	2004	2005	2006
Primary schools	Guangxi	0.32	0.382	0.442	0.463	0.531	0.47
	Hubei	0.441	0.267	0.427	0.435	0.444	0.666
	Zhejiang	0.418	0.587	0.405	0.216	0.548	0.58
	Heilongjiang	0.418	0.348	0.59	0.31	0.447	0.392
Junior secondary schools	Guangxi	0.439	0.625	0.522	0.469	0.412	0.277
	Hubei	0.425	0.334	0.221	0.495	0.435	0.571
	Zhejiang	0.702	0.525	0.414	0.316	0.48	0.455
	Heilongjiang	0.318	0.429	0.417	0.356	0.191	0.203

Table 4.19 The elasticity of per student average regular expenditure with per capita recurrent fiscal revenue

	Province	2001	2002	2003	2004	2005	2006
Primary schools	Guangxi	0.251***	0.352***	0.302***	0.375***	0.313***	0.267***
	Hubei	0.414***	0.201***	0.386***	0.292***	0.283***	0.32***
	Zhejiang	0.213***	0.285***	0.263***	0.12***	0.201***	0.223***
	Heilongjiang	0.3***	0.183***	0.262***	0.159***	0.184***	0.096***
Junior secondary schools	Guangxi	0.225***	0.282***	0.245***	0.291***	0.204***	0.164***
	Hubei	0.365***	0.195***	0.185**	0.28***	0.259***	0.283***
	Zhejiang	0.308***	0.293***	0.317***	0.201***	0.231***	0.249***
	Heilongjiang	0.256***	0.345***	0.291***	0.272***	0.155**	0.131**

Note The other control variables of all the models are all include the logarithm of number of students, while the OLS model of three provinces data include year and province variables
*, **, and *** represent significance level of 10, 5 and 1 %

4.6.2 The Relationship of the Intra-county Inequity of Regular Expenditure to Per Capita GDP and Fiscal General Revenue

When the Theil coefficient is decomposed by inter-county and intra-county, we found that intra-county inequity made up most of the total inequity. Therefore, we aimed to find out what caused the significant intra-county inequity of education. Many scholars and government officials argue that an underdeveloped economy and weak financial ability are the most important reasons why the government cannot achieve intra-county equity in compulsory education. However, does the intra-county equity of per student average regular expenditure improve after the economy is developed to a higher level and the government has a better financial ability? To examine this question, we designed two regression models.

The dependent variable in both regression models is the intra-county Gini coefficient of per student average regular expenditures. The independent variable of model 1 is the logarithm of per capita GDP, whereas model 2 takes the logarithm of per capita recurrent fiscal revenue as the independent variable. Because of the limitations of the data, we only selected Guangxi, Hubei, and Zhejiang in 2005 and 2006 to estimate these models.

The methods used to estimate these two models were OLS and the difference method. The basic principle of the difference method is as follows: the value of each variable in the regression model is obtained by the value of 2006 minus that of 2005. The benefit of such a method is to eliminate the influence of each county's fixed factors on the inequity of regular expenditure. In addition, when we estimate the two models with OLS, we added year as a dummy variable. In both models, we used the logarithm of the number of students as the control variable. The results of the estimation are listed in Table 4.21. In this report, only the coefficients and the statistical characteristics of independent variables are reported.

First, we examined the relationship between the logarithm of per capita GDP and the Gini coefficient of per student average regular expenditure. Within three provinces, the OLS estimation of model 1, both at primary schools and junior secondary schools, shows that the coefficient of the logarithm of per capita GDP is positive. This demonstrates that the higher the per capita GDP is, the higher the intra-county Gini coefficient is. However, when we use the difference method to estimate model 1, some coefficients of the logarithm of per capita GDP are negative. These minus coefficients may tell us that some intra-county fixed factors have important influence on the inequity of regular expenditures. However, in the estimation of the two models, we cannot find a steady and specific relationship between per capita GDP and the intra-county inequity of per student average regular expenditure.

Secondly, we examine the influence of the per capita recurrent fiscal revenue logarithm on intra-county inequity of per student average regular expenditure. In primary schools, the relationship of per student average regular expenditure with per capita recurrent fiscal revenue displays similar results to those stated previously. However, the model for junior secondary schools is different. Except for Zhejiang, all the other models for junior secondary schools proclaim that if the county government has a greater financial ability, the inequity of per student average regular expenditure for junior secondary schools is also significantly higher.

One conclusion from the above analysis is that there is no stable and definite relationship between intra-county inequity of per student average regular expenditure and economic development level. The other conclusion is that although there is not a stable and definite influence of local financial ability on intra-county inequity of per student average regular expenditure for primary schools, for junior secondary schools, financial ability has a strong influence on the intra-county inequity of per student average regular expenditure. We can say that the local economic development level and financial ability does not affect the intra-county inequity or expand the inequity. Therefore, an underdeveloped economy and weak financial ability is not a true reason for intra-county inequity (Table 4.20).

Table 4.20 Regression results for Model 1 and Model 2

	Three provinces		Guangxi		Hubei		Zhejiang	
	OLS	Diff.	OLS	Diff.	OLS	Diff.	OLS	Diff.
Model 1								
Primary schools	0.0055	−0.0083	0.004	-0.0106^{*}	0.0217^{***}	−0.0197	−0.0065	0.0044
Junior secondary schools	0.0171	−0.0031	0.0015	−0.0016	0.0405^{***}	0.0018	0.0097	0.0029
Model 2								
Primary schools	0.0046	−0.0034	0.0046	0.0062	0.0146^{**}	−0.0094	0.0009	−0.0091
Junior secondary schools	0.0171^{***}	0.0145^{**}	0.0035	0.0321^{**}	0.0358^{***}	0.0018	0.0122	0.0120

*, **, and *** represent significance level of 10, 5, and 1 %

Table 4.21 The regression results of Model 3

	Three provinces		Guangxi		Hubei		Zhejiang	
	OLS	Diff.	OLS	Diff.	OLS	Diff.	OLS	Diff.
Primary schools	1.63E−05***	3.39E−05***	1.9E−05***	2.9E−05**	8.90E−06	1.40E−05	1.7E −05***	4.2E−05***
Junior secondary schools	1.7E−05***	4.3E−05***	2.6E−05***	7.4E−05***	3.9E−05***	4.4E−05***	1E −05***	3.7E−05***

*, **, and *** represent significance level of 10, 5, and 1 %

If an underdeveloped economy and weak financial ability is not the true reason for intra-county inequity, we argue that the formula for fiscal appropriation or education resources distribution may be the true reason. When the formula is not changed, the inequity is going to be expended with the increase of per student average fund input. To prove our argument, we designed the regression model 3 to examine the relationship between per student average regular expenditure and its inequity, based on the precondition that the formula is not improved to a more balanced level. Model 3 adheres to the rules of Model 1 and Model 2. The dependent variable is the Gini coefficient of per student average regular expenditure, and independent variable is the per student average regular expenditure.

Table 4.21 shows the estimated results (only the coefficient of per student average regular expenditure is presented). Firstly, as for the model of three provinces, both the OLS and fixed effect model stably demonstrate a positive relationship between per student average regular expenditure and its inequity, which means that the higher the former is, the worse the inequity is. For example, with an increment of 100 Yuan for average regular expenditure per primary school student, the Gini coefficient will increase by 0.0016; for junior secondary schools, the Gini coefficient may increase by about 0.0017. From the model for each province, we can come to the similar conclusion. In addition, the relationship between per student average regular expenditure and its Gini coefficient is very significant, except in primary schools of Hubei. Hence, we think that a better method to distribute fund inputs or education resources is the key to achieve intra-county equity.

4.7 Vertical Equity: Is the Difference Between Rural and Urban Areas Really Small?

When we decomposed the Theil coefficient of each resource into inter-rural/urban intra-rural/intra-urban Theil coefficients, we found that inter-rural/urban inequity is very small and just gave a small contribution to total inequity. Vertical equity requests that the government provide more education resources for disadvantaged groups. In this study, we define the children and their schools of rural areas as disadvantaged groups. We think that the government should input more funds into rural areas than urban areas. Namely, the government should provide a better education or much more education resources for those rural students and rural schools. However, what excess of disadvantage over advantaged groups is reasonable? We cannot answer this question. However, we hope to see that the difference between rural and urban areas is decreasing gradually, and this has been happening in China since 2000.

To measure the difference between these rural and urban areas, we may use three methods: the absolute difference of the mean of the two groups, the ratio of per-student education resources, and the comparison of growth rate of per-student education resources. However, we only used the ratio of per student education resources in this study. We subtracted the rural mean value of education resources from the urban one; then, this difference was divided by the rural one to compute the ratio. This ratio has three characteristics:

1. The ratio may be positive or negative. The positive one illustrates that the students in urban areas receive more fund inputs and other education resources than rural students; whereas the negative one shows that the rural students receive more fund inputs and other education resources.
2. If the ratio is going up, the growth rate of the urban mean will be faster than the rural one. If the ratio is going down, the growth rate of the rural mean will be much faster.
3. The ratio is the relative difference between rural and urban areas. Suppose the ratio of the fund input mean is 0.5. This illustrates that the government should input another 50 % into rural areas so that the rural students have the chance to receive the same fund input as urban students.

4.7.1 Education Revenue and Fiscal Appropriation

In the same province, there are differences in education revenue between rural and urban areas. The government has a different policy choice for primary schools and junior secondary schools. In Guangxi, the lowest ratio is 0.468 and the highest one is 0.602 for primary schools; for junior secondary schools, the lowest one is 0.191 and the highest one is 0.476. In Hubei, the lowest one is 0.674 and the highest one is 1.009 for primary schools, whereas the lowest one is 0.528 and the highest one is 0.688 for junior secondary schools. The rural and urban difference for primary schools is much higher than that of junior secondary schools in both Guangxi and Hubei. In Zhejiang's primary schools, the lowest one is 0.164 and the highest one is 0.425; for junior secondary schools, the lowest one is 0.22 and the highest one is 0.381. The rural and urban difference for primary schools is lower than that of junior secondary schools in Heilongjiang, where the lowest and highest of primary schools is −0.095 and 0.181 respectively; those of junior secondary schools are 0.553 and 0.957, respectively. Here, −0.095 indicates that the mean of per rural student education revenue is 9.5 % higher than that of per urban student education revenue. We also found that the growth rate of rural education revenue has been

Table 4.22 The ratio of education revenue

Year	Primary schools				Junior secondary schools			
	Guangxi	Hubei	Zhejiang	Heilongjiang	Guangxi	Hubei	Zhejiang	Heilongjiang
2001	0.534	0.964	0.425	0.181	0.239	0.588	0.381	0.739
2002	0.523	1.009	0.248	0.171	0.191	0.533	0.321	0.957
2003	0.602	0.978	0.211	0.132	0.203	0.688	0.22	0.865
2004	0.593	0.755	0.164	0.028	0.25	0.64	0.304	0.787
2005	0.514	0.698	0.218	0.02	0.476	0.528	0.329	0.553
2006	0.468	0.674	0.19	−0.095	0.285	0.566	0.272	0.601

Table 4.23 The ratio of fiscal appropriation

Year	Primary schools				Junior secondary schools			
	Guangxi	Hubei	Zhejiang	Heilongjiang	Guangxi	Hubei	Zhejiang	Heilongjiang
2001	0.437	0.829	0.341	0.077	0.150	0.575	0.399	0.539
2002	0.479	0.855	0.169	0.053	0.119	0.438	0.218	0.726
2003	0.519	0.759	0.127	0.027	0.148	0.466	0.125	0.623
2004	0.526	0.544	0.023	−0.071	0.190	0.521	0.121	0.569
2005	0.402	0.496	0.058	−0.072	0.402	0.381	0.138	0.402
2006	0.347	0.472	0.052	−0.170	0.190	0.417	0.100	0.434

faster than that of urban education revenue in the primary schools of Guangxi since 2003, Hubei since 2002, and Heilongjiang since 2001.

Fiscal appropriation shows the same characteristics as education revenue. In the primary schools of Heilongjiang and junior secondary schools of Guangxi and Zhejiang, the rural and urban difference is the lowest. In 2004, 2005, and 2006, the government of Heilongjiang input more funds into rural primary schools. Additionally, the ratio of Guangxi's primary schools from 2004, Hubei's primary schools, and Zhejiang's junior secondary schools from 2001 was decreasing. This illustrates that the growth rate of rural education revenue is much faster (Tables 4.22 and 4.23).

4.7.2 *Regular Expenditure*

Table 4.24 shows that the characteristics of the regular expenditure ratio are the same as the education revenue and fiscal appropriation. In primary schools, the rural and urban difference in Heilongjiang was the lowest every year, and that of Hubei was the highest. In 2006, the regular expenditure of rural primary schools was 10.9 % higher than that of urban ones in Heilongjiang. However, in Hubei, the

Table 4.24 The ratio of regular expenditures

Year	Primary schools				Junior secondary schools			
	Guangxi	Hubei	Zhejiang	Heilongjiang	Guangxi	Hubei	Zhejiang	Heilongjiang
2001	0.526	0.875	0.328	0.184	0.234	0.593	0.285	0.752
2002	0.521	0.959	0.227	0.158	0.163	0.519	0.26	0.883
2003	0.565	0.949	0.161	0.121	0.181	0.634	0.124	0.882
2004	0.55	0.75	0.162	0.031	0.23	0.62	0.293	0.754
2005	0.514	0.672	0.212	0.013	0.454	0.519	0.307	0.549
2006	0.431	0.659	0.169	−0.109	0.274	0.544	0.243	0.606

regular expenditure of rural primary schools was 65.9 % lower than that of urban ones. In junior secondary schools, the difference between rural and urban areas of Guangxi was the lowest before 2005; then, Zhejiang's was the lowest and Heilongjiang's was the highest. In 2006, regular expenditure for rural areas was 60.6 % lower than that for urban areas in Heilongjiang; in Zhejiang, urban areas were 24.3 % higher than rural areas.

Rural and urban differences in teacher's salary are lower than other education resources in each province. Since 2001, education policy has directly influenced teacher's salary in rural areas. In addition, the guarantee mechanism for teacher's salary was relatively well defined, which can be proven by the analysis of the difference in teacher's salary between the urban and rural areas. At primary schools, the difference of teacher's salary in Hubei was the highest at 38.1 % in 2006, followed by Guangxi at 18.1 %. Compared with 2001, the difference of these two provinces in 2006 showed an ascending trend. At junior secondary schools, the highest difference was still in these two provinces, which were 28.9 and 21.9 %, respectively. The difference in the primary schools of Hubei in 2006 increased to 38.1 %, which is the highest in Table 4.25. In general, the difference in teacher's salary was smaller than that of the other aspects, and the difference in primary schools was less than that of junior secondary schools (Hubei is an exception).

Table 4.25 The ratio of teacher's salary

Year	Primary schools				Junior Secondary Schools			
	Guangxi	Hubei	Zhejiang	Heilongjiang	Guangxi	Hubei	Zhejiang	Heilongjiang
2001	0.026	0.297	0.191	0.135	0.045	0.331	0.207	0.182
2002	0.055	0.277	0.116	0.160	0.102	0.173	0.127	0.238
2003	0.049	0.341	0.119	0.184	0.038	0.276	0.107	0.194
2004	0.059	0.257	0.146	0.138	0.102	0.249	0.128	0.230
2005	0.218	0.316	0.161	0.152	0.298	0.281	0.178	0.181
2006	0.181	0.381	0.160	0.012	0.219	0.289	0.161	0.107

Table 4.26 The ratio of non-personnel expenditures

Year	Primary schools				Junior secondary schools			
	Guangxi	Hubei	Zhejiang	Heilongjiang	Guangxi	Hubei	Zhejiang	Heilongjiang
2001	0.809	1.048	0.839	0.567	0.367	0.519	0.456	0.996
2002	0.678	1.542	0.515	0.413	0.153	0.753	0.314	0.856
2003	0.783	1.153	0.337	0.352	0.25	0.712	0.12	1.442
2004	0.933	1.163	0.241	0.407	0.408	0.488	0.446	0.945
2005	1.093	0.863	0.445	0.45	0.532	0.56	0.441	0.594
2006	0.482	0.91	0.358	0.276	0.208	0.539	0.384	0.741

As for the difference of non-personnel expenditure between the urban and rural areas, the changes in these regions are similar to the above findings, so they are not discussed in detail. The difference of non-personnel expenditure between the urban and rural areas shows a special aspect: Among several indicators of education expenditure, the difference in per-student non-personnel expenditure in primary schools in four provinces was the highest. For example, for primary schools, in 2006 the difference in Guangxi approached 50 %, Hubei exceeded 90 %, and Zhejiang and Heilongjiang were in excess of 27 %. In 2006, the differences of junior secondary schools were 20.8 % in Guangxi and 74.1 % in Heilongjiang, respectively the lowest and highest.

Based on the analysis above, we have found that the difference of regular expenditure, teacher's salary, and non-personnel expenditure between rural and urban areas is still great, although the difference in some provinces was small in some years. The government must make an effort to reduce and eliminate the difference between rural and urban areas. The other finding is that the difference of primary schools is much lower than that of junior secondary schools, or the former is much higher than the latter. This illustrates that the government takes the different policies or models to develop primary education and junior secondary education. One is a balanced model, whereas the other is unbalanced. We can say that the government has the most important role in improving the equity of education (Table 4.26).

4.7.3 *Physical Facilities*

We were startled by the differences in capital equipment value between rural and urban areas. In many years, the difference was greater than 100 % or close to 100 %. In Guangxi and Hubei, the difference for primary schools always exceeded 100 %. The difference for Guangxi in junior secondary schools was the lowest, except for 2005. In 2006, four ratios were higher than 100 %, and the lowest one was 27.5 % (Table 4.27).

Table 4.27 The ratio of capital equipment value

Year	Primary schools				Junior secondary schools			
	Guangxi	Hubei	Zhejiang	Heilongjiang	Guangxi	Hubei	Zhejiang	Heilongjiang
2001	1.637	1.011	0.762	1.374	0.304	0.255	0.294	1.006
2002	1.519	1.470	0.591	1.261	−0.044	0.611	0.424	1.050
2003	1.974	1.447	0.470	0.595	0.230	0.678	0.297	1.352
2004	1.368	1.573	0.640	0.923	0.288	1.023	0.441	1.378
2005	1.608	1.545	0.892	0.896	1.103	0.952	0.548	1.035
2006	1.102	1.178	0.805	1.025	0.275	1.024	0.473	0.792

The difference of per student average books between rural and urban areas reduced our shock in the heart. Only in Guangxi was the difference in primary schools higher. The others were all less than 30 %. Eight ratios in Table 4.28 are less than 0, indicating that a rural student has more books than an urban student on average.

The education policies in recent years have embodied a support system oriented toward rural areas, and our results reflect the effects such policies have created. However, a more detailed investigation found that the implementation of the policies created significant differences in different regions, especially in primary schools and junior secondary schools in different areas. In central and western provinces such as Hubei and Guangxi, junior secondary schools in the rural areas have largely received more policy support than primary schools. At the same time, we also found that the differences between the urban and rural areas presented a decreasing trend in several provinces. Until 2006, the differences in per student regular expenditure between the urban and rural primary and junior secondary schools were all above 20–50 % (except in the primary schools of Zhejiang and Heilongjiang), which demonstrated the permanent difference between the urban and rural areas to some extent.

When we decomposed the Theil coefficients of those resources, we found that the inequity is mainly derived from intra-rural inequity or intra-urban inequity. The inter-rural/urban inequity only gives a small contribution to total inequity.

Table 4.28 The ratio of books

Year	Primary schools				Junior secondary schools			
	Guangxi	Hubei	Zhejiang	Heilongjiang	Guangxi	Hubei	Zhejiang	Heilongjiang
2001	0.564	0.261	0.297	0.096	0.043	0.153	0.071	0.203
2002	0.487	0.172	0.253	0.132	0.083	0.187	0.100	0.283
2003	0.500	0.204	0.295	0.003	0.119	0.291	0.124	0.837
2004	0.459	0.121	0.202	−0.033	0.042	0.181	−0.011	0.134
2005	0.419	0.159	0.187	−0.183	0.123	0.155	−0.063	−0.136
2006	0.439	0.092	0.133	−0.103	0.073	0.054	−0.055	−0.020

However, according to the analysis above, we may say that although the intra-inequity contributes the most of inequity, it is still urgent to reduce the inter-equity. Hence, the government should revise the method to distribute the fund inputs and other resources among groups and within groups to reduce intra-rural inequity, intra-urban inequity, and inter-rural/urban inequity.

4.8 Conclusions and Policy Suggestions

4.8.1 Conclusions

4.8.1.1 The Inequity Is Expanding in Some Provinces

According to the objectives of education policies from 2001, the level of equity should be improved. However, we found that the inequity of education revenue and expenditure in Guangxi and Hubei was increasing in the period from 2001 to 2006. Also, the inequity of fiscal appropriation was increasing after 2004, although it went down before 2004. In the other two provinces, the inequity went up or down irregularly. Additionally, the inequity in some provinces stayed at a higher level, not going up or down.

4.8.1.2 The Inequity Levels in Primary Schools and Junior Secondary Schools Are Different in the Same Province

In Guangxi and Hubei, the inequity in junior secondary schools was lower than that of primary schools, while in Heilongjiang the inequity in junior secondary schools was persistently higher than that of primary schools. Only in Zhejiang was the inequity in primary schools and junior secondary schools quite similar. This illustrates that the government's preference determines the equity or inequity of education resource distribution.

4.8.1.3 The Inequity's Sources Are Different

As fiscal appropriation for education increases, the inequity of fiscal appropriation distribution is main reason for the total inequity. This is found when we decomposed the Gini coefficient. When we decomposed the inequity with the Theil coefficient, we found that the inequity was derived from different sources, such intra-county inequity, inter-county inequity, and intra-rural or intra-urban inequity. For example, the inequity of regular expenditure, teacher's, salary and non-personnel expenditure is mainly from inter-county inequity. However, the inequity of physical facilities is mainly from intra-county inequity.

4.8.1.4 The Intra-county Inequity Is Not Derived from Poor Local Economic Development Levels and Weak Financial Ability

When we examined the relationship of the average regular expenditure per student with GDP and recurrent fiscal revenue, we found that the per student average regular expenditure would rise with the increase of per capita GDP and recurrent fiscal revenue. That is to say, the inter-county inequity increased by expansion of the difference of local economic development and financial ability. However, we came to a different conclusion when we measured the influence of the GDP and recurrent fiscal revenue on intra-county inequity of regular expenditure. Counties with good economic development and financial ability did not have improved equity of education. The method to distribute the fund input and other resources is the most important factor affecting the equity or inequity.

4.8.1.5 The Inequity between Rural and Urban Areas Should Be Given Attention

Although the inequity between rural and urban areas only gives a small contribution to the total inequity and its contribution ratio has been decreasing, this inequity is still very great in some provinces, primary schools, or junior schools. The government should direct more funds and other resources into rural education in order to improve the equity level.

4.8.2 Policy Suggestions

4.8.2.1 The Balanced Distribution of Fiscal Appropriation May Improve Equity

The government should be responsible for providing compulsory education for every child, and every child was born with the right to receive the same education. Since the beginning of the twenty first century, the government has taken the main responsibility for rural compulsory education instead of farmers. The government mainly directs the funds into compulsory education by fiscal appropriation. The balanced fiscal appropriation should be the key to achieving education equity.

Now, the proportion of fiscal appropriation to education revenue is increasing. Also, the inequity of fiscal appropriation distribution is the main reason for education revenue inequity. If we want to improve the equity of education revenue, the best method will be the equity of fiscal appropriation distribution.

4.8.2.2 A Reasonable Transfer Payment System May Reduce and Even Eliminate Inter-county Inequity

In our research, the economic development level—especially the financial ability of the county government—affects the per student average fund input in China. Particularly, the per student average fund input for education will increase with the increase of financial ability. However, we hope that students in every county may receive a similar or identical education using fund inputs and other education resources. If there is no transfer payment, the county government with a strong financial ability will input more funds into education and provide a better education for the students. Those counties with weak financial abilities cannot do this. Therefore, the education received by students in different counties will differ. In order to ensure that all county governments provide a similar or identical education for students, the central, provincial, and municipal governments should supply more transfer payments for counties with lower levels of economic development and weak financial abilities. A reasonable transfer payment system may reduce and even eliminate the inter-county inequity.

4.8.2.3 The County Government Should Design an Equality Formula to Distribute Education Resources in the County

Many scholars and government officials argue that an underdeveloped economy and weak financial ability is the most important reason why the government cannot achieve intra-county equity in compulsory education. However, we find there is no stable, definite, and direct relationship between intra-county inequity and local economic development and financial ability. Although both the economic development and the strength of financial ability are at a higher level, the county government does not improve education equity. We cannot help but think that the reason for intra-county inequity is the unbalanced distribution of fund inputs and other education resources. If the government wants to improve intra-county equity, the county government should be responsible for designing a formula to distribute education resources equally, especially fund inputs.

4.8.2.4 The Government Should Provide More Fund Inputs and Other Education Resources for Rural Compulsory Education

Compared with urban compulsory education, rural compulsory education is still lacking fund inputs and physical facilities. The inequity between rural and urban areas still urgently needs to be reduced. The government should revise the method to distribute the fund inputs and other resources and input more funds and other resources into rural compulsory education.

4.8.2.5 The Standard of Education Input Is Good for Reduction of the Inequity

One institutional reason for the education inequity is that the government does not determine the standardized benchmarks for education input and school operation. Since 2000, teachers' salaries have been standardized. Therefore, the inequity of teachers' salaries is the lowest. It is crucial for the government to design a higher minimum standard for education input and school operation, which is beneficial to reduce the inequity. The high minimum standard will make the government supply the more education input for rural schools or other disadvantaged schools than before. After the education inputs for disadvantaged schools improves, the Gini coefficient will decrease. Hence, the inequity is going to be reduced.

Appendix: Methodology for Measuring the Degree of Equity

The Measurement of Horizontal Equity

In the study of education finance, the common indicators to measure the difference in education resources include adjusted H/L difference (the difference between the higher 95 percentile and lower 5 percentile of the distribution), adjusted range ratio (the ratio between the higher 95 percentile and lower 5 percentile of the distribution), coefficient of variation (standard deviation divided by mean value), Gini coefficient (total equity index GE equals 1), and Theil coefficient. This section introduces the calculation methods for each indicator used in the research.

Adjusted Range ratio

$$\text{Adjusted range ratio} = 95\,\%\,\text{quantile}/5\,\%\,\text{quantile}$$

Coefficient of Variation

Coefficient of variation is also known as variation coefficient, dispersion coefficient, or difference coefficient. It is the ratio of standard deviation of a set of data with its mean value and is the relative indicator used to measure the dispersion level of data. The formula is as follows:

$$V = \frac{\sqrt{\frac{\sum_{i=1}^{n} (y_j - \bar{y})^2}{N}}}{\bar{y}},$$

where: y_j and $\bar{y}$ respectively represent j sample's individual number of certain indicator and the mean value of certain indicator of the total sample. N is the sample number.

The Methods of Calculating and Decomposing the Gini Coefficient

1. Calculation method

At the dawn of twentieth century, Italian economist Gini found the indicator to decide the revenue distribution degree of equity on the basis of the Lorenz curve (see the figure below). If the area between the line of actual revenue distribution curve and revenue distribution perfect equity curve is A, and the area under the actual revenue distribution curve is B, the degree of inequity is represented by the quotient of A/(A + B).

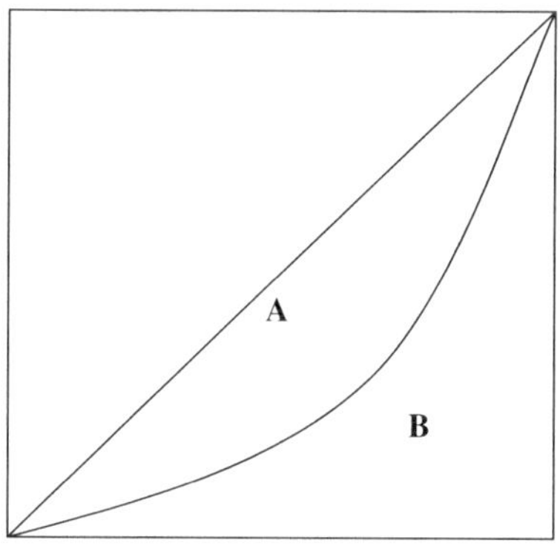

Although the calculation method based on the above figure is an extremely plain mathematical expression, it is not practically operational. At present, for calculation and decomposing of the Gini coefficient, there are many formulas and algorithms, from which we list the most direct calculation formula as follows:

$$G = \frac{1}{2n(n-1)u} \sum_{j=1}^{n} \sum_{i=1}^{n} |x_j - x_i|$$

where $|x_j - x_i|$ is the absolute value of any pair of sample difference; n is sample capacity, and u is mean value.

In addition, there is a method to calculate the Gini coefficient that is more direct and simple. If the sample population can be divided into n group, and w_i, m_i and p_i respectively represent the per capita revenue quotient, average per capita revenue, and population frequency of ith ($i = 1,2,\ldots n$) group, after sorting all the samples on the basis of low and high per capita revenue (m_i), the Gini coefficient (G) can be calculated with the following formula:

$$G = 1 - \sum_{i=1}^{n} 2B_i = 1 - \sum_{i=1}^{n} p_i(2Q_i - w_i)$$

where $Qi = \sum_{k=1}^{i} W_k$ is total revenue proportion from 1 to i; $\sum_{i=1}^{n} B_i$ is the approximation area below the Lorenz curve; $\sum_{i=1}^{n} p_i = 1,, \sum_{i=1}^{n} w_i = 1.$

2. Method for Decomposing the Gini Coefficient

Method 1 decomposes the Gini coefficient on the basis of revenue sources. The specific decamping method is as follows: if total revenue Y is composed by F terms of revenue, it is possible to divide the Gini coefficient into F parts. By this method, it is possible to investigate the contribution value of the revenue difference and each revenue source under various terms to the revenue difference. C_f represents concentration rate of f sub-term, u_f and u respectively are the per capita revenue of f sub-term and sample total per capita revenue, $w_f = u_f/u$ is the weight of f revenue source in the sample total revenue, then C_f can be obtained by the following formula:

$$C_f = 1 - \sum_{i=1}^{n} 2B_{ft} = 1 - \sum_{i=1}^{n} p_i(2Q_{ft} - w_{ft})(f = 1, 2, \ldots, F)$$

where $Q_{ft} = \sum_{k=1}^{f} w_{fk}$ is f revenue source total revenue weight from 1 to i, p_i is the ith sample population's weight in total population, and $w_{ft} = p_i m_i / u_f$ is the ith sample f revenue's weight in the total F sub-term revenue. The calculation formula of C_f is similar to that of G; however, in the calculation, the sample shall be arranged according to the sequence of small to large of the per capita.

After obtaining the F concentration rate (C_f) of F revenue sources, the overall sample Gini coefficient can be decomposed according to the following formula:

$$G = \sum_{f=1}^{F} w_f C_f,$$

where F is the number of sources of revenue and w_f is the weight of f revenue source in the sample revenue. The Gini coefficient is the weighted average of all the sub-term revenue concentration index, and the weight number is the weight of each revenue in the total revenue. $(w_f C_f / G) \times 100\ \%$ is used to measure the fth revenue's contribution on the percent basis to Gini coefficient.

When $C_f > G$, and the per capita revenue of the sample is constant, the weight (w_f) increase of f revenue source in the revenue will result in an increase of the Gini coefficient—that is, even larger revenue inequity. It is possible to determine f revenue source's contribution trend to the Gini coefficient through the calculation and comparison of C_f and G.

In Method 2, decomposition of the Gini coefficient is determined on the basis of time change. Although the decomposing method of the Gini coefficient introduced above is effective, a certain term of revenue has a smaller contribution to the Gini coefficient, and it is still possible for such a term to become a key factor and result in a change of the resident revenue difference or Gini coefficient. For this consideration, through decomposing Gini coefficient on the basis of time change, it may be helpful to figure out the cause of such change. Because the concentration index change may be independent of the change in revenue weight, the expanding or shrinking of revenue difference represented by the Gini index may simply result from the weight change of single-term revenue in the total revenue rather than the change of concentration level of single-term revenue.

If subscript t and $t + i$ are used to represent time, the change of the Gini coefficient is as follows:

$$\begin{aligned}\Delta G = G_{t+1} - G_t &= \sum_{i=1}^{F} w_{t+1}C_{t+1} - \sum_{i=1}^{F} w_t C_t \\ &= \sum_{i=1}^{F} (w_t + \Delta w)(C_t + \Delta C) - \sum_{i=1}^{F} w_t C_t \\ &= \sum_{i=1}^{F} \Delta w C_t + \sum_{i=1}^{F} \Delta C w_t + \sum_{i=1}^{F} \Delta w \Delta C\end{aligned}$$

The above formula denotes that the change of difference can be decomposed into three major parts, where the first part represents the Gini coefficient increase or decrease resulting from weight change; the second part represents the Gini coefficient increase or decrease resulting from the change of the concentration level. The third part represents the Gini coefficient increase or decrease resulting from joint changes in weight and concentration level. Because the change of weight is closely related to the adjustment of economic structure, we refer to $\sum \Delta w C_t$ as a structural effect, $\sum \Delta C \Delta w_t$ as a concentration effect, and $\sum \Delta w \Delta C$ as a synthetic effect.

The Calculation and Decomposing of the Theil Coefficient

The expression of the Theil coefficient (T) is:

$$T = \frac{1}{n}\sum \frac{x_i}{u}\log\left(\frac{x_i}{u}\right)$$

where x_i is the per-student education expenditure of ith county level unit. The overall Theil coefficient may be decomposed into inter-group and intra-group inequity. If the minimum observed unit in the sample may be divided into groups, the intra-group inequity coefficient (T_w) is:

$$T_W = \sum \left(\frac{n_k u_k}{n_u}\right) T_k,$$

where T_k is the overall Theil coefficient of *k*th group; and n_k, u_k respectively represent the observed value in the *k*th group and per-student expenditure level of *k*th group. It is obvious that the intra-group inequity coefficient is actually the weighted mean value of overall inequity coefficient of each group. The inter-group inequity coefficient (*Tb*) is actually the difference between the overall inequity coefficient with intra group inequity coefficient: $Tb = T - T_w$.

2. Introduction of the Method for Measuring Fiscal neutrality

Methods	Definitions
1. Simple correlation (Sim Corr)	Pearson correlation coefficient between X with w
2. Slope coefficient of simple regression (SLOPE1)	Coefficient b_1 in $X_1 = a + b_1 w$ (weighted and averaged with student number)
3. Slope coefficient represented by quadratic function (SLOPE2)	Coefficient of $b_1 + 2b_2\bar{w}$ in $X_1 = a + b_1 w + b_2 w^2$
4. Slope coefficient represented by cubic function (SLOPE3)	Coefficient of $b_1 + 2b_2\bar{w} + 3b_3 w^2$ in $X_1 = a + b_1 w + b_2 w^2 + b_3 w^3$
5. Elasticity of simple regression (ELAST1)	(SLOPE1) × (*W*/*X*), (*X*, *W* is the mean value)
6. Elasticity of quadratic function (ELAST2)	(SLOPE2) × (*W*/*X*), (*X*, *W* is the mean value)
7. Elasticity of cubic function (ELAST3)	(SLOPE3) × (*W*/*X*), (*X*, *W* is the mean value)
8. Constant elasticity (ELASTC)	B_1 in $Lnx = a + b_1 \ln w$
9. Adjusted simple regression coefficient	$(2 \times SLOPE1 \times \delta_w)/\bar{x}$
10. Adjusted quadratic function relationship	$(2b_1\delta_w + 4b_2\bar{w}\delta_w)/\bar{x}$
11. Adjusted cubic function relationship	$(2b_1\delta_w + 4b_2\bar{w}\delta_w + 6b_3\delta_w\bar{w}^2 + 2b_3\delta_w^3)/\bar{x}$

Note In this formula, the population is not weighted

References

Du, Y. H. (2000). *Research on unbalanced education development*. Beijing: Standard University Press.

Milanovic, B. (2007). Globalization and inequality. *Global Inequality*, Cambridge, 26–49.

Odden, A. R., & Picus, L. O. (2000). *Schools finance: A policy perspective* (2nd ed.). New York: McGraw-Hill.

Tsang, M. C., & Ding, Y. Q. (2005). Research on unbalanced utilization and deployment of compulsory education resources in China. *Education and Economics*, *2*, 45–47.

Wang, R. (2001). Research on regional difference in China's compulsory education expenditure. Conference Paper of Provide Sufficient Resources for Education—International Symposium of Education Economics, 327–341.

Wang, R. (2003). Research on input equity in China's compulsory education expenditure. *Economics Quarterly*, *2*(2), 1–17.

Chapter 5
Rural Compulsory Education Finance Monitoring and Evaluation System

On December 24, 2005 the State Council issued the Notice on Reforming Fund Guarantee Mechanism for Rural Compulsory Education, symbolizing the rural compulsory education finance system striding into a new era. One of the core elements of the new mechanism is that the financing responsibility of governments at all levels for compulsory education is clarified clearly (see Table 5.8). Do central and local governments fulfill their responsibility? What responsibilities should be further clarified? Are various funds sufficiently prepared and allocated pursuant to predetermined amounts and directions? These are important issues in compulsory education financing. How can we know more information about these issues, especially in detail? We need to design a monitoring and evaluation system.

Monitoring and evaluation are the keys to ensuring that any system is implemented smoothly and developed continuously. Hence, the task of this chapter is to design a monitoring and evaluation system for the new mechanism. The focus of the monitoring system is whether the budget is implemented, and the key problem of the evaluation system is what the output is after the resources are inputted. In the report, we design a monitoring system to collect detailed information about the implementation of the new mechanism and design an evaluation system to measure the education financial effort and "crowding-out effect" of the government at various levels.

In this chapter, we first define the concept and framework of the monitoring and evaluation system. Secondly, we design a monitoring system for rural compulsory education finance, especially monitoring indicators for TEOS, non-personnel expenditures, school building repair and maintenance, and teacher salary. Thirdly, we design two evaluation systems at the provincial and county levels to evaluate the government's financing effort and the crowding-out effect. Finally, we present a case study and apply a pilot survey to analyze and discuss the micro-foundation of the monitoring and evaluation system—school budgets.

Y. Du and Z. Sun, *Research on Compulsory Education Financing in China*,
New Frontiers of Educational Research, DOI 10.1007/978-3-662-47830-1_5

5.1 The Framework of a Monitoring and Evaluation System for Compulsory Education Finance

A monitoring and evaluation system is an important part of improving and perfecting compulsory education finance, which is conducive to enhancing education quality. Compulsory education is covered by public finance because of the implementation of the new mechanism. This guarantees the fund supply for compulsory education to some extent. However, some problems still exist and must be solved during the implementation of the new mechanism, such as whether the transfer payments from the central to local government are allocated in a timely fashion, whether the responsibilities taken by the local government are distinctly clarified, and whether the local governments have assumed their responsibilities.

To resolve these problems, it is necessary to establish a monitoring and evaluation systems to collect and analyze information in order to monitor and evaluate the finance system. This study attempts to design a finance monitoring and evaluation system for compulsory education finance so as to strengthen input monitoring, process monitoring, and output evaluation to provide the decision maker with supports.

The monitoring system tracks the process of the finance system or policy implementation according to the objectives. The core mission of the monitoring system is to collect and analyze information about the finance system or policies. It plays an irreplaceable role in policy analysis and has four important functions: supervision, auditing, final accounting, and interpretation. In detail, monitoring may help decision makers to find out whether the implementation of the finance system and policies is consistent with the objectives, whether and why the finance system and policies deviate from the original objectives, and whether the target groups truly benefit. The monitoring system may help decision makers to learn the social and economic effects of the finance system and policies.

The evaluation system analyzes the output, cost, and efficiency of the finance system, policies, and responsibilities of governments at different levels, based on some certain value judgment. Only a scientific evaluation system makes it possible to identify whether a policy has reached the predetermined objectives and whether this policy should be continued, adjusted, or terminated.

A policy should be evaluated by the following:

1. Effect—whether the output of the policy is valuable
2. Efficiency—what the cost of the output is
3. Adequacy—to what extent the target problems have been resolved
4. Equity—whether the benefit is distributed among target groups equally
5. Response—whether the output of the policy complies with the demand, preference, or values of the targeted groups
6. Suitability—whether the outputs (targets) are really worth more effort or resources.

The standards and content are the most important core aspects of an evaluation system and are the basis of designing the evaluation indicators.

Furthermore, the monitoring and evaluation system can analyze policies to find out what is gained, what is lost, what we can learn, and so on. These findings will give decision-making support to implement and develop the policies in future.

5.2 Rural Compulsory Education Finance Monitoring System

As shown in Table 5.1, the monitoring system contains monitoring principles, bodies, contents, and results sorted out from several new mechanism provisions. However, these provisions are very abstract. The urgent problems of the monitoring system lie in ambiguous monitoring principles and inadequate publicity and transparency. Most of the existing provisions do not reflect the features of the new mechanism. Additionally, there are some shortcomings of current monitoring: singular principal part, excessive reliance on administrative department, insufficiency in operability stipulation of the functions in top-down monitoring at

Table 5.1 Current rural compulsory education finance monitoring system in China

Monitoring principles	Monitoring bodies	Monitoring contents	Monitoring results
1. Finance disclosure 2. Supervision reporting system, set up and make public the supervision and report telephone number 3. Specific audit system 4. Enhance finance management and improve fund usage efficiency	1. Local education administration department 2. Local government, planning, auditing, supervision, regulatory, monitory and other departments	1. Arranging budget for rural compulsory education 2. Recruiting and assessing teachers for rural schools 3. Defining rural indigent students 4. Charging situation of primary and junior secondary school 5. Using and managing rural compulsory education expenditures	1. The central government will strengthen appraisal 2. Render recognition and awards to excellent areas 3. Adopt relevant measures in areas unduly deploying, retaining, delaying, crowding out, and/or misappropriating funds

educational authorities at various levels and the same-level monitoring system and their cooperation, no bottom-up monitoring principal parts being involved in consideration, excessive macro items set under monitoring, failure to set up monitoring indicators, hardships in systematic and in-depth data analysis, lack of responsibility track-down, improper responsibility track-down methodology, and a shortage of specific criteria for reward and punishment.

The basic objective of establishing a rural compulsory education finance monitoring system is to ensure that the government at various levels can input adequate funds into rural compulsory education. A complete monitoring system should define the monitoring principles, define the objectives of compulsory education finance monitoring and its basic responsibility, select monitoring items and key points in the light of actual situation, and finally choose the methods for using monitoring results.

5.2.1 Principles

Rural compulsory education is very important in terms of its foundation, guidance, and overall functions. Good and sustainable rural compulsory education is vital to national development and new rural construction. To better popularize and consolidate nine-year compulsory education, enhance the quality of education, and promote rural education development, it is necessary to strengthen the government's guarantee responsibility for rural compulsory education and mobilize enthusiasm for all parties concerned. Rural compulsory education finance monitoring is a necessary measure to achieve this objective, and monitoring should be carried out in compliance with national education guidelines and policies in order to accurately understand rural compulsory education's input situation, reasonably analyze the problems, and provide an accurate and effective basis for education management and decision making.

Rural compulsory education finance monitoring should adhere to the following principles:

- *Monitoring by law and serving policy-making:* Monitoring should be based on laws as well as various policies and provisions issued by its finance, education, and other departments, to provide the basis for national education decision making by setting up reasonable monitoring indicators and accurately understanding rural compulsory education finance situations.
- *Disclosure, transparent, and multiparty participation:* Disclosure is the origin of monitoring. Monitoring bodies can perform their duties in a targeted manner to improve monitoring effects only if they have obtained adequate information. Information disclosure may be further extended to the monitoring bodies to enable timely detection of problems, correction of deviations, and improvement of monitoring effects. As issued in 2007, Regulations of the People's Republic of China on Disclosure of Government Information stressed that "disclosure is

the universal principle, and non-disclosure is exceptional," which embodies the national will and legal authoritativeness and provides a legal basis for the implementation of such principles.

- *Scientific monitoring, emphasis on directive function:* Monitoring should be conducted under the principle of reasonable and normative judgment throughout the process of setting up a monitoring body, selecting monitoring items, and collecting, sorting, and analyzing the data. At the same time, the monitoring should combine predetermined targets to strengthen the monitoring effect and guiding effect.

5.2.2 Executive Bodies

The most important executive body of the monitoring system is the State, and the Office of Fund Guarantee Mechanism for Rural Compulsory Education has the power to represent the State to perform the monitoring. Under the lead of the Office, a national monitoring network will be designed in order to provide services for developing compulsory education.

The Office is responsible for the macro-governance in the monitoring system, designing a monitoring program and indicator system, conducting investigations and research on the project on a yearly basis, and training and coordinating. The People's Congress at various levels should, as the executive body, participate in monitoring to expand and improve the monitoring; the National People's Congress has the highest power, and the local People's Congress also has a similar station in local areas. The People's Congress has the power to monitor and govern government's behaviors.

Additionally, the media, schools, students, and families should be taken as executive bodies and participate in monitoring. One mission of the media is to report the government's behaviors, and schools, students, and families are the final beneficiaries. Therefore, they are the main information providers for a monitoring system.

5.2.3 Monitoring Contents and Indicator System

The most important objective of a compulsory education finance monitoring system is to collect relevant information on compulsory education finance at the micro-level, and such information is also very important to evaluate whether the policy achieved its predetermined objectives. Here, we design a monitoring system for the fund guarantee mechanism for rural compulsory education: (1) whether the new mechanism is implemented according to requirements of the policy; (2) whether the governmental appropriation, the share-mechanism, per student appropriation standard, and appropriation date are carried out according to the requirements of the policy; (3) whether the new mechanism benefits the target groups; (4) what problems exist in the implementation of the new mechanism and what caused these problems. If we can find out the answers to these questions, we will give policy suggestions to improve and perfect the new mechanism.

According to the contents of the new mechanism, we have designed monitoring indicators for Two Exemptions, One Subsidy (TEOS), non-personnel expenditures, school building repair and maintenance, and teacher salary to monitor the government's behaviors. Theoretically, it is also required to obtain fundamental information from the schools, such as enrollments, beneficiaries of TEOS, the teachers and other staff, school buildings, and others. In this study, only monitoring indicators for government were designed.

5.2.3.1 "Two Exemptions and One Subsidy" Policy

The TEOS policy is one core content of the new mechanism. As early as 2001, the State Council required that governments at various levels should implement and perfect a student assistance system in compulsory education in order to mitigate the burden of indigent students. Meanwhile, the central government commenced a pilot system to provide free textbooks for primary and junior secondary school students from poor families in the poverty-stricken regions, which was the starting point of TEOS. In recent years, under the background of the "people oriented" concept and constructing a harmonious society, the TEOS policy has been developed rapidly, especially the coverage and assistance standards.

To ensure that the policy benefits all targeted groups, the governments at various levels should input sufficient funds pursuant to the share mechanism and their responsibilities. The objective of monitoring indicators for TEOS is to monitor whether the executive bodies perform their responsibilities. The indicators mainly focus on the following: the number of beneficiaries, assistance standards (i.e. appropriation standard), appropriation date, and the use of various appropriations. This information will determine whether governments at various levels assumed their responsibilities, whether the fund is sufficient, and whether the targeted students receive the assistance in time.

1. **Miscellaneous Fee Exemption**
   According to the provision of the new mechanism, in western China since 2006, the students in compulsory education in rural areas are exempted from miscellaneous fees. The expenditure for the miscellaneous fee exemption is jointly funded by the central and the local government at the proportion of 8:2 in western China and 6:4 in central China. In eastern China, the proportion is determined by the financial ability of the local government. Beijing, Tianjin, and Shanghai directly under the central government should shoulder all financial responsibilities.
   We designed four indicators to monitor the miscellaneous fee exemption: the number of beneficiaries, the standard of miscellaneous fee exemption, the amount of expenditures for the miscellaneous fee exemption, and the appropriation date. These indicators are grouped by the type and location of the school (see Table 5.2).

Table 5.2 Monitoring indicators for miscellaneous fee exemptions

Monitoring indicators		Primary schools			Junior secondary schools		
		Urban	Town	Rural	Urban	Town	Rural
Enrollment (student)							
Standard for exempting tuition and miscellaneous fees (Yuan per student a year)							
The amount (ten thousand Yuan)							
The budgetary appropriation from upper government[a]	Appropriation standard (Yuan per student a year)						
	The number of beneficiaries (student)						
	Appropriation amount (ten thousand Yuan)						
	Appropriation date						
The budgetary appropriation of local government	Appropriation standard (Yuan per student a year)						
	The number of beneficiaries (student)						
	Appropriation amount (ten thousand Yuan)						
	Appropriation date						

[a]Upper-level appropriation includes appropriations to the local government by all upper-level governments

2. **Free Textbooks**
   In 2006, free textbooks were provided to indigent students in rural compulsory education, and from autumn 2007, free textbooks were available to all students in rural compulsory education. According to the Notice on Adjusting Fund Guarantee Mechanism for Rural Compulsory Education jointly issued by Ministry of Finance and Ministry of Education in 2007, the requirement for the provision of free textbooks to all students in rural compulsory education commenced in the autumn semester 2007. The textbooks for the national curriculum are provided by the central government and the textbook of the local curriculum by the local government.

Table 5.3 Monitoring indicators for free textbooks

Monitoring indicators			Primary schools			Junior secondary schools		
			Urban	Town	Rural	Urban	Town	Rural
Enrollment (student)								
Standard for free textbook (Yuan per student per year)								
Total fund (ten thousand Yuan)								
National curriculum	Central government	Appropriation standard (Yuan per student per year)						
		The number of beneficiaries (student)						
	Appropriation	Appropriation amount (ten thousand Yuan)						
		Appropriation date						
Local curriculum	Upper-level appropriation[a]	Appropriation standard (Yuan per student per year)						
		The number of beneficiaries (student)						
		Appropriation amount (ten thousand Yuan)						
		Appropriation date						
	Local appropriation	Appropriation standard (Yuan per student per year)						
		The number of beneficiaries (student)						
		Appropriation amount (ten thousand Yuan)						
		Appropriation date						

[a]Upper-level appropriation includes appropriations to the local government by all upper-level governments

We also designed four indicators for free textbooks: the number of students receiving free textbooks, the appropriation standard for free textbook, the amount of expenditure for free textbooks, and the appropriation date (see Table 5.3).

3. **Living Subsidy for Indigent Boarding Students**
   The living subsidy program focuses on indigent boarding students in rural compulsory education. Because there is no uniform standard for the living subsidy of poor boarding students, the standard varies in different regions. The living subsidy standard in most provinces is about 1 Yuan per student per day, or even less than 1 Yuan. It commenced in the autumn semester of 2007 to increase the minimum living subsidy standard to 2 Yuan per primary school student per day and 3 Yuan per junior secondary school student per day. The central government provides 50 % of the fund for provinces in western and central China. The local government undertakes the other 50 %. If the standard implemented by local governments in western and central China is higher than the minimum standard, the excess fund needed will be borne by the local government. At the same time, the central government requires the local government in eastern China to strengthen the poor boarding student living subsidy policy; the funds needed should be borne by the local government. The central government will provide a reasonable reward for these provinces and municipalities.
   Providing a living subsidy for indigent boarding students was the responsibility of local governments. There is big difference among the standard of living subsidy implemented by local governments before the autumn of 2007. Until then, there was no clear share mechanism to provide the funds for the implementation of this policy. Therefore, the monitoring indicators for the indigent boarding student living subsidy not only include the number of the beneficiaries, appropriation and subsidy standard, the amount of expenditure for living subsidy, and appropriation data, but also the fund-sharing mechanism (see Table 5.4).
   The major objective of the TEOS policy is to mitigate the burden of the farmers. It is also necessary to collect information at the individual level if we want to know the actual effect of this policy. However, it is difficult to make the students and their parents become participants of the monitoring system, and we should make more efforts to resolve this difficulty in the future.

5.2.3.2 Non-personnel Expenditure

Since 2001, the State has issued relevant policies that require local governments to determine reasonable non-personnel expenditure standards and gradually improve the non-personnel expenditure guarantee level for rural primary and junior secondary schools. These policies also clarified the responsibilities of the government at each level. To improve the non-personnel expenditure guarantee level for rural compulsory education, the new mechanism requires that rural primary and junior secondary school should begin to implement school budgets and provincial governments should determine non-personnel expenditure appropriation standards. By 2008, the non-personnel expenditure standard for rural primary and junior secondary schools in each province (region and municipality) should increase to the

Table 5.4 Monitoring indicators for indigent boarding student living subsidy

Monitoring indicator		Primary schools			Junior secondary schools		
		Urban	Town	Rural	Urban	Town	Rural
Definition of indigent student: student from the family with per capita income lower than Yuan							
Enrollment (student)							
Of which: indigent students							
Boarding students							
Students from agriculture and forest							
Reflow student number							
Dropouts							
The standard of living subsidy (Yuan per student per year)							
Total amount (ten thousand Yuan)							
Upper-level appropriation[a]	Appropriation standard (Yuan per student per year)						
	The number of beneficiaries (student)						
	Appropriation amount (ten thousand Yuan)						
	Appropriation date						
Local government appropriation	Appropriation standard (Yuan per student per year)						
	The number of beneficiaries (student)						
	Appropriation amount (ten thousand Yuan)						
	Appropriation date						

[a]Upper-level appropriation includes appropriations to the local government by all upper-level governments

standard determined before the beginning of the autumn semester in 2005 by provincial government. By 2009, the central government will determine the national standard of non-personnel expenditure for primary and junior secondary school. If the standard determined by each province (district, municipality) is lower than the national one, 50 % of the gap should be eliminated in that year and should be jointly funded by central and local governments according to the share-mechanism for miscellaneous fee exemptions.

Non-personnel expenditure is an important requirement for school operation, and the amount of non-personnel expenditure has a direct influence on whether the teaching activities and other activities are carried out successfully. The guarantee level of non-personnel expenditure for rural compulsory education is determined by the non-personnel expenditure appropriation standard. The other factor that determines how many non-personnel expenditures a school can get is the school scale. The non-personnel expenditure is jointly funded by the central and local governments on the basis of the sharing-mechanism miscellaneous fee exemption. Therefore, the monitoring indicators for non-personnel expenditures consist of the number of enrollments, appropriation standard or non-personnel expenditure standard, sharing-mechanism, and appropriation date (see Table 5.5).

To monitor non-personnel expenditure guarantee levels, we should know whether the non-personnel expenditure is adequate for a school to provide enough required activities and curriculums to students. However, this is a difficult job. In the future, we should spend much time and effort in overcoming this difficulty.

Table 5.5 Monitoring indicators for non-personnel expenditure

Monitoring indicators		Primary schools			Junior secondary schools		
		Urban	Town	Rural	Urban	Town	Rural
Enrollment (student)							
The non-personnel expenditure standard (Yuan per student per year)							
The amount (ten thousand Yuan)							
Upper-level Appropriation[a]	Appropriation standard (Yuan per student per year)						
	The number of student (student)						
	Appropriation amount (ten thousand Yuan)						
	Appropriation date						
Local government Appropriation	Appropriation standard (Yuan per student per year)						
	The number of student (student)						
	Appropriation amount (ten thousand Yuan)						
	Appropriation date						

[a]Upper-level appropriation includes appropriations to the local government by all upper-level governments

5.2.3.3 School Building Repair and Maintenance

Rural primary and junior secondary school buildings were repaired and maintained mainly by various national special projects before the new mechanism, such as the National Compulsory Education Project for Poverty Stricken Regions in 1995 and the National Dilapidated School Building Renovation Project for Rural Primary School and Junior Secondary School in 2001. However, these projects are not a long-term and stable guarantee mechanism. The new mechanism requires that the central government should measure the cost of school building repair and maintenance. The central government affords 50 % of the cost for every province, region, and municipality in western and central China. In eastern China, provinces and municipalities shoulder all the costs. However, the central government will give some rewards according to their financial ability and outcome achieved in school building repair and maintenance. The new mechanism is a long-term and stable mechanism. To make it more effective, it is necessary to monitor the fund demand, fund resource, and outcomes (see Table 5.6).

Table 5.6 Monitoring indicators for school building repair and maintenance

Monitoring indicators		Year ××
The total floor areas of school building (m^2)		
of which: the floor areas of dilapidated school building (m^2)		
the areas of D Grade dilapidated school building (m^2)		
Total floor areas needed to be repaired and maintained (m^2)		
The total fund needed (in ten thousand Yuan)		
School building	The floor area of new school building (m^2)	
	The cost of new school building (Yuan)	
	The floor area of repair and maintenance (m^2)	
	The cost of repair and maintenance (Yuan)	
	The floor area of renovation (m^2)	
	The cost of renovation (Yuan)	
The appropriation standard for repair and maintenance (Yuan per square meter)	Upper government	
	Local government	
The total appropriation for repair and maintenance (ten thousand Yuan)	Upper government	
	Local government	
Appropriation date	Upper government	
	Local government	

5.2.3.4 Teachers' Salaries

During the middle and late 1990s, the local government delayed paying salaries for teachers in rural areas. The financial ability of the local government was weakened due to tax-shared reforms, tax-fee reform, and other changes of finance system, so the local governments, especially county governments and township governments, could not afford teachers' salaries. In 2001, the State Council issued the Decision on Basic Education Reform and Development, which proposed a county-centered system. Under this system, the county government takes the responsibility for salary and personnel management for rural education. The problem of delaying the teachers' salaries was resolved in time.

Since the new mechanism was implemented, the rural primary and junior secondary schools have lost the right to charge fees to students. Meanwhile, various funds must be used for predetermined purposes, which must not be paid for teachers' allowances. Therefore, many local governments and schools are not able to pay for teachers' allowances, causing the actual income of the teachers to decrease. In addition, some local governments are unable to implement the "Three Insurances, One Fund" (i.e. medical insurance, pension insurance, unemployment insurance, and housing fund) for rural teachers, while such expenditures are fulfilled by charging fees. If these problems cannot be resolved in a short time, teachers' teams will become unstable and the effect of the miscellaneous fee exemption policy will be discounted. Hence, the indicators we designed for monitoring teachers' salaries focus on a teacher's actual income (see Table 5.7).

5.2.4 Accountability and Intervening of Monitoring Results

The final mission of this monitoring system is to promote the development of compulsory education. In a complete monitoring system, we not only collect and analyze the information about the progress of the policy but also do some necessary accountability and intervening. The latter two are integral parts of the monitoring system. The precondition of accountability is clearly defined government's responsibilities. However, the government's responsibilities of financing compulsory education have not been clarified clearly. Thus, it needs to be studied further. The evaluation, reward, and punishment should be based on relevant studies so as to strengthen accountability and intervening.

Finally, the bodies of the monitoring system should report the results of monitoring to the upper government and the public. This is a better way to let the public participate in the social administration.

Table 5.7 Monitoring indicators for teachers' salaries

Monitoring indicators		Year × ×
The number of staff	Total	
	Full-time teacher	
	Substitute teacher	
The total rural teachers' salaries (in ten thousand Yuan)	Total	
	Primary school teacher	
	Junior secondary school teacher	
Average salary (Yuan per teacher per month)	Urban primary school	
	Town primary school	
	Rural primary school	
	Urban junior secondary school	
	Town junior secondary school	
	Rural junior secondary school	
Average allowances (Yuan per teacher per month)	Urban primary school	
	Town primary school	
	Rural primary school	
	Urban junior secondary school	
	Town junior secondary school	
	Rural junior secondary school	
Average "Three Insurances, One Fund" (Yuan per teacher per month)	Urban primary school	
	Town primary school	
	Rural primary school	
	Urban junior secondary school	
	Town junior secondary school	
	Rural junior secondary school	

5.3 Rural Compulsory Education Finance Evaluation System

It is a harder and more complicated job to design an evaluation system for rural compulsory education finance. In this report, it is possible to evaluate the urgent problems focused on by the central government. One problem close to the new mechanism is that the change happens in the input into rural compulsory education. The change shows two characteristics:

1. The government has provided more and more inputs for rural compulsory education. In 1997, budgetary appropriation for rural compulsory education was 43 billion Yuan, accounting for 54.8 % of the total input of rural compulsory education; in 2002, it was 99 billion Yuan, or 78.2 % (Xin 2003); in 2006, it reached 188.05 billion Yuan, or 86.4 %.
2. Responsibilities between the central and local governments are clarified more clearly. The central government and provincial governments have undertaken more financial responsibility. The more underdeveloped the province is, the more responsibility the central government has taken. Before 2003, the funds inputted into rural compulsory education by the central government mainly consisted of transfer payments for teachers' salary and tax-fee reform and special fiscal appropriation. In 2002, the central government inputted 35.9 billion Yuan into rural compulsory education, which accounted for 36.3 % of the total budgetary expenditure for rural compulsory education. In 2004, the central government required governments at all levels to input yearly increased educational expenditures into rural education in the future. The central government spent 70.4 billion Yuan on rural compulsory education, occupying 43.7 % of the total budgetary inputs.

After the new mechanism, the central government increased the fiscal appropriation for rural compulsory education year by year. However, the total budgetary expenditure did not increase significantly. Did the local government reduce expenditures for rural compulsory education? Did a "crowding-out" effect emerge? It is necessary to evaluate the degree of efforts made by local governments to develop rural compulsory education, especially fiscal input.

This section focuses on the degree of efforts made by local governments and the crowding-out effect. If we want to evaluate the two issues, it is necessary to clarify the responsibilities of the local government at each level under the new mechanism. This is our starting point to design an evaluation system for compulsory education finance. Our evaluation system embodies an executive body, evaluation content, and evaluation indicators.

5.3.1 Executive Body

The executive body of a compulsory education finance evaluation system mainly includes the NPCs, government, and agencies:

1. *NPCs*. According to the Education Law, the central government and other levels of government should report to NPC or Standing Committee at the same level on the budget and final accounting of educational expenditure. This law endows the NPC at various levels with the power to monitor and evaluate.

2. *The government at various levels.* The government has the responsibility of monitoring and evaluation of educational inputs of lower level governments. The education department, financial department, and bureau of statistics are mainly responsible for the monitoring and evaluation of the education input. These departments of the government are the core executive bodies of the evaluation system.
3. *Agencies.* When the departments of the government evaluate the government's behaviors or their own behaviors, objectivity and justness may be ignored. Therefore, the agencies, like non-government organizations, should participate in the evaluation system as the executive body.

5.3.2 Evaluation Contents and Indicators

After the implementation of the Fund Guarantee Mechanism for Rural Compulsory Education, the two characteristics of rural compulsory education financing were presented. The first one is that the government takes all responsibility for funding rural compulsory education; the second one is that the financial responsibility for rural compulsory education between the central and local government has been clarified. This shows that China has made huge progress in developing compulsory education. However, one urgent problem exists in the new mechanism: how to clarify the local responsibility of funding rural compulsory education among local governments at different levels. Under the situation that the local responsibility cannot be clarified clearly, provincial governments and county governments will shift their responsibility to others. Now, the objectives of the evaluation system for compulsory education finance are to find out whether the local government completes its responsibility and whether the crowding-out effect emerges at the county level.

To introduce the evaluation system in detail, we designed the evaluation content and indicators for provincial and county governments. We introduce the relationship among the governments at different levels under the current finance system, explain the responsibility of education input after the new mechanism, design the indicators to evaluate efforts made by the government, and finally define and explain the crowding-out effect at last.

5.3.2.1 Evaluation Contents and Indicators for Provincial Governments

1. **Current Finance System**
   Since tax sharing reform, which was the shift from a decentralized financial system to a centralized one in 1994, the financial ability of the central government has been intensified increasingly. On the contrary, the local government

has been weakened. Under the tax sharing reform, the central government expanded its resources of fiscal revenue. From 1994, the value-added tax, as a main resource of fiscal revenue, has been defined as a sharing tax with 75 % for the central government and 25 % for the local government. In 2002, 50 % of the increment of enterprise income tax and individual income tax was submitted to the central government from the local government, which used to be the resource of fiscal revenue for local governments. In 2003, that proportion became 60 %. Currently, except for business tax, other resources of fiscal revenues for local governments feature unstable and high collection costs. Although the revenues from these two taxes have been increased significantly, the local governments do not increase their fiscal revenues accordingly.

The central government's financial ability increased for 13 consecutive years from 1993 to 2006, and the proportion of its fiscal revenues in the national total fiscal revenues increased to 52.8 % from 22 %. While the central government centralized the financial power, it transferred more responsibilities to local governments. In 1993, the fiscal revenue of local governments accounted for 78 % in total revenue and decreased to 44.3 % after 1994. Meanwhile, the proportion of the fiscal expenditures in the national total spent by local governments was growing, from 67.4 % in 1990 to 75.3 %[1] in 2006.

It is obvious that after tax sharing reform, the central government has increased fiscal revenue, occupying about 50–60 % of the national total fiscal revenue. However, this did not necessarily mean that the fiscal expenditure of the central government was expended. Actually, 60–70 % of the fiscal revenue as transfer payment was transferred to the local government. The local government's fiscal revenue accounts for 40 % of the national total revenue, while its fiscal expenditure exceeded 70 % of the national total expenditure. The gap between fiscal revenue and expenditure was settled by transfer payment from the central government. Therefore, the transfer payment began to play an increasingly important role in the financial system.

Under the tax sharing system, the provincial government also strengthened its financial ability. Because there was no distinct provision for financial relationships among local governments in the tax sharing reform, the provincial government prefers to share more fiscal revenue in order to meet the fiscal expenditure. There is a common phenomenon that the government at the upper level chooses to share more fiscal revenue from the lower government. Under the drive of benefit, the concentration of fiscal revenue made by the provincial government was growing at an annual average rate of 2 % (16.8 % in 1994 and 28.8 % in 2000). The municipal governments also were trying to share more fiscal revenue from county governments. In 2000, the net surplus of local governments was 13.4 billion Yuan, while the fiscal deficit of county and township governments increased. This situation actually demonstrated the fact

[1]National Bureau of Statistics of China. Statistics Yearbook (2007). Beijing: China Statistics Press. 2007.

that financial ability was being centralized to the provincial and municipal governments.[2]

2. **Financial Responsibilities of Compulsory Education Taken by the Provincial Government under the New Mechanism**
In 2005, the State Council issued the Notice on Reforming Fund Guarantee Mechanism for Rural Compulsory Education. In the new mechanism, rural compulsory education would be funded jointly by the central government and local governments. In 2006, the Notice on Strengthening Budgetary Management for Ensuring Rural Compulsory Education Fund provided that:

> The fund for rural compulsory education borne by the central government as transfer payment should be allocated to [the] provincial government. The provincial government should be responsible for raising the fund afforded by local governments. The provincial government has the power to clarify the financial responsibility among local governments, based on the financial ability of each government. Every government's educational inputs at present mustn't be lower than the inputs before the new mechanism.

Specifically, local governments undertook the following financial responsibilities together with the central government at a certain proportion: student exemptions from miscellaneous fees in rural compulsory education, non-personnel expenditures for rural primary and junior secondary schools, guarantee mechanism for repairing and maintaining school buildings, and guarantee mechanism for teachers' salaries. The responsibilities of the governments at various levels are shown in Table 5.8.

3. **The Indicators to Evaluate the Fund for Rural Compulsory Education Input by the Provincial Government**
The financial ability, especially fiscal revenue and expenditure, of the provincial government is the basis of evaluating the provincial government's fund input for rural compulsory education. The fiscal revenue of each provincial government consists of budgetary revenue, fund revenue, and transfer payment.
Under the current finance system and the new mechanism, the provincial government should take more financial responsibility for rural compulsory education. Therefore, we designed the following indicators to evaluate the provincial government's fund inputs for rural compulsory education, as shown in Table 5.9.

We divide the indicators into two categories: (1) static indicators, which represent the fund inputs for rural compulsory education by provincial governments in a certain period; and (2) dynamic indicators, representing the changes of the fund input for rural compulsory education by provincial governments at different periods. Both static and dynamic indicators include absolute and relative indicators. The absolute indicators may reflect the absolute magnitude of the fund for rural

[2]Jia Kang and Bai Jingming. County and Township Finance Resolution and Finance System Innovation. Economic Research. 2002(2).

Table 5.8 Financial responsibilities of the governments at various levels and individuals before and after the implementation of the new mechanism

	Before 2005	From 2005 to 2007
Tuition and miscellaneous fee		
Central government	Exempting miscellaneous fees for student in poverty areas	Western China, 80 %; Central China, 60 %
Local government	Some provincial governments afford the expenditure of miscellaneous fee exemption	Western China, 20 %;Central China 40 %; Eastern China, 100 %
Individual	Miscellaneous fees	0
Free textbooks		
Central government	100 % of fund for free textbooks in pilot areas	100 % Undertake the books for poor students in the central and west China
Local government		
Individual	Textbooks	Textbooks
Living cost of boarding student		
Central government		
Local government	Provided by some provinces	100 %
Individual	100 %	Part
Non-personnel expenditures		
Central government		Western China, 80 %; central China, 60 %
Local government	One part of non-personnel expenditure burdened by county government	Western China, 20 %; central China,40 %; eastern China, 100 %
Individual		
Repair and maintenance for school buildings		
Central government	Supply special fund for poverty areas	50 %, for central and western China
Local government	The provincial government supplies the fund according to the special fund from the central government. The county government supplies the fund for new school buildings	Central and western China 50 %; eastern China, 100 %
Individual		
Teachers' salary		
Central government	Supply the subsidy for poverty-stricken counties	Supply the subsidy for poverty-stricken counties

(continued)

Table 5.8 (continued)

	Before 2005	From 2005 to 2007
Local government	The provincial government supplies the subsidy for poverty-stricken counties	The provincial government supplies the subsidy for poverty-stricken counties
	The country government is responsible for paying teachers' salaries	The country government is responsible for paying teachers' salaries
Individual		

Table 5.9 Evaluation indicators of provincial government's fund input for rural compulsory education expenditures

Static indicators	Absolute indicators	Total fund input for rural compulsory education
		Per student fund input for rural compulsory education
	Relative indicators	The ratio of the fund input for rural compulsory education input to the fiscal expenditure
		The ratio of per student fund input for rural compulsory education to per capita fiscal expenditure
Dynamic indicators	Absolute indicators	The growth rate of the total fund input for rural compulsory education
		The growth rate of per student fund input for rural compulsory education
	Relative indicators	The ratio of the growth rate of the total fund input for rural compulsory education to the growth rate of total fiscal expenditure
		The ratio of the growth rate of per-student fund input for rural compulsory education to the growth rate of per capita fiscal expenditure

compulsory education inputted by provincial governments. The relative indicators may offer relationships between the fund inputs for rural education input and financial ability.

Absolute indicators reflect the absolute magnitudes and changes of the total fund input for rural compulsory education and resources acquired by each student directly. However, these cannot tell us whether the total and per-student fund input is commensurate with the financial ability of the provincial government. To know this, we designed relative indicators to evaluate the provincial government's fund input for rural compulsory education.

In the relative indicators we designed, the numerator is those absolute indicators respectively, and the denominator is the total fiscal expenditure, per capital fiscal expenditure, the growth rate of total fiscal expenditure, and the growth rate of per capital fiscal expenditure correspondingly. When these relative indicators decrease, we can say that the provincial government has reduced the fund input for rural compulsory education. The fiscal revenue and expenditure must be increased year by year. If these relative indicators decrease, the reason will be as follows: the growth of fund input (per student) for rural compulsory education does not catch up with that of fiscal expenditure (per capital). If the central government makes more of an effort to fund rural compulsory education while the effort made by provincial government decreases, it can demonstrate the fact that a crowding-out effect happened to the provincial government.

The advantage of these indicators is that their growth rate may evaluate whether the new mechanism has a long-term effective impact on rural compulsory education.

5.3.2.2 Evaluation Contents and Indicators for County Governments

1. **Responsibilities of a County Government after the Implementation of the New Mechanism**
   In 2001, the State Council decided to implement a county-centered system for rural compulsory education, requiring the county government to list the insufficient part of both teachers' salaries and non-personnel expenditures in the budget. After the funding body shifted from the township government to the county government, it was possible for the county government to transfer funds at the county level. However, the huge gap of the education expenditures is still difficult to fill. Because the personnel expenditure occupies a large portion of the expenditures for compulsory education, the county government still undertakes considerable responsibility to raise the funds. The county government also plays an important role in funding rural compulsory education. The financial responsibility of the county government in the new mechanism is shown in Table 5.10.
2. **The Indicators to Evaluate the Funds for Rural Compulsory Education Inputted by County Governments**
   The county government's fiscal revenue mainly includes budgetary revenue, fund revenue, and transfer payments. The fiscal expenditure is similar to the revenue. Aiming at the fiscal revenue and expenditure and financial responsibilities of the county government, we designed indicators to evaluate the fund input for rural compulsory education by county governments. The indicators are shown in Table 5.11.

To evaluate the county government's fund input for rural compulsory education accurately, we eliminated the transfer payment afforded by central, provincial, and municipal governments from the total fund input. For the absolute amount, the total fund input for rural compulsory education and per student fund input for rural compulsory education can be used to evaluate the amount of fund input for rural compulsory education, which directly and clearly demonstrates the situation of fund guarantee for rural compulsory education.

Table 5.10 The proportion of the local government's financial responsibilities of compulsory education taken by the county government in the new mechanism

		Miscellaneous fee exemption	Free textbooks	Living subsidy for Indigent boarding students (%)	Non-personnel expenditures (%)	Maintenance and repair of school buildings
Zhejiang	Linan (1)	50 %	50 %	50	50	100 %
	Anji (2)	30 %	30 %	30	30	70 %
	Jiangshan (3)	0	30 %	30	0	40 %
Hubei	Chibi (1)	0	0	100	50	50 %
	Wuxue (2)	0	0	100	50	50 %
	Xiaochang (3)	0	0	100	0	0 %
Guangxi	Yongfu (1)	0	0	100	30	0
	Rong'an (2)	0	0	100	30	0
	Guiping (3)	0	0	100	30	0
Heilongjiang	Mishan (1)	0	0	30	20	The insufficient part will be settled by budgetary fiscal expenditure or non-personnel expenditure
	Tangyuan (2)	0	0	30	0	
	Keshan (3)	0	0	30	0	

Note In the table, (1), (2), and (3) respectively represent the economic development of each county in the province as high, marginal, and low

Table 5.11 Evaluation indicators of the county government's fund input for rural compulsory education expenditures

Static indicators	Absolute indicators	Total fund input for rural compulsory education
		Per student fund input for rural compulsory education
	Relative indicators	The ratio of the fund input for rural compulsory education to the fiscal expenditure
		The ratio of per student fund input for rural compulsory education to per capita fiscal expenditure
Dynamic indicators	Absolute indicators	The growth rate of the total fund input for rural compulsory education
		The growth rate of per student fund input for rural compulsory education
	Relative indicators	The ratio of the growth rate of the total fund input for rural compulsory education to the growth rate of total fiscal expenditure
		The ratio of the growth rate of per-student fund input for rural compulsory education to the one of per capita fiscal expenditure

The ratio of the fund input (per student) for rural compulsory education to the fiscal expenditure (per capital) link the financial ability of the county government with the fund input for rural compulsory education. It is possible to evaluate the fund for rural compulsory education inputted by the county government.

The crowding-out effect is more likely to emerge in the county government because both the central government and provincial government increase transfer payments for rural compulsory education. It is very likely that the county government will use transfer payments from the central and provincial governments to substitute for the fund that was originally inputted into rural compulsory education. The fund saved will be spent on production and public expenditures, among others.

5.4 Micro-Foundation of Monitoring and Evaluation System: School Budget

The mission of the Fund Guarantee Mechanism for Rural Compulsory Education is essentially to supply sufficient funds for primary and junior secondary schools in rural areas. One core of the new mechanism is the school budget—the basis of the monitoring and evaluation system. It is crucial for the new mechanism to develop a school budget system.

A complete budget includes preparation, approval, implementation, and final accounting. However, primary and junior secondary schools have not ever had budgets before the new mechanism, so the budget is a new item faced by schools. In this section, we discuss the problems faced by schools in preparing and implementing budgets.

5.4.1 Research Design

5.4.1.1 Problems

There are three problems needed to be resolved in school budgets. The first problem is how to prepare a budget for a school. This problem is given more attention by principals and other managers of the schools. The government and policy makers are interested in the next two problems: who will participate in preparing budgets in schools and what the outcomes after the budget implementation are. We focus our attention on these three problems and aim to resolve them.

5.4.1.2 Methodology

An interview and questionnaire are the main methods we used to collect data and information. Our survey staff interviewed school principals, other managers, and teachers from 36 junior secondary schools and 36 primary schools sampled from sample townships. The principal or other manager completed a copy of the questionnaire designed by our experts. In the survey, the survey staff also examined the draft budget in some schools.

5.4.1.3 Interviewees

The interviewees include principals, other managers, and teachers from schools and governors or officials from educational departments.

In every sample county, the survey staff interviewed officials who were in charge of school budgets in the education department. In a few counties, such as Yongfu of Guangxi and Jiangshan of Zhejiang, the survey staff also interviewed officials in charge of educational budgets who are from finance departments. From the education departments of provincial governments, we know that within the same province or region, the education department of the county government varies in their understanding of the significance of the school budget. Because the school budget is under the guidance of the education department and finance department, these two departments' understanding of the school budget directly influence the implementation of the policy.

In each of the 72 schools, the survey staff interviewed principals, teachers, and other participants in the budget. The principals were asked to fill out one copy of the questionnaire on the school's budget. The staff also collected some text materials relevant to preparing the budget, implementing the budget, and final accounting at the same time.

5.4.2 Findings

5.4.2.1 Problems in Budgets

1. **Findings at the County Level**
   All 12 sample counties implemented the schools' budgets after a push from both the education department and finance department. However, we found two opposite opinions on the school budget. Education departments of some counties believed that under the limitation of educational expenditure and relevant benchmarks, the school budget is just an expenditure plan for regulating schools' expenditure spending, which is unable to really reflect the school's demand for expenditures. A budget based on actual demand may be just a factor when the education or finance department allocates the expenditures among schools. In this situation, the schools are unwilling to budget scientifically. The budgeting is just to fill out a table and then submit it to the administration department.
   However, the opposition argues that schools cannot use a budget just as a pretext for asking for more expenditures from the finance department. Otherwise, when the financial ability is unable to meet the expenditure demand of the schools, the schools' positivity to budgeting will decrease. The education department and finance department should teach schools how to use the budget and the expenditure. Based on the budget, schools should learn the technology of financial analysis to find a way to use the limited expenditures efficiently.
   The second finding is that the budget procedures are different in 12 sample counties. As a requirement of the policy, the budget procedure should be composed of four steps, named "Two Up, Two Down." The first step is the first "up," which means that the school prepares the draft budget and submits it to the education department. The next is the first "down"—that is, the education department proposes a budgetary amount of expenditure for the school, based on the draft budget. The third step is the second "up": The school prepares the final budget, according to the proposed budget, and the final budget needs be submitted to education department. The fourth step is the second "down"—namely, the education department examines and approves the final budget. However, in reality, there are only three counties of Hubei where the procedure of the school budget follows "Two Up, Two Down." In the other 9 counties, the procedure is "One Up, One Down"—the first and the fourth steps are omitted. These two different procedures are the reflection of the above-mentioned two opposite opinions.
   The third finding is the equity in preparing a school's budget. That is to say, the education department gives more support to disadvantage, weak, and small schools and teaching points. This is very important for balancing the development of the rural schools.
   The school budget still faces other problems. For example, the education department does not approve the budget based on the expenditure demand of schools. The education department does not approve the budget for each school.

Expenditures for some items are not included in the budget. The budget for personnel expenditures is always supplemented in the implementation. The method to allocate the funds out of the budget from a county government to a school is subjective.

In the survey, we also intended to know that how the education or finance department carries out a performance evaluation of the budget. However, at present, the administration department only supervises and audits the use of the expenditures. Although the administration department may want to carry out a performance evaluation for school budget, the technology is not available. The budget cannot truly reflect the complete demand for expenditures.

2. **The Findings at a School Level**

In the 72 schools, what we found is the same as the findings at the county level. These schools also agree that the budget is not a reflection of the true and complete demand for expenditures. For example, the budget does not include a salary for temporary staff. Actually, schools have to use non-personnel expenditure to pay for these staff's salary. Also, the budget for training, equipment, and repair and maintenance cannot meet the demands for school operation.

Secondly, although the education or finance department of a county government has different opinions for the school budget, these two opposite opinions do not influence the school budgeting. One reason may be that the budget is a good way for principals to improve school administration. The other reason may be that although the education or finance department has a biased understanding of the school budget, it will still emphasize the importance of the school budget.

The third finding is that the budget prepared by schools was low quality, perhaps for two reasons. First, the schools may have limited time to prepare the draft budget—about one week to prepare and submit the draft budget to the education department. The time is so short that schools cannot clarify their basic information, such as the capital, revenue, and expenditure from the previous year, as well as personnel and student scale, in order to analyze the implementation of the budget from the last year. Furthermore, schools need to collect the relevant policies that influence the schools revenue and expenditure. All of these are necessary to prepare a scientific and complete budget. The other reason is that schools lack a professional accountant or financial staff. To improve the quality of the budget, the administration department should give schools more time to prepare the draft budget and supply training for accountants or other financial staff.

In the 72 schools, we also discovered that the schools have posted detailed expenditures from last year in a prominent position. However, when we ask the teachers, students, and parents whether they pay attention to that, most of the answers were "rarely." The public's indifference also makes the decision makers of the budget neglect the effect of the budget.

5.4.2.2 Who Participate in Preparing the Budget in a School?

At the school level, we focused on who participates in preparing the budget and what role they play. According to policies, the school's budget should be decided jointly by the staff from the office of teaching affairs, office of logistic affairs, and finance office and the representatives of teachers under the lead of the principal. Only the principal and the accountant prepare the budget in 42 % of the 72 schools. In some schools, the budget is just decided by the accountant. Only in 33 % of the schools do personnel from the office of teaching affairs participate in budgeting. The office of teaching affairs generally is the department familiar with the teaching activities, student activities, and their demand. However, this office does not have much power to affect the resource distribution.

We also discovered that more than half of the schools have teachers' representatives take part in budgeting. That is to say, the principal should report the budget to the teachers' representatives committee. Sometimes, the representative's suggestions will be adopted. However, their preferences directly decide who the beneficiaries are. Some representatives pay attention to the benefits of the teachers, and the others focus on the development of the student and the school. In Heilongjiang, when we asked during the interview of the school principals why the teachers do not participate in the school's budget process, their replies were that the teachers are not interested in participating in the management of the school's expenditure, which is consistent with the conclusion from the interview with the teachers. The teachers are more interested in teaching and student management. They do not like participating in the school's management, especially the school's finance. Generally speaking, these staff members know the school's actual needs better than the principal, especially physical facilities. Therefore, the principals should generally consult these staff members in the budget process. However, the survey shows that only 33 % of the schools have the staff members from the office of logistic affairs participate in budgeting. This proportion is very low because there is no special personnel in charge of logistic affairs or because interviewees have different understandings of these staffs. In addition, in some schools, the labor union will also participate in budgeting.

5.4.3 Conclusions and Policy Suggestions

In the survey, we learned that no matter the economic background, schools do not prepare their budgets in strict accordance with the budget requirements of the policies. The reasons are as follows:

1. The importance of the school's budget is still not recognized clearly by the decision makers. They believe that the school's budget is only a tool used by the administration department to regulate and control the use of expenditures, or only a tool to ask for expenditures from the administration department.

2. Primary and junior secondary schools in China, especially rural schools, lack high-quality accountants. This is a very serious problem. The accountant position is occupied by a teacher or older accountant. The former does not have much time to prepare, implement, and supervise the budget. Although the latter is familiar with the accounting of schools, they may lack new skills such as office automation, which is also required by modern accounting in addition to professionalism.
3. The school budget item design and standards are unable to satisfy the actual operation demands of the schools, because no attention is paid to some objective factors, such as boarding students, the adjustment of school distribution, etc. In recent years, in order to resolve the obstacle of receiving education for children in remote and poverty-stricken areas, the government made great efforts to adjust school distribution and establish boarding schools. However, the government did not increase the funds for these schools accordingly. For example, the relevant expenditure standards for electricity, water, and heating were not increased. Also, personnel expenditures do not include salaries for temporary staff hired to be caretakers and managers for boarding students and dorms in the budget; thus, these schools have to use non-personnel expenditure to pay for the temporary staff's salaries.
4. The public indifference to expenditure usage is also an important factor leading to the insignificant effects of a school's budget. The teachers, students, and parents are all integral parts of the school's management; however, they pay little attention to it, especially to expenditure usage, which means that the budget decision makers have no pressure to use the expenditures effectively.

On the basis of the above, we put forward three policy suggestions. First, under the macro-background that the government increases the fund input for education continuously, the school's operation should gradually transform from an input model to an output-cost model. Also, the school should take student achievements as the final objective. That is to say, the school should supply students with better education with limited expenditures. The education department should train the principal how to use the expenditure effectively.

Second, the government should adjust the budget items and revise the benchmarks and expenditure standards of school that run promptly and continuously. Reasonable demands for the expenditures should be listed in the budget.

Finally, the government and schools should make great efforts to train a special team of finance staff for rural schools.

Reference

Xin, J. (2003). Press conference by Ministry of Education on some issues of current educational reform and developments. *China Education Daily*, 10-22-2003.

Chapter 6
International Experience

6.1 Non-personnel Expenditures in Compulsory Education and Benchmark Standards: International Experience

This section is written in fulfillment of the Asian Development Bank contract for project TA-4363 PRC Support for Reforms in Compulsory Education Financing (SRCEF). The report starts by setting out international classifications of education expenditures, thereby identifying what constitutes non-personnel expenditure (NPE). It then outlines key indicators on NPE in relation to other education expenditures drawn from Organisation for Economic Co-operation and Development (OECD) and United Nations Educational, Scientific and Cultural Organization (UNESCO) statistics. As NPE finances the acquisition by schools of learning and other physical resources, the measurement of these is considered next, focusing on surveys. The next section of the report summarizes evidence on the importance of non-staff resources for achieving educational outcomes in middle- and low-income countries. This shows that the provision of learning and other physical resources generally matters for students' educational attainment. The next section considers international practice in the allocation of NPE for compulsory education, focusing on experience with specifying benchmark standards for adequacy. A short discussion of general principles or criteria for designing formulae for the allocation of funding for school resources follows. The report concludes with recommendations for the SRCEF project drawn from international experience.

6.1.1 Defining Non-personnel Expenditure in Education

Expenditure is classified into current and capital according to the length of time the item acquired lasts. A strict definition of capital expenditure is that it is on items that

Y. Du and Z. Sun, *Research on Compulsory Education Financing in China*,
New Frontiers of Educational Research, DOI 10.1007/978-3-662-47830-1_6

last for more than one year. This definition is used by the OECD (2006, p. 250). Capital expenditure comprises spending on assets that last longer than one year and includes spending on the construction, renovation, and major repairs of buildings. Current expenditure comprises spending on school resources used each year for the operation of schools. Current expenditure can be further sub-divided into three broad functional categories: the compensation of teachers, the compensation of other staff, and other expenditures (e.g. teaching materials and supplies, maintenance of school buildings, preparation of student meals, and renting of school facilities).

It is, in fact, impossible to draw a precise line between current and capital NPE. Teaching materials and supplies, such as books and mathematics equipment, can last longer than a year. In many educational systems (e.g. UK and Sri Lanka), low-cost equipment is purchased out of current revenues and therefore recorded under current NPE. Furniture purchased for a new school is classified as capital expenditure, but quite often the purchase of a few items of replacement furniture is included under current expenditure. In the OECD definition, school maintenance is classified as current expenditure, whereas major repairs are capital. It is therefore useful to classify NPE for schools into four categories, the first three of which are current expenditure:

1. Consumables: expenditure on items that last less than a year and for which the expenditure has to be repeated each year, such as stationery and electricity;
2. Low-cost and medium-life materials and goods and equipment, such as books, laboratory equipment, computers, record players: these need to be replaced every few years;
3. Small capital works, including maintenance of school buildings and minor refurbishments;
4. Capital expenditure: major renovations and repairs, new buildings including the equipping of new schools with learning resources.

Countries with extensive financial delegation to schools, such as Australia and England, include categories 1, 2, and 3 in the budgets allocated to schools, whereas less extensive delegation, such as Sri Lanka's Norm Based Unit Cost Resource Allocation Mechanism, delegates 1 and 2. In the case of the PRC financial reforms, it is intended to include items 1–3 in the benchmark standard.

When the amount that an education system spends on NPE is considered in relation to the quality of education provided by this spending, it is essential to consider both the annual flow of NPE and the stock of learning resources that the flow has built up at schools over time. The term *learning resources* as used here refers to stocks of books, materials, and equipment, including furniture and blackboards, used by teachers and students in conducting learning activities. Teachers' professional development (in-service training) is usually included as a consumable, although it could be included in staff expenditure. The term *school resources* is used here—as in the general literature—for all resources, both physical and human. Student learning is supported by the school's existing stock of learning resources, not just the current annual flow of NPE. There are also stocks of physical resources that are not used directly in supporting students' learning, but they are required to administer the school and operate the school building. However, annual flows of NPE are easier to measure than stocks of learning and other physical resources; consequently, there are more readily available data on annual flows of NPE than on stocks of resources. One of the most commonly published learning resource stock data indicators is students per computer, but even this is incomplete as it does not indicate the quality of the computers. In recent years, more international country-level indicators of NPE are available that show the variations nationally in the proportions of capital expenditure in total and the percentage of NPE in total current spending for primary and secondary sectors aggregated.

6.1.2 How Much Is Spent on NPE?

The OECD indicator of educational spending distinguishes between expenditure on the provision of educational instruction, called core education, and on ancillary services. Core educational provision is split between direct costs, which include teaching and materials, and indirect costs, which include administration, support services, teachers' professional development, student counselling, and the construction and maintenance of school facilities. Ancillary services include transporting students from home to school and students' boarding at school. Hence, NPE includes both core educational provision and ancillary services.[1] On average, OECD countries devote 5 % of education spending for primary, secondary, and post-secondary non-tertiary institutions on ancillary services,[2] making up 0.2 % of gross domestic product (GDP; OECD 2006, p. 247).

It will be necessary in the SRCEF project to define which ancillary services (in particular for students who board at school, and for meals and transport), are included in the benchmark standard for NPE.

OECD countries vary in the proportion of capital spending in total spending, as can be seen in Fig. 6.1. At the top end, countries spend almost 20 % on capital expenditure for primary and secondary education, falling to under 3 % at the other end of the spectrum. The average in 2003 was 8.2 % of total spending on capital expenditure. Capital spending is often variable over time as it is affected by the buoyancy of public revenues, ability of the public sector to borrow, the policies of the government of the day toward the school infrastructure, and demand, which depends on the growth of the student population or shifts in its location.

[1]Research and development is included in ancillary services, but this is relevant only for tertiary institutions.

[2]Ancillary services include only public expenditures and exclude private expenditures.

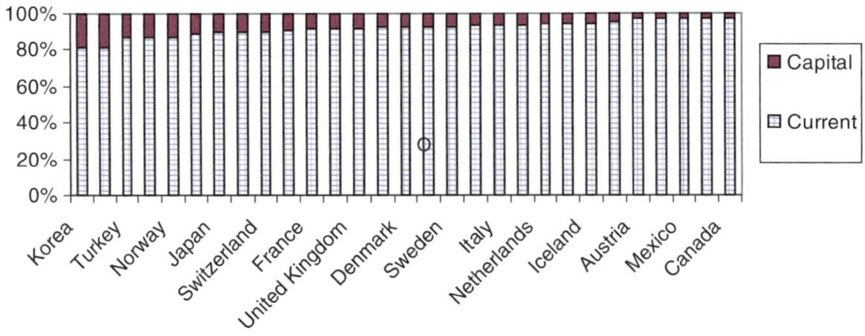

Fig. 6.1 Percentage of capital and current expenditure in total expenditure on primary, secondary, and non-tertiary postsecondary institutions (OECD countries 2003). *Source* OECD (2006). Table B6.2. There are 29 countries: not all are named on the chart

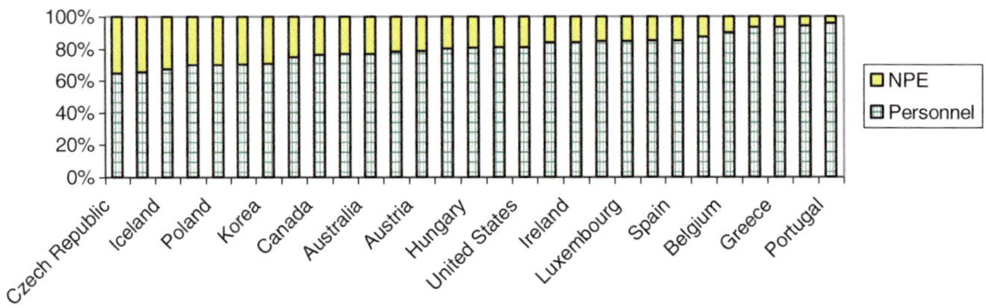

Fig. 6.2 Personnel and non-personnel expenditure as a percentage of current expenditure on primary, secondary and non-tertiary postsecondary institutions (OECD countries 2003). *Source* OECD (2006)

There are also equivalent education indicators published for 19 middle-income counties, not including China in 2006,[3] referred to as World Education Indicators (UNESCO Institute for Statistics 2006). While the average percentage of capital expenditure in total expenditure for primary and secondary education at 8.6 % is very similar to the OECD's, the range is much larger. The percentage varies from 34 % for Malaysia to 0.5 % for Zimbabwe. Current expenditure can be split into expenditure on personnel (teachers and other types of staff) and NPE. In OECD countries in 2003, NPE was on average 19.8 % of current primary and secondary expenditure. As can be seen in Fig. 6.2, the percentage varied from 35 % in the Czech Republic and Finland to 4.3 % in Portugal. The highest spenders on NPE in percentage terms are either high-income countries or transition states, which are

[3]PR China appears in a few statistics in the 2005 edition of WEI. UNESCO Institute for Statistics (2005). *Education Trends in Perspective: Analysis of the World Education Indicators.* Paris: UNESCO Institute for Statistics.

catching up on the underfunding of education in the decade following the collapse of communism. The lowest spenders are relatively low-income countries.

For the twelve WEI countries for which there are data, NPE was on average 13.8 % of total current spending. This percentage varied from an enormous 45 % in Uruguay to 5.3 % in Jordan. Malaysia as a successful Asian economy may be a good comparator for PRC: its NPE is 21 % current expenditure.

The NPE measures examined above are all national averages. Variable averages at the national level can be consistent with very large variances within the country. These, of course, can only be revealed by within-country studies of representative samples of schools. However, large variations in NPE per student within a country generate useful data for testing whether the amount of NPE has an effect on student outcomes.

6.1.3 Measuring Schools' Physical Resources and the Equity of Their Distribution

NPE is an annual flow that, as noted above, finances not only consumables but schools' learning resources and other physical resources with a medium-term life span in excess of a year. Thus, in order to assess how much NPE per student is needed, one must examine the stock of schools' physical resources and their quality. NPE is needed both to maintain an existing stock of resources at their current value through replacement and updating, while additional flows are required to build up a deficient stock of resources to an adequate level. When researchers wish to measure the stock of school resources, they are faced with the problem of how detailed to make their investigations. This is clearly a judgment that must depend on the purpose, context, and research resources of the investigation. I have selected the research instruments developed by the South African Consortium for Monitoring Education Quality (SACMEQ) as these are well tried, tested, and statistically sound, thereby creating an excellent database. The consortium was formally established in 1995, with support from the International Institute for Educational Planning and consists of 15 countries: Botswana, Kenya, Lesotho, Malawi, Mauritius, Mozambique, Namibia, Seychelles, South Africa, Tanzania (Mainland and Zanzibar), Uganda, Zambia, and Zimbabwe.

The SACMEQ consortium has enabled educational researchers and planners to develop important technical skills related to the design and implementation of large-scale data collections, as well as to the application of a wide variety of computer-based techniques for the preparation, management, analysis, and reporting of educational planning data. SACMEQ's research program has resulted in the preparation of research reports that have contributed to the conduct of informed debates concerned with equity in the allocation of human and material resources among regions and schools, and literacy and numeracy levels for important sub-groups of pupils defined by gender, socio-economic background, and geographic location (Onsomu et al. 2005).

An example is the use by the Ministry of Education, Science and Technology in Kenya of its SACMEQ study to address specific questions on schools' physical resourcing (out of 21 questions in all) (Onsomu et al. 2005, Chap. 1), which are given below.

Do Standard 6 pupils have sufficient access to classroom materials in order to be able to participate fully in their lessons?
Do Standard 6 pupils have access to library books in their schools, and (if they do have access) is the use of these books maximised by allowing pupils to take them home to read?
What is the availability of classroom furniture and classroom equipment (for example, chalkboard, dictionary, maps, book corner, and teacher guides) in Standard 6 classrooms?
What are the school heads' views on general school infrastructure and the condition of school buildings?
Are material resources being allocated in an equitable fashion among regions and schools within regions?

The SACMEQ research instruments include a number of items on school learning resources. The pupil questionnaire contains questions on the following:

Personal materials (exercise books, notebooks, pencil sharpener, eraser, ruler, pen, folder);
Seating arrangements;
Library books;
Access to reader and math textbooks.

The head teacher questionnaire includes items on:

Classrooms (permanent, temporary, open air);
Condition of school building, including toilets;
Accommodations (library, hall, staff room, head teacher office, storeroom, first aid kit, sports area or playground, garden, fence or hedge round school, cafeteria or shop, water, electricity, telephone, fax, typewriter, duplicator, radio, tape-recorder, projector, TV, VCR, photocopier, computer).

The teacher questionnaire has questions on:

Pupil seating arrangements;
Number of books in the classroom;
Resources in classroom (black/white board, wall chart, cupboard, bookshelves, classroom library, teacher's table and chair);
Whether the teacher can access school items (map, English dictionary, geometry, instruments, teacher's guidebooks for maths and English).

These data are used to report frequencies of the possession of the resources and also to construct indices by scoring 1 for each item possessed, then summing and expressing the sum as a proportion of the maximum score if all items are possessed. In this way, indices are produced at the school and provincial level. For some questions, such as the condition of the school buildings, the responses were scored on a Likert scale, such as from 5 (good condition) to 1 (needs complete rebuilding), and the responses are summed to give an indicator (Nzomo et al. 2001). In the report of the second survey (Onsomu et al. 2005), equity indicators for the distribution of various school resources are reported. One indicator compares the variance of the resource measure for schools in the province with the national variance, as shown in Table 6.1. The second measure is the intraclass correlation, *rho*, for the distribution of the resource measure. Rho measures the extent to which the variation in the distribution of the resource is due to inequality between provinces or is due to inequality between schools. The higher rho is, the more the differences in resource distribution are due to inequalities between provinces rather than between schools. If rho is 0, then all of the variance is between schools. The descriptive statistics are used to compare actual resourcing with the Ministry of Education's benchmark standards (Nzomo et al. 2001). This will be discussed further in the section on benchmark standards.

Table 6.1 Equity of material resource allocation as assessed by (a) Variation among schools within provinces, and (b) Variation among provinces (SACMEQ II)

Material resources	Variation among schools within provinces								Variation among provinces (rho × 100)
	1	2	3	4	5	6	7	8	
Classroom furniture index by reading teacher	84.0	124.5	81.6	32.7	65.1	87.4	97.0	84.9	26.4
Classroom furniture index by mathematics teacher	88.2	127.4	70.7	31.6	58.7	89.3	94.6	74.3	31.9
Toilets per pupil	14.1	107.2	56.5	27.5	274.6	32.3	32.9	48.1	17.7
Classroom library by reading teacher	91.8	98.1	103.1	106.6	101.1	105.0	96.1	103.4	0.0
Classroom library by mathematics teacher	88.8	101.7	103.9	99.1	106.1	84.5	97.2	106.6	3.5
Classroom space per pupil	171.9	147.5	24.7	35.8	66.5	147.4	28.1	36.1	0.0
Reading teacher housing quality	87.5	91.5	87.4	95.0	93.3	106.9	104.9	109.1	4.0
Mathematics teacher housing quality	97.5	91.3	100.3	101.8	92.1	105.5	101.4	106.0	0.0
School resources index	92.5	98.2	68.4	52.3	91.4	74.1	88.8	49.2	41.5

Note 1 = Coast, 2 = Central, 3 = Eastern, 4 = Nairobi, 5 = Rift Valley, 6 = Western, 7 = Nyanza, 8 = North Eastern. *Source* Onsomu et al. (2005); Table 6.4

6.1.4 The Importance of Non-personnel Expenditure and Learning Resources for Student Attainment in Developing Countries

Concern about low levels of NPE, and hence low stocks of learning resources and poor school facilities, stems naturally from the possible negative impact of inadequate learning resources and poor school physical environments on student learning. This is a matter for empirical verification. Compared to developed countries, developing countries have both a much lower average level of school resources as well as greater variability in the quality of school learning resources within their national borders. Consequently, the empirical evidence on positive effects of learning resources on student attainment is stronger for developing countries than for developed countries. In the latter, the empirical evidence that additional school resources raise student attainment is equivocal (Hanushek 1998, 2005; Laine et al. 1996).

The empirical evidence on the effect of learning resources on student attainment is mainly derived from econometric education production function studies. A major methodological problem in education production function studies is *endogeneity*—the tendency for the amount of resource per student to be dependent on factors that affect student attainment, which confounds the causal relationship from additional school resources to improved attainment. School resources depend on student attainment when parents with higher attaining children choose better resourced schools or when governments' compensatory policies give more funding to schools with low-attaining students. Two-way causality between resourcing and student attainment leads to biased estimates of the size of the effect of resources on attainment and whether it is statistically significant. When using data from natural settings, two main approaches are used to tackle endogeneity (Levacic and Vignoles 2002). One is collecting a large number of control variables so as that there are no important omitted variables and the other is to use the available data to create variation in the resourcing variables, which is independent of student attainment. Thus, the effects of learning resources on student attainment can only be properly tested for when other key variables, in particular class size, and teacher quality variables are controlled for, as well as the student family background factors that influence cognitive attainment.

Two influential reviews of developing country education production studies both concluded that the impact of additional learning resources on student attainment was stronger than that of additional teacher resources. Fuller and Clarke's review (Fuller and Clarke 1994), summarised in Table 6.2, showed a greater proportion of studies with significant effects for physical inputs than for teacher inputs, other than class instruction time. Sixteen out of 18 studies found that the presence of a school library had a positive and statistically significant effect on student attainment, while 73 % of studies found the possession of school textbooks enhanced student learning.

Table 6.2 Summary from Fuller and Clarke (1994) of positive and significant resource effects on student attainment

	Number of studies	Positive and significant effects	Confirmation of findings percentage
Primary schools			
Teachers' salary	11	4	36.4
Teacher pupil ratio	26	9	34.6
Teachers' education	18	9	50
Teachers' experience	23	13	56.5
Class instruction time	17	15	88.2
Frequency of homework	11	9	82
School library	18	16	89
School textbooks	26	19	73
Secondary schools			
Teachers' salary	11	2	18
Teacher pupil ratio	22	2	9
Teachers' experience	12	1	8.3
Class instruction time	16	12	75
School textbooks	13	7	54

Fuller and Clarke (1994)

Pritchett and Filmer (1999), examining empirical evidence from a range of education production function studies, argued that there is a misallocation of resources in developing countries towards excessive expenditure on teachers and insufficient expenditures on physical inputs. The supporting evidence is the preponderance of findings that the marginal product of additional physical inputs is much greater than that of teacher salaries or class size. Pritchett and Filmer attributed this inefficiency in resource allocation to the political influence of teachers on education bureaucrats and politicians.

A study using non-experimental data from Ghana (Glewwe and Jacoby 1994) found that school inputs enhance learning, but that not all types were statistically significant. Conditions of classrooms (leaking and unusable classrooms) had a strong effect on reading and mathematics scores for middle school pupils. Among instructional resources, only blackboards were significant for math and reading attainment. Teacher experience and length of schooling of teachers had no effect. For the Philippines, Bacalod and Tobias (2005) found that schools with basic facilities, in particular electricity, achieved much better student progress, while

Table 6.3 Cost-effectiveness ratios for additional spending on primary education in rural Northeast Brazil (achievement gain per US dollar spent)

Input	Portuguese	Math
Hardware (water, bookcase, teacher table, pupil chair, desk, 2 classrooms, large room, director's room, kitchen, toilet)	0.37	0.39
Textbook usage	3.73	2.50
Writing materials	1.3	1.52
Alternative teacher education strategies		
Curso de Qualificacao (a remedial program for teachers who did not complete 8 grades of primary school)	0.13	0.27
Logos (a program to give teachers with complete primary education a qualification equivalent to 3 years secondary schooling)	0.91	0.75
4 years primary school education	0.93	1.45
3 years secondary school education	0.28	0.43
Teacher salary	0.11	0.11

Note The outcomes are test scores in Portuguese and mathematics for second-grade pupils averaged over the years 1981, 1983, and 1985. *Source* Harbison and Hanushek (1992); Table 6.2, p. 138

Tan et al. (1999) reported that the availability of textbooks improved student attainment. An extensive evaluation of a primary school development project in rural Northeast Brazil in the 1980s (Harbison and Hanushek 1992) found that additional physical resources were generally more cost effective than teacher inputs, although both had positive effects, as shown in Table 6.3. Higher teacher salaries were the least cost-effective.

The SACMEQ datasets contain a sufficient range of variables for statistical regressions (using multilevel modelling) of pupil attainment on indices of school resources, including learning and physical as well as human, and controlling for family background factors. A Kenyan analysis of data covering 3299 pupils in 185 school in all 8 provinces sought statistically significant factors that explain student attainment (Onsomu et al. 2005). The number of resource variables to include in the regressions was reduced by using factor analysis to create constructs from a set of observed variables assumed to measure the same latent variable. The construct or composite variables for physical resources are a pupil learning material factor, a pupil working place in classroom factor, and a school resource factor. In Kenya, it was found that pupil-level resource variables, namely having most of the personal materials and a workplace, were positively and significantly related to attainment in math and reading at grade 6. The school-level variables found to be significant in explaining reading and math attainment were average pupil home background, pupil behavior, teacher qualifications, and average number of days pupils were absent from school. The composite resource variable at the school level was not significant. It could be that poor school-level resources are quite highly correlated with poor pupil level resources, so any independent effect is not picked up by regression analysis.

A cross-country study by Wößmann (2003) used pupil level data from the Third International Maths And Science Study on 260,000 students from 39 developed countries on the pupils' school and its decision making, resources at school level, and pupils' family background, supplemented by data on the decentralization of decision-making concerning the curriculum, assessment, and management as well as private sector involvement. Resource variables included expenditure per student, class size, pupil–teacher ratio, head teachers' reporting of adequacy of materials, instruction time, and teachers' age, gender, experience, and years of education. The major finding of the study is that institutional variables mattered more for pupil attainment than resourcing variables. Of the institutional variables, centralized examinations, curriculum, and textbooks had a positive significant effect on attainment, as did the decentralization of decision making on purchasing supplies and hiring teachers. The pupil–teacher ratio was insignificant. Instruction time had a small positive and significant effect. Head teachers' rating of resource adequacy was significant, with better resourcing positively related to student attainment.

On balance, the empirical evidence supports the view that the quantity and range of learning resources and standard of school facilities is a factor in determining pupils' educational achievement in developing countries. Moreover, the provision of such resources in schools in developing countries tends to be unevenly distributed and hence inequitable. This stems from the inability of governments to fund sufficient provision of physical resources since spending on these is a residual after teacher salaries have been paid. Consequently, schools are forced to rely on funding these resources from fees and contributions from parents and the community. This brings about a close association between the quality and quantity of the school's physical resources and the wealth of the local community. The situation can be remedied if governments can mobilise increased funding for NPE. At this point, the question arises as to how much additional funding governments need to provide for ensuring an adequate standard of learning resources and the physical environment of schools and how such increased funding should be allocated to regional or local education authorities and to schools. The issue of standards or norms for NPE and for schools resources is considered in the next section.

6.1.5 Benchmark Standards for Non-personnel Expenditure and Schools' Physical Resources

By a standard or norm with respect to school resources is meant a specification of what resources should be provided to schools for some specified purpose. An absolute resource standard (in contradistinction to a relative one) defines the resource inputs required for a school to achieve specified educational aims for students. At the national level, these aims are usually set out in general terms in legislation and in more detail in a national curriculum or learning goals. Thus, an absolute standard for resourcing schools must be linked to a prior standard for educational aims, set out as learning goals.

There are two approaches to the question of determining what a resource standard should be: top-down and bottom up. The top-down approach is the simplest. It starts from the premise that the political system, which in some fashion resolves the competing claims between public and private spending and between the different claims on public spending, generates a sum of money that is available for basic education and, in particular, for NPE. In addition, there may be a stated policy to increase the proportion of education spending that is for non-personnel resources. The problem of setting a standard in the top–down approach is to determine an allocation mechanism for dividing up a cake of pre-determined size. The top–down standard does not specify the absolute amount that NPE per student should be or provide a recipe for what should be the stock of resources available to schools catering for specific grades or curriculum content.

In contrast, the bottom–up approach starts from the premise that it should be possible to work out a list of ingredient resources that schools need in order to be able to achieve the educational goals for their pupils that the government, representing society, expects of them. The bottom–up approach is concerned with determining the size of the cake as well as with its distribution. Educational outputs are specified and then the types and quantities of resources required to achieve those outputs are identified and costed, given information on input prices. Given the basic standard of education expected to be acquired by students, the resource standard is the types and mix of resources required to achieve it. However, the link between the educational output goals and the resource inputs schools need to achieve those goals is made complex by the mediating effect of the characteristics of the students, which are highly dependent on factors arising from their home background and community. One of the most consistent and robust findings from educational research is that individual student characteristics are by far the most important source of variance in students' cognitive attainment, greatly exceeding the influence of schools on attainment. Thus, a resource standard defined using the bottom-up approach needs to take account of the mediation of student characteristics between the input of school resources and the achievement of educational goals. This may be as simple as defining a standard for the students who do not have severe learning difficulties or are not socially disadvantaged and then increasing it for those who fall into these categories.

6.1.5.1 Top–Down Approach: Some Examples

South Africa is an example of a country with an explicit policy of improving the physical resourcing of basic education schools by increasing the proportion of current expenditure in non-personnel items. The post-Apartheid government inherited an education system with vast differences in the quality of schools and hence in standards of education. These differences were both racial and regional. In 1998, NPE was on average 10 % of total current expenditure and in some provinces less than this.

In 1999, the policy on New National Norms and Standards for School Funding was implemented with the aim of gradually bringing a uniform standard of NPE to all provinces. In South Africa, NPE is classified into three kinds: (i) maintenance of buildings; (ii) utilities (water, electricity, etc.); and (iii) learner support materials. Provincial education budgets were increased by at least 1 % in real terms per year and any additional revenue was to be allocated to NPE. Equity in the allocation of NPE is being achieved by progressively redistributing the funding available for NPE between schools (Wildeman 2003). Public schools are ranked in order of poverty using two indices—the wealth level of the local community and the conditions at the school. Schools in the poorest quintile receive 35 % of the province's NPE funding, the next quintile 25 %, while the top quintile receives only 5 %. In South Africa, public schools are able to charge fees, reflecting the political reality that the white population would react against deterioration in the quality of schooling received by their children. Consequently, schools in wealthier communities can secure a higher level of NPE. However, the policy has made the public funding of NPE vertically equitable and is gradually reducing the inequity in overall non-personnel resources.

Another country with an explicit policy to address improvements in 'quality inputs' in schools is Sri Lanka. In the late 1990s, NPE was 9 % of recurrent expenditure in the primary sector and 11 % in the secondary sector, which was relatively low for south and east Asia (Word Bank 2005). Furthermore, in 1996, less than 1 % of recurrent expenditure was devoted to *quality inputs*—defined as educational materials, consumables, and equipment. International aid agencies, in particular the World Bank and the Asian Development Bank, were concerned at the inequitable distribution of schools' learning resources and their absence in a high proportion of the less advantaged schools, clearly identified in a World Bank commissioned study (Aturupane 1997) as shown in Table 6.4.

Therefore, the General Education Project II, commencing in 2000 and funded by the World Bank, included the formulation and implementation of a Norm Based Unit Cost Resource Allocation Mechanism (NBUCRAM) (World Bank 2005). Expenditure allocated under NBUCRAM is split into three categories (World Bank 1999):

(i) Consumables: provinces were required to allocate 2 % of their recurrent education budget to this category;
(ii) Low-cost equipment (capital) on which provinces must spend 25 % of their Provincial Special Development Grant (PSDG) from the central government;
(iii) Maintenance of equipment on which provinces must allocate 10 % of their (PSDG).

From the total amount allocated to NBUCRAM expenditures, the province must set aside 5 % for the most deprived schools, these being the schools in the worst conditions as classified on a five-point scale by the central Ministry of Education. Schools are defined as disadvantaged to the extent that they experience recurring teacher shortages (weight 40 %); access for students is difficult (weight 6 %); lack

Table 6.4 Availability of teaching aids and medium- and high-level learning equipment in schools, by type of schools in Sri Lanka (1996)

Type of Teaching Aid or Equipment	National Schools (%)	Type 1AB Schools (%)	Type 1C Schools (%)	Type 2 schools (%)	Type 3 Schools (%)
Globes	100	83	100	20	33
Charts for teaching	100	100	100	0	0
Duplicating machines	100	100	50	20	0
Photocopying machines	25	33	0	0	0
Radio sets	100	83	33	40	0
Television sets	100	100	33	20	0
Video cassette players	100	83	0	20	0
Typewriters	100	100	83	80	33
Printers	50	17	0	0	0
Computers	75	33	0	0	0
Overhead projectors	25	0	0	0	0

Source Aturupane (1997)

of basic school facilities (weight 30 %); and the poverty of the local community (weight 24 %) (Balasooriya 2004).

The rest of the funding is allocated to individual schools by a formula that includes the number of pupils enrolled (above a certain number the allocation is capped), primary or post-primary phase, and the type of school (these vary by age range and curriculum covered). Because it was observed that schools biased their spending to the upper grades, the NBUCRAM formula weights the per student allocation to schools according to grade categories, as shown in Table 6.5. The funding for consumables and low-cost equipment is allocated to schools for the principal, advised by a development committee representing staff, to determine how to spend. Thus, an element of school-based management was also introduced.

Table 6.5 Weight of funds allocation for each school sections

School section	Weight of consumables allocation (%)	Weight of equipment allocation
Grades 1–5	25	15
Grades 6–9	35	35
Grades 10–11	25	30
Grades 12–13 (arts/commerce)	5	5
Grades 12–13 (science)	10	15

Source Balasooriya (2004)

It is evident that the NBUCRAM policy was successful in improving the adequacy of learning resources in those schools that had been neglected by the previous method of allocation, which had favoured larger and more prestigious schools, and consequently NBUCRAM improved equity (World Bank 2005). A survey of school principals and provincial administrators by Balasooriya (2004) found that the majority of respondents thought that the ability of schools to determine their own purchases had improved efficiency, although there were some problems regarding bottlenecks in purchasing.

These two examples show how countries can pursue policies of improving the adequacy and equity of the allocation of NPE by focusing on the allocation mechanism alone and leaving the sum available to be generated by what the government decides it can make available. This approach has the advantage of relative simplicity as it does not require the establishment of a standard for schools' resourcing defined in absolute terms. When the government places a strong emphasis on making NPE per student more equitable between schools, then a formula that ensures horizontal equity plus additional vertical equity for disadvantaged schools achieves this goal without the need to specify a standard for NPE in absolute terms. The issues raised by a bottom-up approach to defining an absolute standard are considered next.

6.1.5.2 Bottom–Up Approach

The concept of a benchmark standard for non-personnel resources and expenditure should be interpreted as equivalent to the concept of an 'adequate' level of spending on education. When this link is made, the benchmark standard is connected to the long-standing and well-worked topic in education finance of the adequacy of school financing. This has received by far the most attention in the United States, where education policy is made through litigation that challenges a state for violating its or the federal constitution. Over the years, a considerable number of states have been forced to respond to court judgments that their school funding system was unconstitutional because it did not guarantee adequate funding for all students. Consequently, much effort has been expended in the United States for defining adequacy in ways that can be made operational and applied in practice.

Initially, the US courts defined adequacy rather simply by comparing actual expenditures to average. Using this admittedly crude indicator, a country can compare its average percentage of NPE in total current education spending on a particular phase of education with the average of other countries. If the comparison is made with OECD countries, then adequate NPE is around 20 % of total current spending; or if World Indicator Countries are used (Fig. 6.2) the adequate level is 14 %.

However, as Odden and Picus (2000) pointed out, the US courts have over the years moved from using average expenditure per student as a criterion of adequacy to defining adequacy in terms of the minimum funding needed to sustain educational programmes and school designs that provide a defined adequate standard of education, although this need not be for all students, given there is an irreducible number that cannot achieve the minimum standard. The key point is that contemporary definitions of adequate funding links it to the achievement of specified educational outcomes for students. The problem is to make this definition of adequacy operational. Four approaches have been used by US states in seeking to establish adequate funding for schools (Picus and Blair 2004). These are outlined below.

1. **Professional Judgment Approach**
   The professional judgment approach involves a group of educational experts, perhaps also working with finance specialists or economists, deciding what resources are needed by schools to ensure that the majority of children attain the required basic educational standards. The resources are then cost to reach a total amount per student. The 1992 standards issued by China's Ministry of Education probably belong to this category. The professional judgment approach is also known as the activity-led funding model that identifies the activities required to deliver a specified curriculum to pupils of various ages and costs the resources required to produce the activities (Abu-Duhou 1999).
   Absolute resource standards that concern the quality of the physical environment can be based on technical knowledge, such as the amount of space needed per student taking into account health and safety factors, or the recommended ambient temperature range. Standards regarding learning resources, however, require the professional judgment of educationists.
   The drawback to this approach is that it relies on the professional judgment of educationists who are likely to bias upwards the amount of resources needed. This approach often produces a level of adequate funding that is in excess of current funding and fails to convince politicians and policymakers that the additional resources demanded by educationists are in fact needed for adequacy.
   Once accepted standards have been specified using the professional judgment approach, surveys of schools' resourcing can produce data on the actual standards in schools, which in developing countries are likely to be below the standards in a considerable proportion of schools. The SACMEQ surveys provide data for the relevant ministries of education to compare resourcing standards with actual practice, as in the study by Nzomo et al. (2001).
2. **Best Practice Schools or School Districts**
   In this method, adequacy is defined as the cost of the resources used by those schools or school districts with the best educational outcomes for students. For the best practice method to be valid, it is essential that the family background characteristics that determine children's academic attainment are controlled for when selecting best practice schools. If this is not done, then at least part of the better performance of schools with higher results is due not to additional resourcing but to family background characteristics.
   The problem with the best practice model is that even if family background factors are controlled for, the best practice schools or school districts may not share features in common with all the schools or districts to which the adequacy

criterion must apply. In particular, it is difficult to assess how much additional resource is needed for students with specific characteristics of disadvantage or learning difficulties. The best practice model requires a common measure of student outcomes, in particular test scores, across all schools, which may not be available, as is the case in China where examinations within the compulsory age range of schooling are set at the county not national level.

3. **Cost Function Approach**
   This approach estimates the cost of achieving a specified educational standards (e.g. in terms of passing standardised tests) from data collected from a sample of schools (Reschovsky and Imazeki 1998; Ruggiero 2007; Duncombe et al. 1996; Duncombe and Yinger 1999). The data should include not only the per student cost of the educational outcomes but also the other variables that determine student outcomes, namely family background and student characteristics as well as school context variables (size, percentage of disadvantaged students, single sex, etc.). One method is to estimate the cost function as a statistical regression equation. Since the education cost function is the dual of the education production function, it is beset by the same endogeneity problem that costs are a function of student attainment as well as student attainment depending on the amount spent. Endogeneity results in biased estimates of the impact of attainment on costs. It can be avoided if there are no omitted explanatory variables or if there are variables which predict student attainment that are independent of costs (i.e. instrumental variables). The alternative is to use data envelopment analysis (DEA), which is a linear programming technique. This treats student socio-economic variables as well as expenditure per student as an input. The DEA method can include several output and input measures, although the computer programming becomes more complex as more variables are added. It also provides a measure of the efficiency of each unit (e.g. school or school district) by comparing its costs with those of the least cost unit that uses the same combination of inputs.
   The cost function approach, in particular the DEA variant, has been used with school district data in the United States. For example, as Ohio's school finance system was ruled unconstitutional for failing to provide adequate education, Ruggiero (2007) used DEA for 607 Ohio school districts to calculate the minimum per student cost of providing Ohio's specified standard of education in school districts classified into 3 groups according to their median per capita income. This study showed that some of the highest performing districts in terms of absolute pass rates in state tests were inefficient and could produce the same results for less expenditure if managed as well as the most efficient districts. A low achieving and lowest income district was found to be efficient, but some low-income districts needed more funding to achieve adequacy while others were very high spenders and might not be able to achieve adequate education even with more spending. Overall, Ruggiero concluded that it would be possible to obtain adequate education by reallocating existing funding from inefficient to more efficient districts, provided that the inefficient districts could

raise their efficiency. The advantage of the DEA method is that it provides evidence on how much additional funding schools with socially disadvantaged students require. However, it has not been possible to locate a study that costs the provision of NPE separately from staff expenditure. This reflects the fact that the vast majority of these studies are for the United States, where states define educational standards for adequacy and where there is good quality data and a large number of quantitative educational researchers. In principle, since DEA can handle several inputs, it is possible to estimate adequate and efficient spending on different kinds of inputs.

4. **Evidence-Based Approach**
   An evidence-based approach uses educational research evidence to identify best practices in organising and resourcing student learning. Professional judgment is then used to create a school design that reflects these best practices so as to achieve the education authority's benchmark for student attainment. An example of a school design is 'Success for All' (Slavin et al. 1996). The resources required for the school design are then costed, and this becomes the standard for adequacy. The strength of the approach is that it is evidence based and more readily understandable by educationists and the general public than the cost function method. This approach can be applied in the United States, where there is considerable evidence on effective school designs, but this evidence could not be transferred to China without further testing out on actual school designs. A further problem, even for the US context, is that the school designs specify particular patterns of resource use, so this raises the question of whether these designs should be mandated for all schools funded using this standard of adequacy or whether schools should be free to determine their own pattern of resource use (Picus and Blair 2004).

6.1.6 Using Research Evidence to Establish a Financial Standard for Basic Education: Indonesia

An interesting example of undertaking research to inform policy on funding basic education is the study commissioned by the Ministry of National Education in Indonesia with support from UNICEF (McMahon et al. 2001). This study included both personnel and non-personnel resources but considered them separately. Both the professional judgment and best-practice models were used to derive a recommended financial standard expressed as a funding formula.

It is interesting to note that McMahon et al. offered a definition of adequacy that, unlike US definitions, is not linked to an explicit educational standard defined in terms of outcomes. An adequate education from an educational point of view requires that there should be adequate books and teaching materials, teachers with enough formal education and teaching experience to have knowledge of their subjects and how to teach, desks for all in the class, and a class size that is not necessarily small but that is not so large that the class is unmanageable and students get no individual attention. An adequate education also requires a school physical environment, including a school building that should be well maintained to ensure that proper teaching and learning takes place.

The cost of these necessary inputs can be estimated based either on judgment by experienced educators and economists or based on what has been done by "best practice schools" in our sample. Both will be used here to arrive at the cost of an adequate education for each child. Then, this will be compared side by side with the average costs of each of these inputs based on our UNICEF/MONE survey of the resources available at school level (McMahon et al. 2001, p. 5).

The professional judgment estimates adequate spending per student for teaching and for categories of NPE, as shown in Table 6.6.

To obtain data on both for "best practice" schools and to assess equity in the distribution of funding for primary schools in Indonesia, a survey was carried out. Ninety-five schools were selected using a stratified random sample that deliberately oversampled madrasah (private) schools to obtain an adequate number of these. Fifty-three of the schools were in a UNICEF school-based management pilot project and a matching set of 42 non-pilot schools was added. The main respondents to the survey were teachers and the principal of each school. The respondents were invited in groups of 7–15 to attend a two-day workshop to which they brought school records and were briefed by the researchers. District officers were also interviewed. A 100 % response rate was achieved. Data on school resources, teaching, and teachers costs' and also on the national grade 6 examination results (NEM) were collected.

Table 6.6 McMahon et al.'s professional judgment of adequacy in per pupil funding

Type of resource	Assumptions regarding specification of the resource	Professional judgment 2000–01 (Rp)	Actual level 2000–01 (Rp)
Teacher	One teacher per pupil. 25 pupils per class. Qualifications: at least diploma II	444,000	400,000
Books	5 books per pupil for the major subjects plus 1 book per 2 children for 3–4 additional subjects	35,000	32,000
Teaching aids and schools supplies	6–8 group teaching aids per class (e.g. maps) + 3–4 personal aids per pupil. Chalk, coloured paper, paper, ink, paints, other consumables	22,000	15,000
School maintenance	To repair leaking roofs and improve sanitation; desks, chairs, blackboard replacement, light bulbs	20,000	14,000
Utilities	Water, electricity, telephone	3000	3000
	Total adequate foundation level for NPE	529,000	467,000

Source McMahon et al. (2001)

The cost-effectiveness of the schools' current expenditure components was evaluated by their performance in NEM 6th grade examinations in language, math, and science and in changes from the previous year in these results, which were generally declining in Indonesia at this time. The researchers also estimated education production functions based on school level data, including parental socioeconomic status 'to capture the net effects of each input' (McMahon et al. p. 29). They also looked for the costs of the inputs used by the most effective schools in terms of their examination results from descriptive data and also from the estimated coefficients of the production functions. They acknowledged the problem of multicollinearity between the inputs and between inputs and SES, so that the 'true effect of each input in not always easy to sort out' (p. 30). These estimated coefficients are not reported and it is not clear how they were used in reaching the conclusions about funding adequacy. Best practice schools were those with the highest NEM scores and those that had improved their scores over the previous year. The 'best-practice' schools turned out to be the pilot schools, and these had about 11 per cent additional funding per student. This was associated with a 5 % higher NEM score level. The pilot schools spent a higher proportion of their budgets on learning resources—3.1 % compared with 1.5 % in the less effective schools. The study concluded:

"About an 11 % per pupil increase in expenditure per pupil nationwide, perhaps focused mainly on teaching aids, books and to some extent teacher salaries, appears to be necessary to arrest and turn round this decline [in NEM scores] as well as to provide a foundation-level "adequate" education based on costing- out "adequate" education inputs. This does not include the cost of … libraries and computer skills" (McMahon et al. p. 113).

While this study has an interesting exemplar research design for similar research in China, the conclusions warrant further comment. As the pilot schools turn out to be the 'best-practice' schools, it may well be that their better educational outcomes are due not only to higher expenditure per pupil but to other aspects of the school-based management reforms being piloted or to the effect of selection of these schools into the pilot project. The absence of clear reported findings from the education production function analysis confirms that such analysis is of limited use unless the data are of high quality so that its statistical analysis can avoid endogeneity bias.

The McMahon et al. study devotes considerable space to elaborating a proposed funding formula for primary schools because they recommend that to improve both efficiency and equity 'all funding needs to be shifted from a per school to a per pupil basis' (p. 116). Once a financial standard for spending per student has been determined, the next step is to decide how it should be allocated to schools. Moving from a traditional historically based and incremental method of allocating funding to school districts (counties) and schools to a funding formula is a natural and relatively easy step once the standard itself has been determined. Indeed, governments often first decide on a policy of introducing formula funding of schools and then as part of implementation determine a per student financial standard. The next section, therefore, considers what the desirable characteristics of a school funding formula are.

6.1.7 Desirable Characteristics of a School Funding Formula

A funding formula can be used to allocate funding both from central government to local districts that administer schools as well as from the district to the schools. The latter formula can be simpler as it does not need to take account of the detailed school level factors that are beyond the control of schools but nevertheless affect their unit costs. Ross and Levacic (1999) provide a set of criteria for the design of a school funding formula, and these are applied here to the consideration of a formula for allocating NPE to school district level and then to school level.

A fundamental criterion is adequacy: the formula should deliver to schools the amount of funding needed for them to provide an adequate education for their students. Given that this has been extensively discussed above, no more will be said here.

A key criterion is efficiency. A funding formula should not give perverse efficiency signals to the recipients of the funding. For this reason, the majority of funds need to be allocated on a per student basis. Furthermore, the formula should not contain indicators that encourage the school district or school to be inefficient. So, while small schools have higher fixed costs per student (e.g. utilities and the running costs of buildings do not vary proportionately with the number of students but tend to be higher for smaller schools), it is inefficient to fund a school district according to the number of small schools it has because this provides a disincentive to close or amalgamate schools in order to reduce unit costs.

Another important criterion is equity. A funding formula by its nature is horizontally equitable as it allocates the same amount of money to every recipient with the same characteristics. It is usually desirable for a funding formula to promote vertical equity by giving additional funding to socially disadvantaged students and/or to schools serving socially disadvantaged groups, the main indicators being poverty, disadvantaged ethnic minorities, or individual students with specific forms of learning difficulty. Efficiency signals are again crucial. It is necessary to fund additionally according to indicators of variables that predict low educational attainment, not measures of low attainment, as this would reward poorly performing districts and schools. In the case of NPE, indicators that predict inadequate stocks of school resources should be used in order to allocate additional funding to districts with particularly poorly resourced schools to enable them to reach parity with adequately resourced schools.

Another aspect of equity is adjusting the formula to additionally fund those districts and schools with higher structural costs that are caused by factors beyond local control, such as climate, topography, and sparse populations. Climate clearly affects heating costs. The additional costs due to lower winter temperatures and longer heating seasons can be calculated from technical information on energy consumption and knowledge of fuel prices. Estimating how much smaller schools need to be because of sparse populations and mountainous terrain or islands can only be done roughly be comparing areas in terms of these factors and the associated average school size, then excluding those which are judged to have too many small schools relative to need. To prevent the inclusion of perverse efficiency incentives, the additional funding for small schools or for transport of students to larger schools or boarding students should be related to factors such as population density, distance between settlements, and topographical features and not the existing number of small schools. The usual practice is to determine weightings for school districts with these features, which multiply up the basic unit of adequate funding for areas without these features.

The relative simplicity of the formula is another consideration that is particularly important for good accountability and transparency of funding. The simpler the formula, the easier it is for all stakeholders, especially parents and the general public, to understand the formula. However, the criterion of simplicity often conflicts with that of vertical equity. The more indicators a formula contains that take account of factors causing schools' costs to vary for reasons beyond the control of schools (from structural cost factors to social disadvantage in its various manifestations), the more complex the formula becomes. It is easier to devise a simpler formula for allocating NPE to the school district (county) level than to the school level because there is a wider variation of factors affecting school level costs. If NPE per student is allocated to counties then the counties can be instructed to allocate to schools partially on a per student basis and partially according to other factors such as school size, isolation, and concentrations of socially disadvantaged students.

McMahon et al. (2001) include a further factor to encourage school districts to mobilize their own resources to add to those provided by higher levels of government. The suggested indicator is the amount of local money raised by the district for schools divided by the local per capita income, so that fiscal effort is rewarded. Other possibilities for efficiency incentives are including an additional element for improved outcomes. A formula can only signal appropriate efficiency and equity incentives if the data for school districts and schools that determine how much funding they receive are accurate and not corrupted at the local level in order to obtain more funding. Locally collected data may require careful auditing. If such corrupt practices are likely, the bias should be toward a simple formula with few indicators and concentrating on indicators that do not depend on local collection by schools and school districts.

6.1.8 Conclusion: Suggestions, Drawing on International Experience, for the Development of a Benchmark Standard for NPE in China

The definition of a benchmark standard in terms of adequacy provides a direct link to the international school finance literature on defining and measuring adequacy. This defines adequacy as the minimum expenditure per student required for achieving defined learning outcomes for students. When these learning outcomes are defined in terms of pass marks or pass rates in standardized tests for certain key grades (e.g. at end of the primary phase or at school leaving age), it is easier to ascertain the cost of achieving these standards by comparing the resourcing and costs of school districts and schools with different unit costs and attainment and taking account of socio-economic differences. The most sophisticated method for doing this is DEA, but it is very demanding of high-quality data. Alternatively, the resourcing and costs of 'best-practice' schools can be examined and these defined as 'adequate.' If best practice schools represent different ranges of socio-economic status, then it is possible to ascertain roughly what additional resourcing is needed in areas of greater social deprivation. The most commonly used method, as it is less data intensive and less demanding of statistical or econometric analysis, is that of professional judgment.

For the SRCEF project, the two viable methods for determining adequacy are professional judgment and best practice schools. Standards based on professional judgment already exist as defined by the Ministry of Education and some provincial level governments and can therefore be used in comparing actual resourcing and NPE expenditure derived from the survey of schools in 12 counties in 4 provinces. To use the best-practice model, the research team will need to determine what criteria to use for selecting schools as best practice, given that there is no national or even provincial level external examination or standardized test in the compulsory phase of schooling. It would appear that participation and dropout rates are not sufficiently variable to be used to differentiate between schools and the project budget does not run to administering a standardized test and collecting student level socio-economic data.

In these circumstances, probably the best way of defining adequacy is to combine the professional and best practice models. This would use the judgment of professionals who are asked to identify some schools in the sample that they consider to offer adequate education and to be just adequately resourced at a basic level. The resourcing of these 'best-practice' schools is then compared with the other schools in the sample to ascertain differences in resourcing levels. Another approach is to use the 1992 resource standards defined by the Ministry of Education and/or its more recent standards for resourcing science and technology subjects and to find out respondents' views as to the necessity of these items and whether their school possesses them.

Devising an appropriate research instrument to collect data to use in measuring schools' actual resourcing and NPE and assessing adequate amounts of these is a challenging task. A difficult balance must be struck between asking for information in too much detail or setting categories that are too broad for a satisfactory assessment of adequacy and for recommending a funding model to the MOE. It is crucial that the instrument collects information on the stock of resources as well as on the flow of NPE. Given the definition of NPE this report began with, only adequacy in consumables can be assessed by the annual flow of NPE. Many of the learning resources, which research shows are important in affecting student attainment, are in the form of stocks (books and equipment) or in the form of the physical condition of the school building and its facilities. The SACMEQ questionnaires on school resourcing provide good examples of questions on stocks of learning resources and the conditions of school facilities, although the actual questions may need to be modified to reflect higher existing standards in Chinese rural schools. The questions need to be pitched so that they will pick up inadequacies in Chinese schools resourcing relative to what are currently professional judgments about adequacy.

When the data collected are analyzed, the project team will be making recommendations about the following.

(i) An adequate level of resourcing and NPE per student in 'best-practice' schools will be determined, and this defines the benchmark. This assessment is likely to be informed by professional judgment as well. International experience shows clearly that an adequate funding level is not amenable to precise scientific definition and is a matter for judgment informed by empirical evidence.

(ii) The benchmark is used to assess the inadequacy of resourcing and NPE per student in schools which are below the benchmark standard. Analysis of the data will indicate the factors that are associated with particularly high degrees of inadequacy. These factors can then be recommended as additional indicators to the number of students in a formula for funding counties for NPE. As with South Africa and Sri Lanka, factors associated with particularly poor resourcing will trigger a higher level of per student NPE to improve the equity of schools' resourcing and hence educational provisions in China. The purpose of this additional funding is for inadequately resourced schools to catch up with adequately resourced schools.

(iii) The project team will also need to make recommendations about additional NPE funding needed on a permanent basis [as opposed to addressing the need to equalise resourcing between areas in (ii)] due to factors at county level that result in higher structural costs above the basic minimum. Structural costs that exceed the norm are caused by factors that are beyond the control of counties and schools, such as sparse populations, topology, and climate. Another factor causing structural cost differences between areas is regional differences in the prices of schools' inputs. To correct for this, indices of input costs need to be developed (see Chambers and Parrish 1994; Chambers 1997). Structural costs in excess of the norm may be particularly difficult to assess from the statistical data collected in the SRCEF project survey because schools whose costs are raised by these structural factors may also be inadequately funded, in which case the data will not reveal what these schools' unit costs would be if they were adequately funded. Some costs, such as heating costs, can be estimated from technical information on energy needs in relation to climatic conditions; others, such as the relationship between population density and an average efficient school size for the area, taking into account transport costs for young children or boarding costs, may not be available from the data collected. It is therefore advisable to collect some data on professional judgment on these issues.

The international experience with respect to funding NPE for compulsory education offers useful guidance at the macro level, when Chinese data on NPE as a proportion of total current expenditure and capital expenditure as a proportion of final can be compared with international indicators. The research literature on the relationship between schools' physical resources and students' learning points clearly to their importance in developing countries (and hence in rural areas of China where resourcing is at lower level than in its more developed areas) and hence the validity of the policy of raising NPE per student in rural areas in China. Apart from giving a variety of approaches to defining adequacy, the international literature also provides the SRCEF project team with some useful examples of research designs and instruments from studies conducted for similar purposes. There is every reason to expect that the SRCEF project will make its own valuable contribution to the international knowledge on school resourcing and its adequacy.

6.2 Financial Disparities and Intergovernmental Grants in Primary and Secondary Education: An International Review

Significant disparities in the financing of basic education (primary and secondary) are a major concern in many countries. Such disparities contribute to unequal education opportunities among population groups and present particular difficulties for groups from poor and other disadvantaged backgrounds. Reducing financial disparities is an important policy in basic education across countries to promote equity and enhance access to quality basic education for all population groups, thus contributing to stability and harmony in society. In countries with a decentralized education system, multiple levels of government are involved in varying extents to achieve the reduction of financial disparities in basic education.

This section provides a cross-national review of financial disparities in basic education, focusing particularly on OECD countries with decentralized financing and a large population. It consists of two parts. Section 6.2.1 presents recent trends in financial disparities in basic education and identifies measures undertaken by the government to reduce financial disparities. Section 6.2.2 presents recent trends in the intergovernmental financing of basic education and identifies factors that influence the financial roles of different levels of government.

6.2.1 Reducing Financial Disparities in Primary and Secondary Education

6.2.1.1 Recent Trends

Recent trends in financial disparities in primary and secondary education are presented for Australia, Germany, Japan, Spain, United Kingdom, and the United States. These countries were selected for this study based on several criteria:

(1) they are economically developed countries with a significant national investment effort on education (at least 3.5 % of their GDP); (2) their primary and secondary education system is financed by two or three levels of government (national/federal, regional/state/province, local/counties/districts); and (3) they have a relatively large population (at least 20 million). Brazil is also added to this study because it is a large decentralized and highly unequal system that has been making some effort in recent years to reduce education disparities across regions and local areas.

Based on data on sub-national units, per-student total public expenditure on primary and lower-secondary education is computed. Financial inequality among sub-national units is determined using three measures: the federal-range ratio, the coefficient of variation, and the GINI coefficient. These inequality measures were computed for the period from the 1990s to the early 2000s. Because of limitations in data availability, the same time period cannot be used for all the countries. For some countries, expenditure on primary education is separated from expenditure on secondary education; but for other countries, expenditure on primary education is lumped together with expenditure on secondary education. The results are shown in Table 6.7.

Table 6.7 Inequality in per-student recurrent expenditure, selected countries

Country	Measure	Trends in financial disparities by level of education
Australia	Federal ratio	Primary: reduced from 1.80 in 1999 to 1.58 in 2006
		Secondary: reduced from 1.92 in 1999 to 1.67 in 2006
	Coeff. of variation	Primary: reduced from .206 in 1999 to.145 in 2006
		Secondary: reduced from .247 in 1999 to .185 in 2006
	GINI	Primary: reduced from .0847 in 1999 to .0640 in 2006
		Secondary: reduced from .0889 in 1999 to .0791 in 2006
Brazil	Federal ratio	Primary: reduced from 4.91 in 1994 to 2.24 in 1999
		Secondary: reduced from 4.24 in 1994 to 2.00 in 1999
	Coeff. of variation	Primary: reduced from .497 in 1994 to .408 in 1999
		Secondary: reduced from .408 in 1994 to .212 in 1999
	GINI	Primary: reduced from .249 in 1994 to .172 in 1999
		Secondary: reduced from .189 in 1994 to .150 in 1999
Germany	Federal ratio	Primary and secondary: increased from 1.38 in 1999 to 1.63 in 2004
	Coeff. of variation	Primary and secondary: increased from .181 in 1999 to .194 in 2004
	GINI	Primary and secondary: increased from .080 in 1999 to .100 in 2004
Japan	Federal ratio	Primary: reduced from 1.44 in 1998 to 1.43 in 2004
		Lower-secondary: reduced from 1.51 in 1998 to 1.40 in 2004
		Upper-secondary: reduced from 1.46 in 1998 to 1.38 in 2004

(continued)

Table 6.7 (continued)

Country	Measure	Trends in financial disparities by level of education
	Coeff. of variation	Primary: increased from .112 in 1998 to .115 in 2004
		Lower-secondary: increased from .115 in 1998 to .118 in 2004
		Upper-secondary: reduced from .120 in 1998 to .106 in 2004
	GINI	Primary: increased from .062 in 1998 to .065 in 2004
		Lower-secondary: reduced from .060 in 1998 to .059 in 2004
		Upper-secondary: reduced from .063 in 1998 to 0.062 in 2004
Spain	Federal ratio	Preprimary and primary: reduced from 1.81 in 2000 to 1.69 in 2005
		Secondary: reduced from 2.25 in 2000 to 1.73 in 2005
	Coeff. of variation	Preprimary and primary: reduced from .293 in 2000 to .182 in 2005
		Secondary: reduced from .310 in 2000 to .233 in 2005
	GINI	Preprimary and primary: reduced from .139 in 2000 to .098 in 2005
		Secondary: reduced from .159 in 2000 to .114 in 22,005
United Kingdom	Federal ratio	Primary: reduced from 18 in 2002 to 9.5 in 2004
		Secondary: increased from 3.54 in 2002 to 7.48 in 2004
	Coeff. of variation	Primary: reduced from 1.13 in 2002 to 0.933 in 2004
		Secondary: increased from .402 in 2002 to .791 in 2004
	GINI	Primary: reduced from 0.48 in 2002 to .00084 in 2004
		Secondary: reduced from .091 in 2002 to .068 in 2004
United States	Federal ratio	Kindergarten to secondary: reduced from 2.18 in 1993 to 1.80 in 2005
	Coeff. of variation	Kindergarten to secondary: reduced from 0.244 in 1993 to 0.223 in 2005
	GINI	Kindergarten to secondary: reduced from 0.131 in 1993 to 0.120 in 2005

Source Tsang, M., Mizunoya, S., Zhang, Y., & You, Y. (2008). *Financing disparities in basic education in OECD countries*. New York: Center on Chinese Education, Teachers College Columbia University

The key findings of Table 6.7 are:

1. For Australia, Brazil, Spain, the United Kingdom, and the United States, inequality in per-student expenditure was clearly reduced in recent years.
2. For Japan, inequality in per-student expenditure did not change that much. It appeared that inequality had a small increase in primary education, but a slight decrease in lower-secondary education and in upper-secondary education.

3. For Germany, there was a clear increase in inequality in per-student expenditure in primary and secondary education.
4. Inequality in per-student expenditure in primary and secondary education was clearly reduced in most of the OECD countries included in this study.

6.2.1.2 Country Case Studies

This section explains the experience of financial equalization in basic education in four populous middle-to-high income countries: United States, Brazil, Japan, and France. United States and Brazil have a decentralized education system with government funding at three levels and a tradition of local control and funding of basic education. Central control and funding of basic education has historically been a key feature of Japan and France. But over time, public funding of basic education has been diversified to multiple government levels.

1. **The United States**

   The United States has a federal system of basic education (kindergarten to grade 12) consisting of three levels: federal, state, and school district. Constitutionally, basic education is the responsibility of the state government, including policymaking and financing. The state government should guarantee a sound basic education for all children within the state. It requires children in the state to stay in school until at least a given age, which is generally set at 16. Most children do stay in school after 16 to complete high school. The federal government has a very limited financing role in K-12 education; it focuses attention on education issues of national concern.

   There is a tradition of strong local control of basic education. Because of large variations among school districts in their fiscal capacity, the socio-economic backgrounds of parents, property values, and other conditions, there can be significant disparities in per-student spending in basic education among localities. The state government has become more involved in the funding of elementary and secondary education to achieve the equalization of per-student spending, leading to a centralization of funding from the local to the state level over time. For example, in 1919–20, the share of total spending on public schools was, .3 % for the federal government, 16.5 % for the state government, and 83.2 % for the local government. In 1969–70, the share was respectively 8.0, 39.9, and 52.1 %. In 2004–05, the share was respectively 7.0, 50.0, and 43.0 %. Historically, there is tension between local-control and state equalization goals in basic education.

   The great majority of state spending on basic education is for equalization aid to needy school districts. Equalization aid is stable (gradual increase over time, and no large fluctuation year by year), substantial (accounting for almost half of total spending on basic education), transparent (through the use of funding formulas with clear criteria), as well as democratic and open (determined through a political process at the local and state levels).

In general, state equalization aid is funded through the general revenue of the state government, although some states do complement general-revenue funding with revenue earmarked for basic education (e.g. revenue from state-run lottery scheme). State governments have a strong tax base to support public spending on basic education and other services (such as state income tax, state sale taxes, etc.). States do vary among themselves in the design of the funding formula for distributing equalization aid. The most common formula involves the foundation grant, which guarantees a minimum level of per-student spending across all school districts within a state. School districts with local funding per student that falls below the foundation level are entitled to state equalization aid. The state equalization aid for such a school district is equal to the product of adjusted total student enrollment and the gap between the foundation level and the local funding. Total student enrollment is adjusted for the number of students in different grade levels and the number of students with special education needs. It may also adjust for variation in the costs of education in different areas within the state and in the concentration of students from poor backgrounds.

State equalization aid is a block grant which augments the total recurrent revenue for basic education in a needy school district; it is not tied to particular inputs to basic education (e.g. salaries for teachers, or spending on textbooks). Students in public schools pay no school fees and receive free textbooks.

Part of the federal spending on basic education is for equalization purposes. For example, federal categorical grants (tied to specific uses or population groups) are available to school districts to provide compensatory education for needy students (Chap. 1 of Federal Grants) and for improving test scores of disadvantaged students and reducing the test-score gap among racial groups ("No Child Left Behind" funding). Compared to state governments, the federal government has only a limited role in financial equalization. National spending on education has been on a long-term gradual increase: total public spending on education rose from 5.4 % of GDP in 1985 to 6.2 % of GDP in 2004.

2. **Brazil**

Brazil has a federal system of education with government involvement at three levels: federal, state, and local (municipal). In this decentralized system, the state government has the responsibility for compulsory education (children aged six to fourteen are required to complete primary and lower-secondary education) but municipal governments have a significant role in shaping policies and funding compulsory education.

The framework for educational financing in Brazil is determined by the Federal Constitution of 1988, with important amendments in 1996. This constitution stipulates that the federal government spends a minimum of 18 % of its tax revenue on education, and that state and municipal governments spend a minimum of 25 % of their tax and transfer revenues on education. Tax collection is distributed across all three levels of government and non-discretionary transfers are distributed to sub-national entities using funding formulas. The federal government spends the majority of its education funds (over 60 %) on high-education institutions, but it has a significant role in equalization in primary and lower-secondary education through its spending on programs towards improving educational equity and quality. Another role of the federal government lies in the collection of education statistics and in educational evaluation, which are necessary in developing objective and transparent methods for distributing public resources in education.

Brazil has historically been characterized by a high degree of socio-economic diversities and has consistently been one of the most unequal societies in terms of inequality measures (such as the GINI coefficient). The large socio-economic inequalities have been companied by substantial financial inequalities in basic education. Such inequalities in basic education are understandable given a tradition of local control and heavy reliance on local resources for funding schools. To mitigate financial disparities in primary education, the three levels of government have worked together to develop and implement the FUNDEF (Fund for the Development of Primary Education and Valuing of Teachers) program since 1998. This program is basically a fund that collects and distributes aid to state and municipal governments for use in promoting access to and equity in primary education. The program aims to enhance equalization of financial resources among municipalities within a state by distributing aid on a per-student basis. Guidelines for minimum teacher salaries and qualifications are set. The federal government has established a national floor of per student education spending. If the FUNDEF amount for a state is lower than the national floor, the federal government "tops up" the fund for this state from its general revenue. Recent evaluation has shown the program to be effective in raising primary-education enrollment and increasing access for children from poor and other disadvantaged backgrounds.

Thus, three types of intergovernmental grants are used in basic education to reduce financial disparities across local governments: grants from federal to regional governments, grants from regional to local governments, and grants from central to local governments. In addition, the federal government is expanding a minimum income program that is tied to educational attendance with the goal of reducing both income inequality and improving educational attainment. This program provides income subsidy to poor households with school-aged children enrolled in school. To help finance the various equalization efforts, the government has increased its national spending on education gradually over time, from 3.9 % of GDP in 1994 to 4.4 % of GDP in 2004.

In 2004, the federal, regional, and local governments contributed respectively 10.7, 27.3, and 62.0 % of total government funding for public primary schools. For public lower-secondary schools, the respective shares are 8.2, 56.4, and 35.4 %.

3. **Japan**

   Japan has a national system of primary and secondary education that consists of three levels of governmental involvement: central, prefecture, and local. The central government has the responsibility for setting policies, curriculum standards, and the contents of public examinations, as well as authorizing textbooks for all prefectures in the country. The prefecture government operates schools and licenses and appoints teachers; the prefecture education board appoints the superintendent for primary and secondary education. Children aged six to fifteen are required to complete six years of primary education and three years of lower-secondary education; and the great majority of them continue to complete upper-secondary education. Although the local government has administrative responsibilities for primary and lower-secondary education, its financing role is significantly smaller than the central and prefecture governments because of its much weaker fiscal capacity.

Using its general revenue, the central government pays for 50 % of teacher salaries, 50 % of new school buildings, 33 % of school reconstruction, and 100 % of textbook costs. The prefecture government pays for the rest of the costs of basic education from its own tax base. Overall, central and prefecture funding pays for respectively 28 and 70 % of total spending on basic education, with the remaining 2 % from private sources. Thus, financial equalization is built into the public system of financing through the central funding of a significant portion of the spending on key inputs of public education operated by the prefecture government. It is also affected through uniform central policies on school personnel, curriculum, and textbooks that apply to all prefecture-operated public schools. Despite the equalization role of the central government, the prefecture government remains the major source of funding of primary and secondary education. In Japan, public-school students pay no school fees and receive free textbooks. Private-school enrollment accounts for a tiny fraction of total enrollment in primary and secondary education.

Egalitarianism and uniformity have long been valued goals of primary and secondary education, and Japan has been reputed for being relatively more equal in basic education than many other countries. Historically, Japan has had among the lowest inequality measures among OECD countries. Central funds are distributed to prefecture governments on the basis of student enrollment and school personnel to ensure key education inputs are provided and in accordance with uniform standards. However, such centralization allows little room for prefecture governments to change the operation of basic education. In the past several years, Japan has experimented education reform to allow more local decision-making (such as school choice) and funding of primary and secondary education. Japan has kept its national spending on education at a rather stable level in recent years. Total public spending on education was 3.5 % of GDP in 1997 and 3.6 % of GDP in 2004.

In additional to earmarked funds to prefecture governments for compulsory education, the central government also provides "local grants" as general revenue to prefecture governments to adjust for the difference in financial ability among prefecture governments. These local grants equalize the general revenue base of prefecture governments. In 2005, local grants accounted for 18.2 % of the total revenue of prefecture governments.

4. **France**

   Historically, France has a national system of primary and secondary education that is highly centralized compared to those in other advanced industrialized countries. Constitutionally, the central government has responsibility for primary and secondary education and there is little role for local governments (communal assemblies) to alter central policies and financing arrangements. Children aged six to sixteen are required to stay in school and the central government guarantees compulsory education for all children in the country.

   Public basic education is funded by two levels of government: the central government and communal assemblies, which respectively pay for 80 and 20 % of total funding for basic education (in 2004). Central funds are passed to communal assemblies to pay for 100 % of teachers' salaries. This practice ensures that adequate and equal funding is provided for the most important school input across all communes. Communes are responsible for school building, equipment, and maintenance, as well as for non-teaching staff. Students in public schools pay no school fees and are provided with free textbooks.

   Egalitarianism and uniformity have long been valued goals of basic education in France. Equalization is inherent in the French mind and is effected through the application of national education polices and uniform standards, as well as the dominating role of central-government funding of primary and secondary education. The national government has a strong commitment in bring compulsory education to all children, including those in remote and mountainous areas and those that have special education needs.

   Basic education was almost entirely funded by the central government in the past. However, in recent years, the central government has begun requiring communal assemblies to pay for a minor but increasing share of the total cost of basic education. This diversification of government funding reduces the financial burden for the central government and allows for some local initiatives in primary and secondary education. Despite this financial decentralization policy, the primary and secondary education system remains highly centralized and the central government is still the major source of funding and policymaking.

6.2.1.3 Cross-National Experiences

There are a variety of approaches and strategies adopted for resource-related equalization in primary and secondary education across countries. The categorization of these approaches and strategies can be understood with the illustration in Picture 6.1.

Picture 6.1 shows the direction of potential financial flow between and within government stakeholders and non-government stakeholders of primary and secondary education. For equalization purposes, the financial flow generally goes from higher levels of government to the local government which operates local schools. Financial resources may also flow directly from higher levels of government to

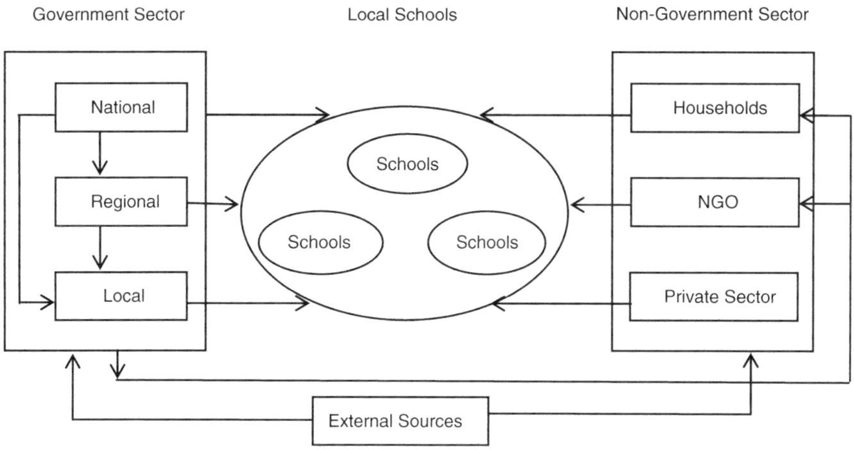

Picture 6.1 Financial flow to reduce disparity in a decentralized system

local schools, bypassing the local government. Some government resources may go directly or indirectly to non-government stakeholders, such as households and non-government organizations. These resources will end up in the production of education services in local schools. External resources from bilateral and multilateral aid agencies may go to government stakeholders and non-government stakeholders. The importance of external aid for financing primary and secondary education varies across countries.

Three broad categories of equalization approaches across countries may be identified: additional intergovernmental resources for equalization, additional equalization resources (from government and other sources) to the non-government sector or schools, and improving efficiency and resource redistribution to promote equalization.

1. **Additional Intergovernmental Resource Transfer for Equalization**
   Allocating additional resources from a higher level of government to a lower-level government to reduce financial disparities among lower-level governments is a common approach for equalization. Within this approach, there are different strategies related to different objectives and designs.

   (a) **Earmarked versus general-purpose intergovernmental grants**
   An intergovernmental grant can be earmarked for compulsory education and given to a fiscally needed local government. The grant can only be used for equalization purpose in compulsory education; it does not allow the local government flexibility in alternative uses that may complement development in compulsory education. An intergovernmental grant may also be given to a fiscally needed local government to augment its general revenue so that the local government may spend it on any needy public services, but the local government may not spend on compulsory

education. An earmarked equalization grant for compulsory education is commonly used in countries with multiple levels of government financing (such as the United States, Japan, and Brazil). In Japan, both types of grants are used by the central government in transferring resources to the regional (prefecture) governments.

(b) **Two or three levels of government financing**

Compulsory education is funded by three levels of government (federal, regional, and local) in some countries (such as the United States and Brazil) and by two levels (central and regional) in other countries (such as France). While there may not be scientific rules for determining the number of government levels for funding compulsory education, a number of observations may be made. First, a diverse, populous, and geographical large country may be more inclined towards adopting a three-level structure. Second, historical development and tradition often affect the structure of government financing. Third, a given level of government must have a stable, substantial, and growing revenue base in order to have a significant role in the financing of compulsory education.

(c) **Relative importance of government levels**

The relative importance of different government levels may change over time. For example, in the United States, the public financing of basic education has moved away from a heavy reliance on the local government to a heavy reliance on both the regional and local governments. In recent years in Spain, the financing of basic education has moved away from a heavy reliance on the central government to a heavy reliance on regional government (see more discussion in Chap. 2). In countries with a long tradition of local control of compulsory education, the local government is a significant contributor to the funding for compulsory education (such as United States and Brazil). Understandably, in countries with a tradition of central control, such as France and Japan, the central or national government is a significant contributor to funding of compulsory education. However, France and Japan differ in the relative importance of the central versus regional governments. The central government is the major contributor in France and the regional government is the major contributor in Japan.

In general, concentrating the financing of compulsory education at a higher-level government (such as the central/federal government) will promote uniformity, standardization, and equalization, but this allows less room for local decision-making and adjustment to local needs. Concentrating the financing of compulsory education at a lower-level government (such as the local government) allows for more local decision-making and adjustment to local needs, but this may contribute to disparities in compulsory education across local areas.

(d) **Variation in education inputs funded**

Intergovernmental grants for financial equalization are often distributed to lower levels of government to pay for spending on inputs to compulsory education. Funding for education inputs can be distinguished into two forms: funding for a basket of education inputs and funding for specific education inputs. An example of funding for a basket of education inputs is the use of the foundation grant per student in some states in the United States. This foundation grant ensures the minimum level of per-student total recurrent cost (including all personnel and non-personnel recurrent inputs) for all school districts within a state. The grant is set equal to the gap between the foundation level and the level raised locally. The grant is not tied to specific education input and thus the school distribute has more discretion in how to spend the grant. In Brazil, a per-student total recurrent cost is specific for distributing funds across municipal governments within a state; and the federal government also sets a national minimum level to equalize spending across states.

An example for funding for specific education inputs is the central funding of 50 % of teacher salaries of compulsory education provided by the prefecture government in Japan. This central funding ensures a strong revenue source for funding a key education input. However, the prefecture government has little discretion in using this grant. Nevertheless, it is still equalizing because teacher costs are the major component of total recurrent costs in compulsory education. In France, the central and commune governments are responsible for the costs of different education inputs.

(e) **Variation in equalization strategies**

Several strategies for financial equalization in compulsory education can be identified. The first is ensuring a minimum level of per-student spending across local governments by specifying a foundation level. This strategy does not put a cap on the spending level of well-endowed local governments; and the spending gap between the high-spending and low-spending governments can be substantial. The second is specifying the minimum level and the top-spending level, thus ensuring a minimum level across all local governments and restricting the gap between the top and bottom spending local governments (e.g. the top level may be set at two times the minimum level). In some situations, it may require a "recapture of excess revenue" of the high spending local governments by the regional government (such as the state government in the USA) for distribution to low-spending local governments. Third, a regional government may attempt to equalize the amount of education revenue across local governments based on tax rates (equalization through "fiscal neutrality") or tax base (equalization through "wealth neutrality"). This strategy is only possible when the local government has a significant tax base for funding compulsory education.

(f) **Variation in adjustment for local needs**

Adjustments in equalization aid are made to reflect variations in local needs. Based on the principle of "vertical equity," local governments with greater needs will receive more equalization aid. Through the use of education cost indexes, adjustments are often made for variations in the number of students by grade level, the number of students with special education needs, the concentration in poverty, and the price of education inputs.

(g) **Variation in determining the minimum per-student spending level**
The minimum level is often determined by a combination of factors related to the demand and supply of funding. On the demand side, consideration is focused on the amount of resources needed to yield an adequate level of learning outcome of compulsory education. There are three methods for making such a demand-based determination: the first based on the resource requirements of a "model school" or "model school district"; the second specifies a learning level (such as a certain test score) and determines the resource level from a statistical analysis of the relationship between learning level and resource level; and the third determines the resource requirement of a "basket of education services" based on the assessment of a group of education experts. On the supply side, the minimum level is influenced by the fiscal capacity of the different levels of government involved in the financing of compulsory education. With rising fiscal revenue, the minimum level can be adjustment upward over time.

(h) **Input-based versus outcome-based funding**
The discussion in this section so far has focused on funding the inputs of compulsory education. However, the amount of intergovernmental equalization grant given to a lower-level of government may be adjusted to reflect some selected outcome of compulsory education, as such dropout rates, graduation rates, and even learning outcomes. Additional resources may be tied to progress in such education outcome and penalty may be imposed on receiving governments not meeting targets of education outcome.

2. **Additional Equalization Resources to Non-government Sector or Schools**

(a) **Additional resources to non-governmental organizations**
The government may provide resources to non-government organizations (NGOs) to run schools to promote equity and equalization in compulsory education. There are several reasons why NGOs may get involved in the provision of compulsory education. First, NGOs may run schools to expand access to compulsory education for disadvantaged population groups who are not already in government-run schools (meeting excess demand for compulsory education). This may occur, in particular, when the local government has a weak administrative capacity (as in the case of El Salvador and Bangladesh), or there is a long and accepted role of NGOs, such as philanthropic or religious organizations, in education (as in the case of Hong Kong and Chile). Second, some NGOs may be able to offer such education programs in a more effective way than the local government (improving efficiency). Third, the involvement of NGOs may bring in additional

resources from the non-government sector for expanding access to compulsory education, which may not be available for government-run schools. There are variations in the management and ownership of schools operated by NGOs. The government may simply ask an NGO (such as a community organization or an education management company) to perform the daily management of schools while the ownership of schools remains in government hands. In another situation, the NGO group (such as a religious organization or a private company) may both own and manage the school. In either case, the NGO will be subjected to operational guidelines and regulations from the government.

These are also variations on how the government provides funding to an NGO-operated school. The government may provide a cash payment to an NGO-operated school to "purchase student places", based on a specific cost per student place. The government may provide a voucher of a designated amount to eligible students and schools that enroll these students can cash in the vouchers from the government. The government may also come to an agreement with an NGO in cost sharing so that the government will pay for specific education inputs (such as a given percentage of teacher salaries).

External resources may be channeled through the government to domestic NGOs to promote education access and equalization. With government approval, external NGOs may also work with domestic NGOs and schools.

(b) **Additional resources to households**

In some situation, the government may provide resources directly to poor households to encourage them to send their children to school. For example, in a "conditional cash transfer program" funded by the government (as in Mexico and Brazil), poor households will receive income subsidies from the program on the condition that they fulfill some specific requirements (such as sending their children to school, having their children receive health-related services, etc.). Such a program has been found to raise school enrollment rates of children from poor background; but the program is not designed to assure the quality of the schooling experience for these children. Another example is giving education vouchers to eligible households for school enrollment. Such a voucher allows the eligible households to choose the school for their children (as in Chile). Vouchers may be a convenient instrument for eligible households on the move (such as migrants).

3. **Improving Efficiency and Redistribution of Resources to Promote Equalization**

This approach aims at using existing government resources more cost effectively in promoting equalization in primary and secondary education.

(a) **Strengthening financial management capacity**

This strategy aims at strengthening the financial management capacity of government education finance units and budgetary personnel at school.

This generally involves providing adequate staff and equipment as well as training these staff in properly recording and reporting financial information. Government monitoring of the distribution and utilization of resources down to the school level is essential in making sure that resources are distributed according to policy and transparent rules, and that resources are utilized as intended. Appropriate public access to and knowledge of budgetary information will also strengthen the capacity for resource monitoring. Such monitoring is essential for minimizing the leakage of resources for unintended uses and thus raising the efficiency of the utilization of education resources in general and for equalization in particular.

(b) **Strengthening accountability of education stakeholders**
Accountability should be instituted and strengthened, in particular, for stakeholders involved in the education of children from marginalized backgrounds. These stakeholders include, in particular, local education officials, school principals and teachers, and parents. They are responsible for their respective duties in the education of children. To be fair, education officials and school personnel should have adequate resources and decision-making power in order to be held accountable for their educational involvement.

(c) **Market-based educational competition**
Some countries allow private schools to compete with government schools for resources from the government (Chile is an example). The basic premise is that in competing for students, schools, both public and private, will improve efficiency in the utilization of education resources for better education outcome. This resource competition may be directed at the compulsory education of children from marginalized backgrounds. However, the empirical record in support of this premise has been mixed.

(d) **Redistribution of existing resources and students**
In additional to financial disparities across areas and regions, substantial disparities in resources and quality often exist among schools in a given area. A number of redistribution strategies are used across countries for equalizing resources and quality among schools and students. The first is to reduce the gap in resources and education quality among schools, especially by strengthening low-performing schools. The second is to rotate effective school principals and teachers among schools so that they do get concentrated in selected schools. The third is to more randomly assign students to schools in a given catchments area (e.g. by computer assignment). Obviously, these strategies are not mutually exclusive; they can be combined to more randomly assign students to equalized schools with improving overall quality.

6.2.2 Changes in the Financing of Primary and Secondary Education by Government Level

This section examines how shares of funding by government level for primary and lower-secondary education have changed in recent years in selected countries and identifies factors that may influence such funding shares.

6.2.2.1 Recent Trends

An estimation is made of the funding shares by government level by level of education in Australia, Brazil, Japan, Spain, the United Kingdom, and the United States. The estimation is based on government education spending before intergovernmental transfer. Also estimated is intergovernmental transfer as a percentage of total education spending by level of education. This following is a summary of the findings, based on studies in Tsang, M., Mizunoya, S., Zhang, Y., and You, Y. (2008). Financial disparities in primary and secondary education: A cross-national study. New York, USA: Center on Chinese Education, Teachers College Columbia University.

1. **Australia**
   Generally speaking, the regional government is the main funding source of education in Australia. Local government does not provide any funding for education.
   Central government spending on primary education fell in 2000 and increased again, and then kept stable at 0.6 %. Regional government spending on primary education accounts for more than 99 % of all the public expenditures on primary education during the 10 years. Central government spending on lower secondary education increased from 1997 to 2001, and fell afterward. Regional government spending on lower secondary education is stable at about 96 % of all the public expenditures on lower secondary education.
   The trends of intergovernmental transfer as a percentage of total public education expenditure differ by levels of education. For primary education, it increased from below 10 % in 1998 to nearly 12 % in 2004; for lower secondary education, it decreased from just below 10 % in 1998 to below 5 % in 2004; for all levels of education, it is stable at just above 5 %. Thus, we can conclude that there is a structural adjustment by levels of education within the intergovernmental transfer. Although the total amount of transfer does not change, more transfer goes to primary education, and less goes to lower secondary education. This means that the government centralized the funding for primary education and decentralized the funding for low secondary. Although public expenditure on education is increasing, the share of spending on public institutions decreased slightly.

2. **Brazil**

This analysis focuses on government spending on public schools, which accounts for 95 % of public spending on all schools. Figure 6.3 shows clear trends in the share of education spending by level of government by level of education. Generally speaking, local government takes more responsibility in financing primary schools and regional government has more responsibility for lower-secondary schools. The financing role of the central government at these two levels is rather limited.

For primary public schools, central government expenditure before transfer increased from 6.16 % in 1999 to 10.69 % in 2004; regional government expenditure fluctuated and decreased from 43.54 % in 1999 to 27.31 % in 2004; local government expenditure increased from 50.39 % in 1999 to 62.11 % in 2004.

For lower secondary public schools, central government expenditure before transfer just fluctuated and showed no clear trend; regional government expenditure became narrow from 69.67 % in 1999 to 56.37 % in 2004; local government expenditure increased from 22.60 % in 1999 to 35.40 % in 2004.

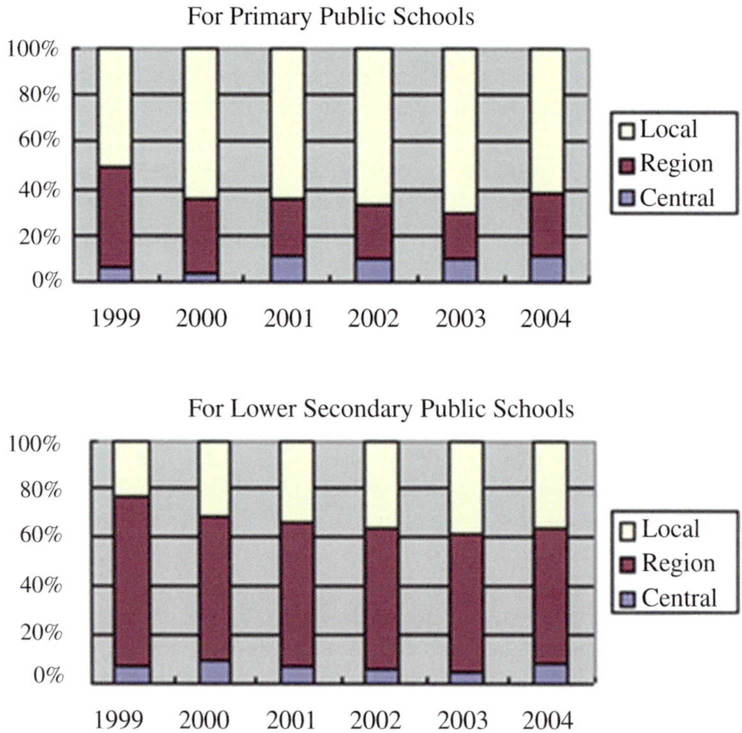

Fig. 6.3 Spending share for public schools by government level in Brazil

These trends reveal that the share of public spending on all levels of education by level of government is stable over time; but for each level of government, the expenditure structure with respect to different levels of education is changing. Basically speaking, the local government is taking more important role in funding primary and lower-secondary education, while regional government is taking less responsibility.

At the primary level, intergovernmental transfer increased for 6.6 % of total spending in 1999 and 14.1 % in 2003. At the lower-secondary level, intergovernmental transfer decreased from 3.7 % in 1999 to 2.3 % in 2003.

3. **Japan**

   In Japan, although the local government has the administrative responsibility for primary and lower secondary, its funding role is significantly smaller than that of the central and prefecture governments because of the relatively weak fiscal capacity of the local government. The funding share by government level was rather stable during the 1997–2004 period. At the primary level, the central share decreased slightly from 30.8 % in 1997 to 29.9 % in 2004, the prefecture share increased modestly from 44.4 % in 2007 to 47.1 % in 2004, and the local (city/town/village) share decreased slightly from 24.8 % in 1997 to 23.0 % in 2004. At the lower-secondary level during the same time period, the central share averaged increased gradually from 30.2 to 33.2 %, the prefecture share decreased modestly from 47.4 to 45.2 %, and the local share also decreased slightly from 22.4 to 21.6 % (Fig. 6.4).

   During the 1997–2004 period, intergovernmental transfer amounted to 30.8 % of total spending in primary education, and 30.5 % of total spending in lower-secondary education. Thus, intergovernmental transfer was a particularly important source of funding in compulsory education, compared to other education levels.

4. **Spain**

   Figure 6.5 showed the share of direct expenditure for all the public institutions by the level of government. At the primary level, there was a large increase in the share of the regional government, from 50 % in 1997 to 76 % in 2004. During the same period, there was a corresponding large drop in the share of the central government, from 40 to 12 %. The share of the local government increased modestly by 2 % points, from 10 to 12 %.

   At the lower-secondary level, there was also a large increase in the share of the regional government, from 50 % in 1997 to 84 % in 2004. During the same period, there was a corresponding large drop in the share of the central government, from 42 to 12 %. The share of the local government also decreased by 4 % points, from 8 to 4 %.

   In short, at both the primary and lower-secondary levels, there was a substantial decentralization of funding from the central to the regional level. There is no intergovernmental transfer in education in the Spanish education system.

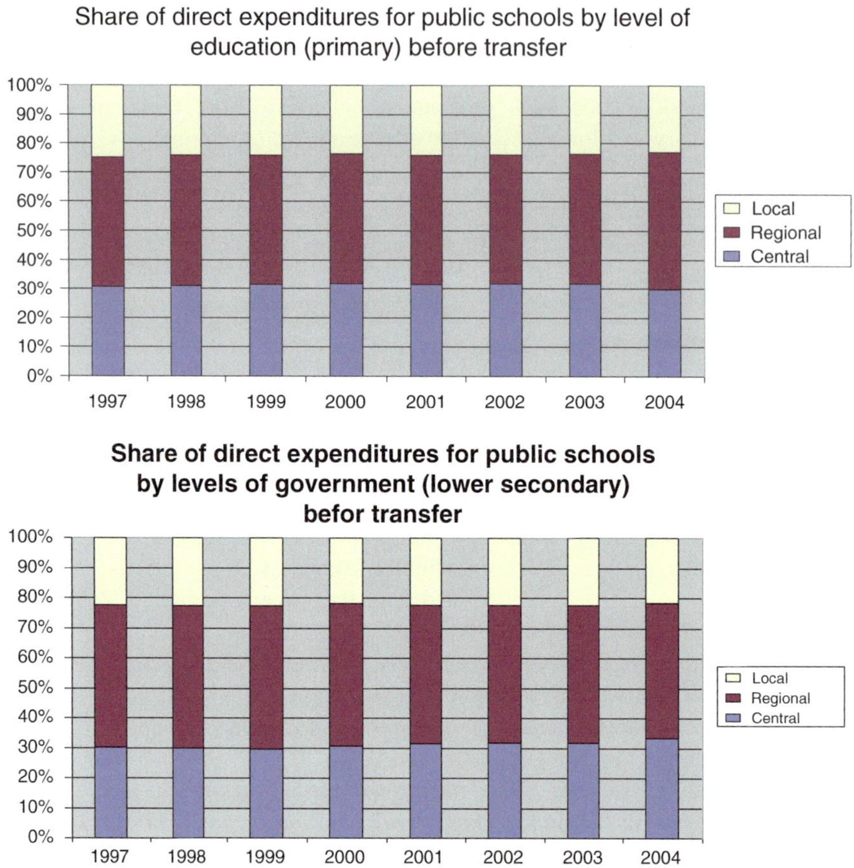

Fig. 6.4 Spending share for public schools by government level in Japan

5. **United Kingdom**

Education in the United Kingdom is primarily funded by the central and local governments, with no role for the regional government. In primary and lower-secondary education, the local government is the major source of government funding, although there has been some increasing central funding in recent years. The local share decreased from 98 % in 1997 to 89 % in 2004 while the central share increased correspondingly from 2 to 11 % in the same period.

For all levels of education, the local share was stable at around 95 % from 1997 to 2003, and decreased significantly to 89 % in 2004. Correspondingly, the share of central government direct expenditures for public schools was kept stable below 10 % from 1997 to 2003, and increased to 10 % in 2004.

At the primary level, intergovernmental transfer as a percentage of total spending decreased from 11 % in 1998 to 6 % in 2004. There was no

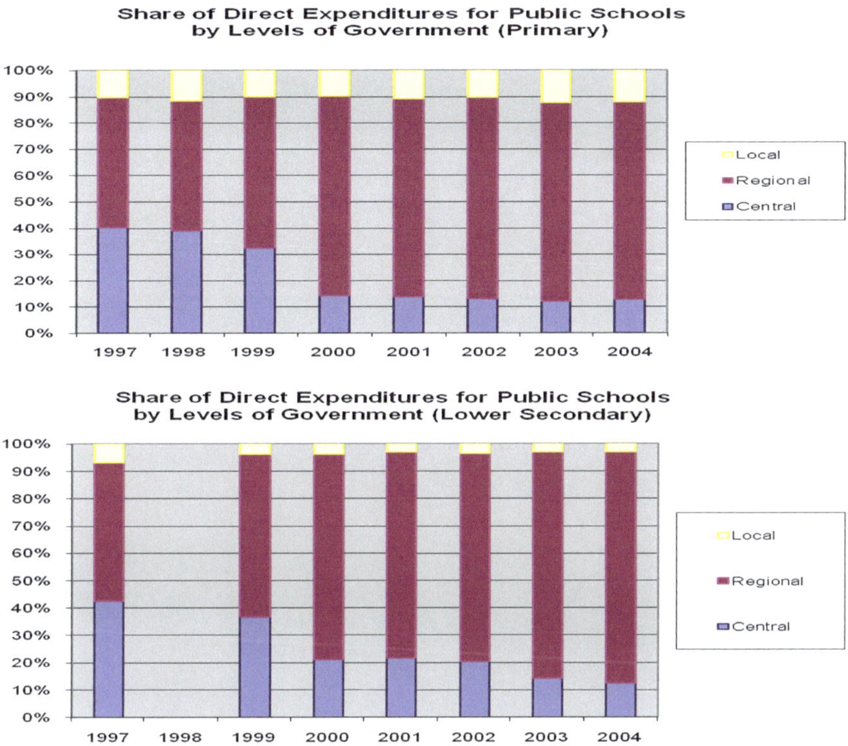

Fig. 6.5 Spending share for public schools by government level in Spain

intergovernmental transfer at the lower-secondary level. All for education levels, the share decreased from 8.6 % in 1998 to 3.4 % in 2004.

6. **United States**

Between 1997 and 2004, the funding share in elementary education averaged 8.3 % for the federal government, 44.4 % for the state government, and 47.2 % for the local government. For lower-secondary education, the respective shares were 8.8, 47.1, and 44.1 %. As shown in Fig. 6.6, at both the elementary and lower-secondary levels, the share of the state government reached a peak in year 2000 and then in a decline during 2001–2004. Compared to the share in 1997, the share in 2004 went up for both the federal and local governments and went down for the state government.

In the 1997–2004 period, intergovernmental transfer amounted to 50.4 % of total spending in elementary education and 54.5 % at the lower-secondary level. Thus, intergovernmental transfer is substantial and is a major part of the funding in elementary and lower-secondary education.

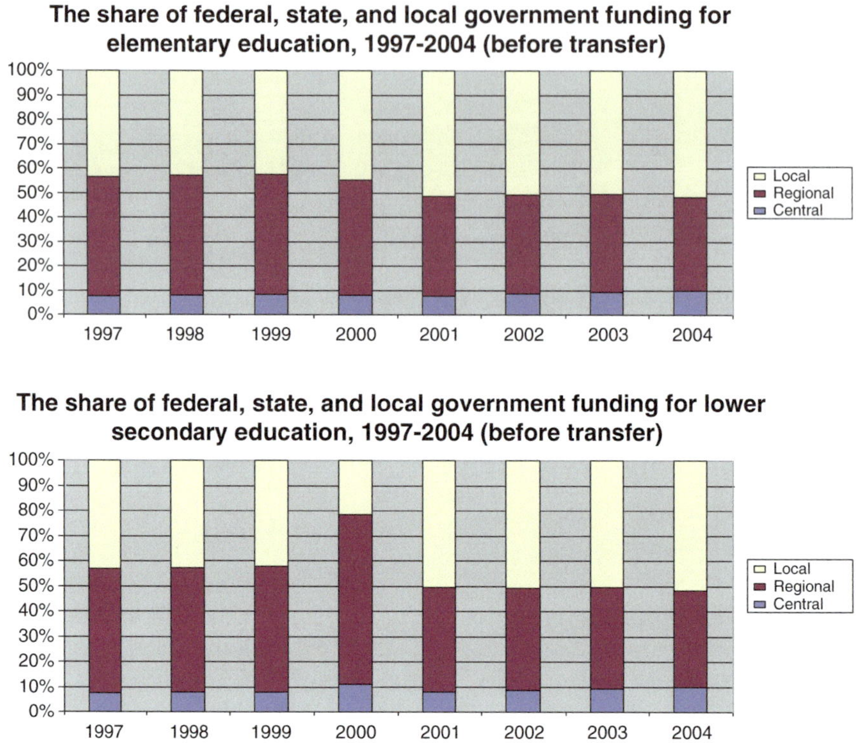

Fig. 6.6 Spending share for on public schools by government level in United States

6.2.2.2 Cross-National Observations

1. **On Sources of Funding**: The regional government is the largest source of government funding for primary and lower-secondary education in Australia, Japan, Spain, and the United States. The largest source for primary and lower-secondary education is the local government in the United Kingdom. In Brazil, the local government is the major source for primary education and the regional government is the major source for lower-secondary education.
2. **Change in Centralization versus Decentralization in Funding**: In Brazil, Spain, the United Kingdom, and USA, there has been an obvious change in the relative share of funding of primary and lower-secondary education by level of government. There has been a centralization of funding in the United Kingdom (more national, less local). In the USA, there was a modest centralization by 2000 and then modest decentralization since 2001. In Brazil, there has been a centralization of funding for primary education (more federal, less regional) and decentralization for lower-secondary education (less regional, more local). In Australia and Japan, the relative share of funding by government level has been

rather stable. Overall, there is no pattern in the changing share of funding for primary and lower-secondary education by government level across countries.

3. **Centralization/Decentralization and Financial Disparities**: From Sects. 6.2.1 and 6.2.2, a mixed relationship can be seen between the reduction in financial disparities and centralization/decentralization of government funding. Reduction in financial disparities appears to be associated with financial centralization in the United Kingdom and the United States at both the primary and secondary education, and in Australia and Brazil at the primary level. However, financial disparities occur in lower-secondary education in Australia and Brazil despite financial decentralization. In primary and lower-secondary education in Spain, reduction in financial disparities and financial decentralization occur at the same time. In Japan, stability in financial disparities was associated with stability in the structure of funding by government level.

6.2.2.3 Factors Influencing the Share of the Funding by Government Level for Primary and Secondary Education

A cross-national review of the financing of primary and secondary education indicates that there is large variation in how the relative share of funding by government level. Each country tends to have its own unique set of factors that shape the distribution of funding shares. It is thus appropriate to say that there is no one single financing model that is most applicable across countries. Nevertheless, there are a number of factors that may account for the governmental structure of financing and its change over time.

1. **Structure of Governance**: For countries (such as France) with a more centralized structure of public administration and finance, higher levels of government tend to have a major role in the financing of primary and secondary education. On the other hand, for countries (such as USA and Brazil) with a more decentralized structure of public administration and finance, lower levels of government tend to have a major financing role. The structure of governance is shaped by a number factors such as tradition (reliance on central versus local control), value (importance attached to standardization and equality versus local discretion and efficiency), size (large versus small population and geography), and diversity (extent of variation in socio-economic and cultural development among regions and localities). A more centralized structure may be associated with a stronger tradition on central control, more importance attached to values of standardization and equality, a smaller population and geographical size, and less diversity in socio-economic and cultural development.
2. **Fiscal Capacity**: Whether a given level of government is a significant source of funding for primary and secondary education depends also on its fiscal capacity. To have a significant role, the government must have substantial, steady, and growing revenue from its tax base. This fiscal capacity is often determined by legislation on what taxes can be raised by different level of government and by

the value of the different tax bases. The pertinent legislation is carried out in the context of the political process of the country, and the tax base is strongly affected by economic conditions (such as income and wealth levels).

3. **The Strength of the Private Sector**: The size of government expenditure on primary and secondary education is affected by the size of the private sector in primary and secondary education and the extent to which the government is allowed to fund private schools. Cross-nationally, the demand for private schooling and thus the size of the private sector has been found to be influenced by three factors: private schools arise to meet the demand for schooling that is not fully met by public schools; private schools arise to meet parents' "taste" for schooling not offered by public schools (such as emphasis on religious learning or a different teaching style); and private schools are operated by non-government organizations (such as civic, charitable, and religious ones) in societies with a strong presence and acceptance of such organizations. Societies differ in whether or not the government can provide funding to non-government or private schools. Such a policy will affect the relative share of different levels of government.
4. **Policy Change**: Changes in education policy may affect the relative government share. Such changes may be brought about by various reasons. For example, in the United Kingdom, the Labour Party in power pushed for reform in education and brought additional national resources to local schools, thus increasing the share of national government relative to the local government. In Brazil, a higher priority for improving access to and equalization in primary education resulted in more federal resources for primary education and consequently a larger federal share. In the United States, the long-term effort to promote financial equalization in elementary and secondary education has resulted, over time, in a centralization of funding from the local to the state level. In Japan and other countries, arrangements for financing are written into education laws or regulations (such as the percentage of funding by government level, the percentage of a government's budget to be spent on education, etc.); these legal arrangements will strongly influence the relative share by government level.

References

Abu-Duhou, I. (1999). Issues in funding basic allocations per pupil by grade level: activity led funding. In K. Ross & R. Levacic (Eds.), *Needs based resource allocation in education via formula funding of schools*. Paris: International Institute of Educational Planning.

Aturupane, H. (1997). *A norm-based unit cost resource allocation mechanism for the education sector, preparatory mission report for the general education project 2*. Colombo: The World Bank (unpublished).

Bacalod, M., & Tobias, J. (2005). Schools, school quality and achievement growth: evidence from the Philippines. *Economics of Education Review, 25*(August), 619–632.

Balasooriya, J. M. B. (2004). *An evaluation of the impact of school based managment and formula funding on the efficiency and equity of school resourcing in Sri Lanka*. Unpublished thesis. Institute of Education, University of London.

Chambers, J., & Parrish, T. (1994). Developing a resource cost base. In H. Walberg, j., & S. W. Barnettt (Eds.), *Advances in Educational Productivity: Cost analysis for education decisions: methods and examples*.

Chambers, J. G. (1997). *Measuring inflation in public school costs*. Washington DC: National Centre for Education Statistics.

Duncombe, W., Ruggiero, J., & Yinger, J. (1996). Alternative approaches to measuring the cost of education. In H. Ladd (Ed.), *Holding schools accountable: performance based reform in education* (pp. 327–356). Washington, D.C.: Brookings Institution.

Duncombe, W., & Yinger, J. (1999). Performance standards and educational cost indices. In H. E. Ladd, et al. (Eds.), *Equity and adequacy in school finance: Issues and perspectives* (pp. 260–297). Washington DC: National Academy Press.

Fuller, B., & Clarke, P. (1994). Raising school effects while ignoring culture? Local conditions and the influence of classroom tools, rules and pedagogy. *Review of Educational Research, 64*(1), 119–157.

Glewwe, P., & Jacoby, H. (1994). Student achievement and schooling choice in low-income countries: evidence from Ghana. *Journal of Human Resources, XXIX, 3*, 843–863.

Hanushek, E. (2005). *Economic outcomes and school quality*. Paris: UNESC/IIEP www.unesco.org/iiep.

Hanushek, E. A. (1998). Conclusions and controversies about the effectiveness of school resources. *Economic Policy Review, 4*(1), 11–27.

Harbison, R. W., & Hanushek, E. (1992). Educational performance of the poor: Lesssons from rural Northeast Brazil. Oxford: Oxford University Press.

Laine, R. D., Greenwald, R., & Hedges, L. V. (1996). Money does matter: A research synthesis of a new universe of education production function studies. In L. O. Picus & J. L. Wattenbarger (Eds.), *Where does the money go? resource allocation in elementary and secondary schools* (pp. 44–70). Thousand Oaks, Ca: Corwin Press.

Levacic, R., & Vignoles, A. (2002). Researching the links between school resources and student outcomes in the UK: A review of issues and evidence. *Education Economics, 10*(3), 312–331.

McMahon, W., Boediono, N. S., & Appiah, E. (2001) *Improving Educational Finance in Indonesia*. Bandung, Indonesia: Policy Research Centre, Institute for Research and Development, MONE, UNICEF and UNESCO.

Nzomo, J., Kariuki, M., & Guantai, L. (2001). The quality of primary education in Kenya: Some policy suggestions based on a survey of schools. Paris: International Institute of Educational Planning. www.sacmeq.org.

Odden, A., & Picus, L. (2000). *Financing Schools: A policy perspective*. McGraw-Hill.

OECD. (2006). *Education at a Glance*. Paris: OECD.

Onsomu, E., Nzomo, J., & Obiero, C. (2005). *The SACMEQ II project in Kenya: A study of the conditions of schooling and the quality of education: Kenya Working Report*. SACMEQ, Harare, Zimbabwe and Ministry of Education, Science and Technology, Kenya. www.sacmeq.org.

Picus, L. O., & Blair, L. (2004). School finance adequacy: The state role. *Insights on Education Policy, Practice and Research, 16*(March), 1–12.

Pritchett, L., & Filmer, D. (1999). What education production functions *really* show: A positive theory of education expenditures. *Economics of Education Review, 18*, 223–239.

Reschovsky, A., & Imazeki, J. (1998). The development of school finance formulas to guarantee the provision of adequate education to low-income students. In W. J. Fowler (Ed.), *Developments in school finance, 1997*. Washington DC: National Centre for Education Statistics, p. 98–212.

Ross, K., & Levacic, R. (Eds.). (1999). *Needs based resource allocation in education via formula funding of schools*. Paris: International Institute of Educational Planning.

Ruggiero, J. (2007). Measuring the cost of minimum educational standards: an application of data envelopment analysis. *Education Economics, 15*(1), 1–13.
Slavin, R., et al. (1996). *Every child, every school: Success for all*. Thousand Oaks, CA: Corwin Press.
Tan, J. P., Lane, J., & Lassibille, G. (1999). *Schooling outcomes in Philippines elementary schools: evaluation of the impact of four experiments*. Sept: World Bank Economic Review.
UNESCO Institute for Statistics. (2005). *Education trends in perspective: Analysis of the world education indicators*. Paris: UNESCO Institute of Statistics.
UNESCO Institute for Statistics. (2006). *Education counts: Benchmarking progress in 19 WEI countries*. Paris: UNESCO Institute for Statistics www.uis.unesco.org.
Wildeman, R. (2003). *Public Expenditure in Education*. Human Science Research Council South Africa. www.hrdwarehouse.hsrc.av.za/educatexpend/educatexpend.pdf.
World Bank. (1999). *Draft aide-memoire: (August 1999): Sri Lanka second general education project, supervision mission report, Colombo*. Sri Lanka: World Bank (Unpublished).
World Bank. (2005). *Treasures of the Sri Lankan Education System*. Colombo: World Bank. http://go.worldbank.org/0.LZ2VZ1960.
Wößmann, L. (2003). Schooling resources, educational institutions and student performance: the international evidence. *Oxford Bulletin of Economics and Statistics*.

Appendix
Sampling and Samples Distribution

According to the requirements of different parts of this study, two kinds of sampling methods were used: investigating sampling and case study sampling. The samples include four tiers: provincial, county, schools, and student. This appendix introduces the sampling method of each tier:

1. For the provincial samples, we select Guangxi, Hubei, Zhejiang, and Heilongjiang as the representatives of western, central, eastern, and northeast China, respectively.
2. For the county samples of each sample province, we first divide the counties with a population of more than 200 thousand and of more 50 % rural population into high, middle, and low categories in light of their per capita GDP, then among each class, randomly select one county as the sample county. According to the above method, there are 12 sample counties in four provinces (regions) with three counties for each province (region).
3. For schools in each sample county, there are two sampling methods: the first is the sampling of sample survey, whereas the second is the sampling of case schools.

   (a) For sampling of sample survey schools, we first selected four towns in each county—one each with a high, middle, and low economic level and one located in the town as the sample town. All the primary schools and junior secondary schools (excluding teaching spot, nine-year schools, and six-year high schools with three-year middle school and three-year high school, etc.) in the four towns were all selected as sampling schools.
   (b) For sampling of case study schools, first we selected three towns as the sample town from the above sampling towns: one located in the township, and one each located in the middle and low economic level town. Then within each town, we selected one independent primary school and one junior secondary school—that is, three primary schools and three junior secondary schools for each sample county. It is required that these six schools all have relatively good physical facilities, and at least one of the primary and junior secondary school is boarding schools.

Y. Du and Z. Sun, *Research on Compulsory Education Financing in China*, New Frontiers of Educational Research, DOI 10.1007/978-3-662-47830-1

Table A.1 Sample distribution

Province (region)	County	Town	Schools			Student sample
			Type	Sampling schools	Case schools	
Guangxi	3	12	Junior secondary schools	13	9	669
			Primary schools	134	9	905
Hubei	3	12	Junior secondary schools	25	9	688
			Primary schools	104	9	1077
Zhejiang	3	12	Junior secondary schools	17	9	774
			Primary schools	40	9	1443
Heilongjiang	3	12	Junior secondary schools	16	9	617
			Primary schools	62	9	700

4. When the students samples were selected, the first task is to select two primary schools and one junior secondary school from the sample schools selected from the four sample towns in each county (that is, eight primary schools and four junior secondary schools for each county), then select a class of the fifth grade of primary schools and a class of the second grade of the junior secondary schools, from which all the students will be treated as the student sample.

According to the above sampling method, there are four provincial samples, 48 town samples, 411 sample survey schools (among which there are 340 primary schools and 171 junior secondary schools), 72 case study schools (among which there are 36 primary schools and 36 junior secondary schools), 6873 student samples (among which there are 4125 students from primary schools and 2748 students from junior secondary schools). The sample distribution is shown in Table A.1.

MIX
Papier aus verantwortungsvollen Quellen
Paper from responsible sources
FSC® C105338

If you have any concerns about our products,
you can contact us on
ProductSafety@springernature.com

In case Publisher is established outside the EU,
the EU authorized representative is:
Springer Nature Customer Service Center GmbH
Europaplatz 3, 69115 Heidelberg, Germany

Printed by Libri Plureos GmbH
in Hamburg, Germany